AMERICAN
HEROES

★ ★ ★ ★ ★ ★ ★ ★ ★ ★ ★ ★ ★

IN THE FIGHT AGAINST RADICAL ISLAM

OLIVER NORTH
EDITED BY CHUCK HOLTON

B&H
PUBLISHING GROUP
Nashville, Tennessee

ISBN: 978-1-4336-7710-6

Published by B&H Publishing Group,
Nashville, Tennessee

Dewey Decimal Classification: 355.3
Subject Heading: TERRORISM \ MILITARY PERSONNEL

1 2 3 4 5 6 7 8 9 10 11 12   17 16 15 14 13 12

For Betsy

With thanks for your patience and prayers
while I keep company with heroes

CONTENTS

★ ★ ★ ★ ★ ★ ★ ★ ★ ★ ★ ★

ACKNOWLEDGMENTS

★ ★ ★ ★ ★ ★ ★ ★ ★ ★ ★ ★

FORWARD OPERATING BASE
DWYER HELMAND PROVINCE,
AFGHANISTAN
15 AUGUST 2008

If our lives are defined by those with whom we keep company, I am in good shape —because my companions are heroes. Shortly before this photo was taken, Chris Jackson, our cameraman, and

Left to right—Andy Stenner, Chris Jackson, Greg Johnson, Oliver North, and Chuck Holton in Afghanistan (August 2008)

three U.S. Marines were wounded by an improvised explosive device. Chris risked his life to save one of the Marines. A few days later, we accompanied U. S. Special Operations Command troops on night raids into Taliban strongholds. Those and many more stories are contained in the pages of this book—all composed during more than a dozen protracted "embeds" with U.S. forces battling radical Islamic terror.

That we have spent so much time accompanying the young Americans and our allies engaged in this fight is a tribute to the vision of FOX News president, Roger Ailes, and David Shepherd and Brad Waggoner at B&H Publishing. Their collaboration made possible this salute to the American heroes who are fighting and winning this war.

Many others contributed to this work as well. Gary Terashita, my friend and editor, made this new account possible. Former Army Ranger and friend Chuck Holton edited my fractured prose and accompanied us to Iraq and Afghanistan to shoot some of the photos for this book.

As for shooting, FOX News cameramen Malcolm James, Christian Galdabini, and Chris Jackson have seen a lot of it in our years covering our troops. They braved improvised explosive devices, suicide bombers, and enemy gunfire to capture some of the most dramatic and dangerous frames and footage from any conflict.

Producers Griff Jenkins, Pamela Browne, Gregory Johnson, and Andrew Stenner all went into harm's way—because that is where the heroes are. Producer Steve Tierney went with us to Afghanistan, and Senior Producer Martin Hinton went with me to document how our Special Operators help their Filipino counterparts track down Islamic terrorists in the southern Philippines.

Much of the work in completing this record of courage and commitment fell on the shoulders of others. My friend and counsel Bob Barnett worked tirelessly with Dianne Brandi at FOX News and David Shepherd at B&H to make this book a reality. War Stories Executive Producer Pamela Browne and Producers Greg Johnson, Steve Tierney, Ayse Weiting, Greg Ebben, Kelly Guernica, and Andy Stenner all pored through miles of our combat video footage to select the best frames for "stills" to illuminate the events described in these pages. And Bill Shine, our immediate boss at FOX News, ensured we would have what we needed to "get it done."

At B&H Publishing Group, Executive Editor Gary Terashita, Marketing Vice President John Thompson, Sales Vice President Craig Featherstone, Art Director Diana Lawrence, Copyeditor George Knight, Project Editor Lisa Parnell, and Managing Editor Kim Stanford all devoted their considerable talent to ensuring that the eyewitness accounts and images in this work will be preserved for posterity.

Marsha Fishbaugh, my incomparable executive assistant and Duane Ward's team at Premiere had to bear the brunt of my frenetic schedule in writing this chronicle. I am grateful for their help in making it a success.

No one gave up more than Betsy, my wife and best friend of forty years, so I could complete this book. She patiently waited and prayed for my safety while I made more than a dozen prolonged trips to cover those serving in Iraq, Afghanistan, the Persian Gulf, and the Philippines. Her support and encouragement and that of our children, their mates, and our eleven grandchildren made this work possible.

None of this would have been documented without the assistance of the soldiers, sailors, airmen, Guardsmen, and Marines with whom we have lived, laughed, and sometimes cried over the course of the seven years they have been fighting this war. Some of their names and pictures are in this book. Most are not. They truly are American heroes. For the opportunity they gave us to let them tell their stories, I am eternally grateful.

Semper Fidelis,
Oliver North

★ ★ ★ ★ ★ ★ ★ ★ ★ ★ ★ ★ ★ ★ ★

HANGING AROUND WITH HEROES

I have the best job in all broadcasting. Soldiers, sailors, airmen, Guardsmen, and Marines—those who fight America's wars—are my only "beat." I hang around with heroes for a living. For some, a hero wears a spandex suit and a cape. My heroes wear flak jackets, flight suits, and combat boots. This book is for and about them.

In 2001 Roger Ailes hired me to host the *War Stories* documentary series on

Front and center, with several of "the remarkable men and women who serve as our guardians against radical Islam"

FOX News channel. Our idea was to present the perspectives of those who had fought America's past conflicts—World War II, Korea, Vietnam—to offer eyewitness participants an opportunity to tell how they made history.

Then came 9/11/01—the day nineteen Islamic radicals hijacked four airliners and killed more than twenty-nine hundred people in America. Within weeks of the attack, I was headed for Afghanistan—with a whole new generation of U.S. warriors. Since then I have been privileged to spend more than an accumulated year of my life documenting the remarkable men and women who serve as our guardians against radical Islam.

In the pages of this book, you will have the opportunity to meet many of those I have encountered in the foothills of Afghanistan's Hindu Kush, the scorching deserts of Iraq, on the waters of the Persian Gulf, in the jungles of the Philippines—and on U.S. military bases and hospitals around the globe. To the extent possible, the accounts here are their words, for no one can tell the story as well as those who live it. This, then, is the first draft of the history they are making.

My purpose is not to glorify war. No one should do that, for war is terrible. Rather, the photos and words in this book are intended to show these brave young Americans as they really are: all volunteers; part of the brightest, best educated, trained, led, and equipped military any nation has ever had. They are young men and women with incredible courage, untiring tenacity, and astounding technical and tactical competence.

There is another dimension to these young Americans that often goes unreported—the extraordinary compassion and faith that they display. I've spent more than forty years either in uniform or around those who are, and I've never seen so many young men and women so willing to demonstrate their faith—by praying before a mission, leading a Bible study, and kneeling beside a wounded comrade in prayer.

Perhaps it's because so many of them have been through the crucible of modern American culture. They've heard the debates over whether they can pray around the flagpole or say "under God" when pledging allegiance to the flag. They've made their decision about what to believe, and they know the peace that comes with a strong faith foundation. Or, as a young U.S. Navy medical corpsman put it, "I know where I'm going and I know why I'm going there." He wasn't talking about a trip to the mall.

Despite the way they are presented by too many in the press and politics, the men and women in uniform today are overwhelmingly *good.* I've seen our troops willingly put themselves at great risk in order to keep from hurting a noncombatant, holding fire until they are sure their target is hostile, and placing themselves in danger to protect innocents during an enemy engagement.

U.S. Army 1SG Todd Hood greets an Iraqi girl in the Dora neighborhood of south Baghdad

Though I have been in more gunfights than I care to count, I never cease to be amazed at the self-discipline of these brave young Americans. They can endure the adrenaline-pumping violence of an enemy engagement—and then, just minutes later, help school children get safely to their classes.

A columnist for the *New York Times* once wrote that our military men and women are "nothing but poor kids from Mississippi, Alabama, and Texas who couldn't get a decent job or health insurance," so they joined the military "because that's all we offered them." A U.S. senator likened those who serve in our armed forces to the armies of Hitler, Stalin, and Cambodia's Pol Pot.

Those opinions are just dead wrong. No nation—ours included—has ever had a military force better than the one we have today. I'm proud of them. You should be, too.

A U.S. Navy corpsman carries a wounded Iraqi soldier to a waiting Marine CH-46 helicopter for evacuation

WHAT IS A HERO?

★ ★ ★ ★ ★ ★ ★ ★ ★ ★ ★ ★

My tattered old *Webster's* defines *hero* as a "legendary figure . . . endowed with great strength and ability . . . an illustrious warrior . . . a person possessing great courage." There's another important characteristic of heroes: they place themselves at risk for the benefit of others.

A firefighter emerges from the smoke at Ground Zero

Nobody doubts that definition fits the first responders who rushed into the twin towers of the World Trade Center and to the Pentagon's flame-filled corridors on 9/11. It certainly includes the passengers who rebelled against the hijackers on United Airlines flight 93 in the skies over Pennsylvania that morning. These are legitimate heroes who knowingly placed themselves in grave jeopardy while struggling to save the lives of others.

Yet, in our celebrity-worshipping culture, the word *hero* has been corrupted to embrace all manner of people who simply aren't heroic. Record-setting athletes, diamond-studded rappers, auspicious movie stars, and intrepid adventurers out to be the first to accomplish some never-tried feat of daring aren't heroes. They may be brave, they may have overcome all odds before making it big—but they don't meet the definition of *hero* if whatever they achieve benefits no one but themselves.

Real heroes are selfless. Those who serve in harm's way in this war have that quality in abundance. And so do their families and loved ones at home. Yet they rarely get the attention, coverage, or press they deserve.

Unfortunately, the negative stories get more ink and air time than they deserve. The U.S. and international press made the aberrant behavior of a few Americans at the Abu Ghraib prison into front-page, lead-story "news" for nine months. The nonstop coverage created the indelible impression that all members of the U.S. armed forces behaved that way.

During the furious fight to liberate Fallujah from the Al Qaeda terrorists who had taken over the city, an edited tape of a U.S. Marine firing at what he thought was a wounded, but armed and hostile, enemy combatant was broadcast countless times by our television networks. Yet when the Marine's court martial resulted in an acquittal, it was barely covered.

When a group of Marines were under investigation for the death of Iraqi civilians in Haditha, a U.S. congressman described the Americans as perpetrators of "cold-blooded murder" and the media beat the story like a rented mule for months. But when a court martial exonerated them, the story was buried—without apology.

There is no doubt that dreadful things happen in war. Ground combat is the most horrific experience a human being can endure. When bad things happen—as they always do in war—they should be reported, and they usually are. But those who persevere, who do the right thing in the midst of shocking violence, who give up personal comfort and safety for what is necessary—these are heroes. They deserve—at the very least—equal time.

Letting their stories be known is important—not just to them, but to all of us. Through self-sacrifice, fortitude, and action—whether they succeed or fail—heroes provide us with an ethical framework for the life of our nation. The deeds of heroes are waypoints on our moral journey, and they encourage us to be better than we otherwise might be.

U.S. Army Staff Sergeant Jonathan Holsey is such a hero. A nine-year Army veteran, SSG Holsey was serving in the 1st Battalion (Bn) of the 503rd Infantry Regiment—one of the units I've been privileged to cover in Iraq for FOX News. A roadside bomb placed by a terrorist—not an insurgent, not a "bomber," a *terrorist*—so severely wounded him that his left leg had to be removed below the knee at Walter Reed Army Medical Center. He now wears a prosthetic leg, yet he plans to stay in the Army. When I asked him why, he replied, "Because my soldiers need me. We have a war to win—and my country needs me."

Marine Lance Corporal Jake Knospler is another hero. On 12 November 2004, Jake was leading his fire team in the 1st Bn, 8th Marines, during the fight to liberate Fallujah from terrorists— not "freedom fighters," terrorists. An enemy grenade hit Jake in the face, blowing away his jaw and part of his skull. He miraculously survived his terrible wounds and more than a dozen surgeries since. Doctors at Bethesda National Naval Medical Center reinstalled part of Jake's shattered skull

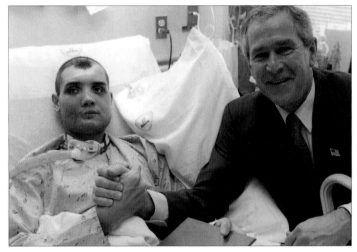

LCpl Jake Knospler gets a visit from President Bush on his birthday

that was removed and sewn into his chest until he was healthy enough to withstand the operation. Jake told me, "I have to get better. My country, my Corps, and my family are counting on me."

At one award ceremony I attended in Iraq, twenty Marines received the Purple Heart for wounds sustained in combat. Their injuries were incurred in some of the toughest gunfights I've ever seen. By the midpoint of their seven-month deployment, 116 Marines in the battalion had been wounded in action, yet seventy of them chose to stay in the fight even though, as a consequence of multiple wounds, they could have gone home.

I asked Lt. David Dobb, who sustained injuries to his hand, why so many of these young men decided to stick it out even though they'd been hurt. "This is what these Marines signed up to do," he told me, "and we're going to see this mission through until the job's done the way it is supposed to be done."

Sgt Kenneth Conde, a squad leader with the 2nd Bn, 4th Marines, was leading a nighttime raid when insurgents tried to ambush the platoon. In the ensuing fight, Sgt Conde was hit in the shoulder by enemy fire.

Though badly wounded, Sgt Conde stayed in the fight and refused to be evacuated until after the engagement. After being patched up at the aid station, he was back with his squad—even though he could have had "a ticket home." I asked him why he decided to stay. "There's no other choice for a sergeant in the Marine Corps," Conde explained. "You have to lead your Marines."

That has been the overwhelming attitude of the young American soldiers, sailors, airmen, Guardsmen, and Marines I have been covering since 2001 all around the globe. They are in harm's way, far from home and loved ones—often in the most arduous conditions imaginable while their countrymen are tucked safely in bed. They are on duty 24/7 for months on end. Though most are too young to buy a legal adult beverage, they have already had more responsibility entrusted to them than their civilian peers will be granted in their lifetimes. And they do it all with grace, humility, and courage that should make anyone proud to be called an American.

That's what heroes do.

Soldiers provide security during a cordon and search in the Jihad area of Baghdad

To see more American heroes and download three of Oliver North's *War Stories* episodes for free, go to http://www.olivernorthheroes.com.

★ ★ ★ ★ ★ ★ ★ ★ ★ ★ ★ ★

1

THE JIHAD

"We love death—
the Americans love life—
that is the difference between us."
—OSAMA BIN LADEN
IN A VIDEOTAPED MESSAGE
FOLLOWING 11 SEPTEMBER 2001

"War is our best hobby.
The sound of guns firing is like
music for us. We cannot live without war. We have no other way except Jihad . . . .
The Americans love Pepsi Cola; we love death."
—MAULANA INYADULLAH, AFGHANI MUSLIM FIGHTING ALONGSIDE THE TALIBAN

"All who hate me love death." —PROVERBS 8:36B

WAKE UP CALL

★ ★ ★ ★ ★ ★ ★ ★ ★ ★ ★ ★

At 0830 on 11 September 2001, when I boarded a Northwest Airlines flight from Detroit to Washington, D.C.'s Reagan National Airport, there wasn't the slightest hint of trouble. As usual, a ticket agent gave my driver's license a cursory glance, to verify that the name on the reservation matched the name on the license, and handed me a boarding pass. As usual, none of the semi-somnolent "security" personnel inquired about the "Leatherman" tool in my carry-on luggage. And as usual, we took off for our destination. Shortly thereafter, "usual" ended forever in the United States.

As our flight approached Reagan National Airport, the pilot suddenly announced over the public address system that we were being diverted to Dulles International Airport, twenty-five miles west of our nation's capital. He didn't tell us what much of the rest of the world already knew until we finally landed amidst scores of other unscheduled aircraft and dozens of police cars:

• that American Airlines Flight 11 and United Airlines Flight 175 had both been hijacked from Boston's Logan Airport and turned into flaming kamikazes, slamming into the twin towers of New York's World Trade Center;

• that American Airlines flight 77, outbound from Dulles to San Francisco, had struck the west side of the Pentagon; and,

• that United Airlines Flight 93 from Newark, New Jersey, to San Francisco had crashed into a field in Somerset County, Pennsylvania.

Passengers disembarking from our flight were told to evacuate the airport immediately. Heavily armed police officers escorted us across the tarmac to a parking lot. They wouldn't even allow checked bags to be retrieved.

When I managed to commandeer a cab, the driver initially refused to take me into Washington, citing radio news reports that the city was being evacuated. The offer of a hefty tip convinced him to at least try.

Shortly before noon we arrived at the Roosevelt Bridge—only to be stopped at a police roadblock, barring traffic from crossing the Potomac into the capital. The westbound lanes of the span were crowded with cars fleeing the city—like an evening rush hour. The eastbound lanes were devoid of cars. Instead, thousands of pedestrians were walking west into Virginia. Off to our right, a plume of black smoke darkened the sky above the Pentagon.

Following the 9/11 terrorists attacks, civilian and military personnel evacuate the Pentagon as injured victims are loaded onto ambulances for transport to a local hospital

When I explained to a Virginia state trooper that I was trying to get to the FOX News Bureau on Capitol Hill, he summoned a police officer who offered me a ride in his cruiser. As I handed the fare to the cab driver, he volunteered in a heavy accent, "Osama must be made to pay for this." I asked the driver, "Where are you from?" He responded, "Afghanistan."

★　　★　　★　　★　　★　　★　　★　　★　　★　　★　　★　　★

The death toll on 9/11 was finally determined to be 2,974. "Experts" tell us that anyone ten years of age or older that day will never forget where they were or what they were doing when the world's worst terror attack was perpetrated in America. Certainly, that's true for me. The horrific images of an airliner tearing into the World Trade Center's south tower, the two 110-story structures collapsing in a cascade of debris while New Yorkers ran for their lives, the scene at the Pentagon when I got there that evening—are all seared in my memory.

A New York City firefighter attempts to clear his eyes of soot during rescue efforts at the World Trade Center

"We've learned the hard way that the global War on Terror will not be short, cost-free, or without losses. But we can reduce our losses by knowing our enemy and acting accordingly."

Three days after the attack, President Bush declared Friday, 14 September 2001, as a national day of "prayer and remembrance" for the victims of the terrorist attacks. Members of the U.S. House and Senate stood on the Capitol steps and sang the hymn "God Bless America" in a remarkable show of unity not seen since.

Sometimes it takes a terrible tragedy for people to see their need for God. Confronted with terrible evil, Americans have sought divine help before. George Washington and Abraham Lincoln both prayed publicly for the nation. President Franklin D. Roosevelt's prayer for America in the opening salvos of D-day is a beautiful example:

". . . for us at home—fathers, mothers, children, wives, sisters, and brothers of brave men overseas, whose thoughts and prayers are ever with them—help us, Almighty God, to rededicate ourselves in renewed faith in Thee in this hour of great sacrifice."

Regrettably, it is also part of the human condition to quickly forget the need for prayer once we perceive that a threat has passed and "normalcy" has been restored. This makes the words penned in 1632 by Renaissance poet Francis Quarles particularly poignant today:

Our God and soldier we alike adore
Ev'n at the brink of danger,
   not before;
After deliverance, both alike requited,
Our God's forgotten,
   and our soldiers slighted.

Military service members render honors as fire and rescue workers unfurl a huge American flag over the side of the Pentagon during rescue and recovery efforts on 13 September 2001

Since that deadly day there have been a multitude of investigations, presidential commissions, reports to Congress, accusations, rebuttals, legislation, and a massive reorganization of the federal government. We have strengthened airport security, expanded our intelligence services, restructured the FBI, increased the size of our armed forces, and engaged Islamic radicals in what has been called a "Global War on Terror." And of course, everyone now knows that the architect of all the coordinated carnage was Osama bin Laden.

Unfortunately, he's just the latest and most visible manifestation of the Jihad being waged against us.

Osama bin Laden

WHO IS THE ENEMY?

★ ★ ★ ★ ★ ★ ★ ★ ★ ★ ★ ★

"Know your enemy" isn't just a hackneyed military slogan; it's an essential survival tool in this new world order of global Islamic terror. We've learned the hard way that the global War on Terror will not be short, cost-free, or without losses. But we can reduce our losses by knowing our enemy and acting accordingly.

Unfortunately, the same American culture that makes blockbuster movies like *Gladiator* and *300* gets squeamish when it comes to pointing out that those who are trying to destroy our way of life are, almost exclusively, radical Muslim males. After 9/11, many people scrambled to assert that Islam was, in fact, a religion of peace. Proponents of such a theory have a delicate dance to perform—one that necessarily skirts around the many references in the Koran that advocate open war against the infidel, which today has become a synonym in Jihadist language for "Westerner."

Millions of Muslim boys are today being "educated" in Islamic religious schools—called Madrassas—that center around the recitation and memorization of the Koran. For many of them, it's their only educational option. These are schools in name only; the vast majority of them teach no math, science, history, or computer classes.

Few of the graduates of these institutions will ever have read a book other than the Koran and texts about the teachings of Muhammed. Unfortunately, hatred fills a large portion of the curriculum. Many of the young men who emerge from these Madrassas have been thoroughly indoctrinated with the belief that America is controlled by Jews, who are in turn controlled by Satan. What's worse, they will have learned that death is their first and best calling in life. They have become "holy warriors," compliant "martyrs" for the Jihad—the "holy war" against the infidels.

To make matters worse, few Westerners seem to comprehend the two dangerous—and perversely synergistic—themes that predominate in modern radical Islam:

1. the apocalyptic belief of Shia scholars, clerics, and political leaders—like Iranian President Mahmoud Ahmadinejad—predicting a violent, "final" clash between Muslims and infidels in which Islam triumphs, by wiping "nonbelievers" from the earth, and

2. the predominantly Sunni Muslim goal of an Islamic Caliphate that extends from Casablanca in the west to Bali in the east.

The vision of a globe-spanning Islamic theocracy is not new. In AD 632, following the death of Muhammed, his followers named Abu Bakr as caliph, or successor. He resolved to spread Muslim theology, with its message of equality and strict rules of behavior, through force of arms. His goal of Islamic dominance has survived a bloody Sunni-Shia schism, the rise and collapse of the Ottoman Empire, two world wars, communism, and the fitful spread of representative democracy through most of the rest of the world.

THE KORAN, ON HOW TO TREAT INFIDELS:

- **al-Anfaal (8):39**—"Fight them, till there is no persecution and the religion is Allah's entirely."

- **al-Taubah (9):123**—"O believers, fight the unbelievers who are near to you, and let them find in you a harshness."

- **Nisaa' (4):91**—"If they withdraw not from you, and offer you peace, and restrain their hands, take them, and slay them wherever you come on them; against them we have given you a clear authority."

- **al-Taubah (9):5**—"Then when the sacred months are drawn away, slay the idolaters wherever you find them, and take them, and confine them, and lie in wait for them at every place of ambush."

- **Nisaa' (4):74**—"So let them fight in the way of Allah who sell the present life for the world to come; and whosoever fights in the way of Allah and is slain, or conquers, we shall bring him a mighty wage."

- **Muhammed (47):4**—"When you meet the unbelievers, smite their necks, then, when you have made wide slaughter among them, tie fast the bonds; then set them free, either by grace or ransom, till the war lays down its loads."

From "Jamal," a former Muslim who converted to Christianity and now lives in Europe.

"I started to regularly visit the mosque for prayer at the age of twelve. Hatred toward the West, mainly the U.S. and Britain, is preached almost in each of the five daily prayers. Islam is indeed a religion that takes its impetus from hatred and anger. It cannot survive without an enemy.

"The first thing I was taught by family, religion and politics in the Mideast is that hating the Jews, or Israel, is the first step of being on the same side of Allah's feelings.

"I remember going . . . on a trip with the mosque; we started singing Islamic praise songs, mainly about the wars and battles Muhammad fought, then about how we will fight the Zionists one day. It soon escalated to shouting death to Israel, America, and the West altogether.

"I remember the euphoria I got out of shouting with anger along with tens of others who were on the same side as me. It didn't matter who the enemy was; what mattered then, to my young mind, is that I belonged to a group. America was a plague with its talons, Israel, in our midst. So were my thoughts back then.

"I later became a Christian. To understand the extent to which we are brainwashed, you only need to learn that this was the hardest single decision I have ever made. I sweated for months before I took that step. We were brought up to learn that Allah is so eager to punish humanity. I was committing an act of treason against a god whom I was told would put burning coal under [a Muslim]'s feet till their brains start to boil for the sin of lying. Just imagine what we were told he wanted to do for those who were not his followers in the first place!

"I lived my whole life thinking I had to work hard to be perfect and powerful so that God would love me and that I should hate non-Muslims so God would love me. Then I realized while I was a Muslim that I would never have God's love because I was not perfect.

"Then my pastor explained that God loves every one, I was amazed that God actually loves everyone because that meant one thing: that God loves me!"

OIL FUELS THE JIHAD

★ ★ ★ ★ ★ ★ ★ ★ ★ ★ ★ ★

President George W. Bush described America's insatiable appetite for oil as an "addiction." He should have included the rest of the planet as well—for all of us are, through this addiction, helping those who hate us.

My old *Webster's* dictionary defines the word *addiction* as an "obsessive dependence" and offers as examples "drugs, alcohol, and gambling." Oil isn't mentioned, but my dictionary is an early 1970s edition—printed before the 1973 OPEC oil embargo.

Neither Webster nor Mr. Bush point out that in order to "feed their habit," addicts must pay out mountains of cold hard cash to very unsavory characters who are often as deadly as the addiction itself. That has always been the case with heroin or crack, and today it's increasingly true of petroleum.

Despite promises of "transparency" in Middle Eastern financial flows since 9/11, there is still no way to track how much oil money is being sent to radical Islamic mosques, "charities," or identifiable terror groups like Hamas, Hezbollah, or Al Qaeda.

Today's fiery leaders of "the religion of peace"—both Sunni and Shia—have instigated and sustained a Jihad, fueled with petro-dollars, paid by the very people they perversely describe as their enemies. Sheiks, imams, mullahs, and ayatollahs routinely expound the virtues of "martyrdom" and vicious treatment for Christians and Jews—and use the money gleaned from petroleum to finance the expansion of their Jihad.

Some political leaders in the U.S. maintain that by becoming "energy independent" we can better protect ourselves from the violence of the Jihadis and the uncertainty and expense of importing oil from the Middle East. To this end, advocates of exploiting our own petroleum reserves, our massive deposits of coal, bio-fuels, and energy sources such as solar, wind, and nuclear power all emphasize that these alternatives will make us safer.

These ideas may or may not make sense from an environmental perspective. But even if the United States achieved total "energy independence" from Middle Eastern oil, it would do little to "de-fund" the Jihad being waged against us.

The cost of drawing a barrel of oil out of the ground is less than $30.00 per barrel. The price on the world market for oil—more than $120.00 per barrel at this writing—is set by supply and demand. The difference between the real cost of oil and the price we are willing to pay means that despots, tyrants, and terrorists are awash in petro-dollars. Even if the U.S. stopped buying Middle Eastern oil tomorrow, the price would likely drop for only a few months, then return to present or higher levels because of demand from China, India, Europe, and Africa.

Until there is a way for the people of this planet to power planes, trains, trucks, and automobiles with something other than petroleum, the world—not just the United States—will continue to finance the Jihad.

THE BARBARY PIRATES: 1804

Presley O'Bannon

Fighting against Jihadist terrorism is by no means a new endeavor for the United States military. Within a year of being recognized as a sovereign nation, American merchant ships were being seized and their crews enslaved by Muslim pirates in the Mediterranean and off the northwest coast of Africa.

At first, diplomats in Washington embarked on a program of appeasement, over the strenuous objections of men like Thomas Jefferson and John Adams, both foreign ambassadors at the time. Treaties were signed and tributes were paid to the government in Tripoli.

But these attempts to buy off the terrorists failed. Despite the treaties, the "Barbary Pirates" continued to capture American vessels and their crews. When Jefferson and Adams met with the Moroccan ambassador and asked for an explanation, his answer could have been taken right from a modern-day Jihadist Web site:

"That it was founded on the Laws of their Prophet (Mohammed), that it was written in their Koran, that all nations who should not have acknowledged their authority were sinners, that it was their right and duty to make war upon them wherever they could be found, and to make slaves of all they could take as prisoners, and that every Musselman [Muslim] who should be slain in battle was sure to go to Paradise."

Incredibly, it took another eight years before the U.S. Congress authorized military action to stop the pirates. In 1794 legislation was finally passed creating the United States Navy. In 1804 during the first of two "Barbary wars" that ensued, a U.S. Marine first lieutenant named Presley O'Bannon led a daring overland raid against Tripoli—modern-day Libya—that at least temporarily stopped the piracy. From that action, the "shores of Tripoli" were immortalized in the Marine Corps hymn.

Interestingly, neither this engagement nor the others that followed were perceived as a "war against Islam." In fact, the force led by O'Bannon was comprised of more Muslims than Marines. After the successful campaign, a Muslim sheik gave the Marine lieutenant his Mamaluke sword in a gesture of thanks. O'Bannon's memento became the model for every ceremonial sword worn by Marine officers to this very day. Notably, O'Bannon realized that the real enemy was hatred, not religion. In his Bible, he reportedly underlined the consoling words of John's Gospel (15:18): "If the world hate you, ye know that it hated me before it hated you" (KJV).

The Barbary wars gave the nascent American armed forces a reputation for courageous initiative under fire that U.S. soldiers, sailors, airmen, Coast Guardsmen, and Marines have upheld ever since. But more importantly, they still carry the tradition of being not just good but just. In the words of William McKinley, "Our flag has never waved over any community but in blessing."

THE "LANDS OF THE PROPHET"

★ ★ ★ ★ ★ ★ ★ ★ ★ ★ ★ ★

The "common ground" for all Islamic radicals is hatred of the United States and Israel. Shia leaders like Iranian Ayatollah Khomeini, Sheikh Nasrallah, and "President" Ahmadinejad of Iran routinely proclaim that Israel, the "Little Satan," must be

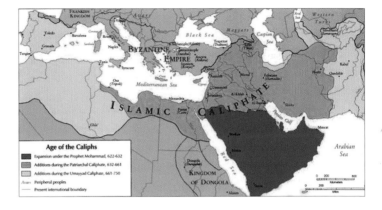

Age of the Caliphs
- Expansion under the Prophet Mohammad, 622-632
- Additions during the Patriarchal Caliphate, 632-661
- Additions during the Umayyad Caliphate, 661-750
- Peripheral peoples
- Present international boundary

destroyed and that the United States, the "Great Satan," must be "driven from the lands of the prophet"—meaning places where Islam is or was practiced as a state religion.

Sunni terror leaders, including Al Qaeda founder Osama bin Laden and his second-in command Ayman al-Zawahiri, have openly pledged to wage Jihad until the establishment of a new Caliphate, bounded by Casablanca in the west and Bali in the east. All who live within this borderless theocracy will be governed by Sharia law.

Then, after a "period of peace," they proudly proclaim that Islam will spread throughout the rest of the world. According to their speeches, writings, and Web sites, the West and its "infidel" religions and cultures will be destroyed.

Ayman al-Zawahiri

Bin Laden has boasted that "the pious Caliphate will start from Afghanistan." Al-Zawahiri envisions a bloody struggle to reestablish the Caliphate, writing that "history would make a new turn, God willing, in the opposite direction of the United States and the world's Jewish government." Fazlur Rehman Khalil, an Al Qaeda apologist, has written, "Due to the blessings of Jihad, America's countdown has begun. It will declare defeat soon" and will be followed by a new Caliphate.

Western political leaders and media elites appear unwilling to acknowledge the threat posed by these two repetitive themes in modern radical Islam—an Armageddon-like final battle and the call for a new globe-spanning Caliphate. The failure of the "international community" to fully support democracy in Afghanistan and Iraq, the unwillingness to challenge and disarm Hezbollah in Lebanon or to stand unified against Iranian efforts to acquire nuclear weapons place all of us—not just Israel—in great peril.

> "Due to the blessings of Jihad, America's countdown has begun. It will declare defeat soon."
>
> **— Fazlur Rehman Khalil**

Instead of confronting radical Islam, the response in the United Nations, most of Europe, and much of the United States has been to preach "tolerance," "understanding," and "dialogue." The belief that poverty, lack of education, or inadequate economic opportunity has incited Muslim rage against the West is totally mistaken.

There are countless poor and uneducated people around the world. The vast majority of them, if they think of America at all, don't want to kill us; they simply want to be here. Many, as we know from both legal and illegal immigration, want to come to the United States to partake in the opportunity that is every American's birthright. They have no interest in flying airplanes into buildings or putting on an exploding vest.

WE DON'T GET IT

★ ★ ★ ★ ★ ★ ★ ★ ★ ★ ★ ★

When I was the U.S. government's counter-terrorism coordinator on the National Security Council staff in the 1980s, we could put a slide on the screen in the White House Situation Room that showed every terrorist organization in the world. We had highly classified "wire diagrams" of the Bader-Mienhoff Gang, the Red Army Faction, M-19, the Popular Front for the Liberation of Palestine, the Red Brigades, Black June, Black September, the Abu Nidal Organization, and the alphabet soup (MNLF, FMLN, MILF, PFLPGC)—the list was practically endless.

We also cataloged state sponsors of terrorism: Libya, Syria, East Germany, Cuba, Nicaragua, and of course Iran. What we didn't see coming was the rise of radical Islam in a way that it would transcend national boundaries to become a global threat to our very way of life.

Part of the problem was that we were looking at the world through Cold War lenses. I, like most Americans—and President Ronald Reagan was no exception—saw the threat of Shia Islam in Iran as secondary to the risks we faced from our most pressing adversary: the Soviet Union.

Second, because our HUMINT (human intelligence) had been so badly debilitated in the Carter administration, we knew very little of the Ayatollah Khomeini's plans for an ascendant Shia empire that could dominate a reestablished Caliphate. Even after we verified Iranian complicity in bombing our embassy and Marine barracks in Beirut and direct involvement seizing American hostages there, no one in Washington wanted to confront the revolutionary Islamic regime in Tehran, out of fear of what the Soviets might do.

Third, and perhaps most important, officials in ours and subsequent administrations were blind to the effect Khomeini's radical Shiite regime was having inside Sunni Islam. Though the Iranians were bled white by the 1980–88 Iran-Iraq war, radical Sunnis such as Osama bin Laden and his Wahhabi supporters in Saudi Arabia saw the rise of Shia Islam in Iran to be every bit as threatening as Soviet troops in Afghanistan, the existence of the state of Israel, or U.S. presence anywhere in the "lands of the Prophet."

By 1990 Sunni zealots around the globe were proclaiming that the collapse of the Soviet empire was their victory. But the sudden arrival of U.S. and other "infidel" troops in Saudi Arabia—after Saddam invaded Kuwait—stunned them all. To prove themselves "worthy" of leading all Islam, the most radical Sunnis declared Jihad against the West in general and the U.S. in particular. By the time our troops returned from Operation Desert Storm, "martyrs" were lining up for the privilege of killing infidels by killing themselves.

Like those who came to America to kill us on 9/11, the thousands of suicide terrorists from Tel Aviv to Madrid to London to Tal Afar who have blown themselves up weren't recruited and indoctrinated by the promise of a square meal. Most of the would-be suicide killers apprehended recently in the United Kingdom had jobs. Like the nineteen hijackers who killed nearly three thousand people in the U.S. on 9/11, several had university degrees. And like the seven who blew themselves to pieces in London on July 7, 2005, they all intended to die. Understanding this is important if we are to prevail against the Jihad that has been launched against us.

"Unfortunately, the same American culture that makes blockbuster movies like Gladiator and 300 gets squeamish when it comes to pointing out that those who are trying to destroy our way of life are, almost exclusively, radical Muslim males"

WHAT DO THEY WANT?
WHY DO THEY HATE US?

★ ★ ★ ★ ★ ★ ★ ★ ★ ★ ★ ★

Khalid Sheikh Mohammed

Khalid Sheikh Mohammed, the mastermind of 9/11 and numerous other terror plots, studied engineering in the United States. Mohammad Atta, the ringleader of the deadly attack on 9/11, lived in America for several years. All of his fellow suicide hijackers lived among us, saw us on our streets, enjoyed our "pursuit of happiness," and had ample opportunity to evaluate who we are. Yet they still hated us enough to want to die killing us. Most Americans don't understand why.

We are practically unique on the planet Earth in wanting to be liked. We're good, decent, generous people. Twice in the last century we armed our sons and sent them around the globe to save others from brutal tyranny. Americans don't fight for gold or oil or colonial conquest; we fight for an idea—liberty. The concept that individual men and women, particularly women, should be free to make their own choices is anathema to radical Islamists.

Those who launched the present Jihad against us don't just hate us because of our wealth and power, though both are certainly factors. Nor do they despise us solely because they perceive our society to be immoral, venal, and decadent—even though those cultural perceptions appear frequently in the rhetoric of radical Islamic writings and broadcasts. And they don't hate us just because of our support for Israel.

If one accepts what they write and say about us—and there is no reason for us to disbelieve their repetitious, very public proclamations—they detest us for all these things, but mostly because we simply will not go away. They curse our presence in the waters they once ruled and for maintaining diplomatic, commercial, and military ties to regimes that we describe as "moderate" and that they call corrupt.

At the heart of this twisted Jihad is a deep-seated belief among its proponents that if they can simply inflict enough pain on us, we will eventually abandon the fight and leave. That's how they defeated the Eastern Roman Empire in Constantinople, how they ultimately prevailed in holding Jerusalem during the Crusades, and how they conquered most of the Mediterranean littoral.

With bloody carnage and armed conquest occupying such a central theme in the sacred texts and history of Islam, it should not be surprising that violence is so prevalent among those who subscribe to modern Salafism, the most intolerant strain of Islam.

Yet despite this historical record and the bloody evidence of contemporary events,

many Western political leaders still persist in describing Islam as a "religion of peace." But if Islam is a religion of peace, the facts show that it is a one-sided, uneasy peace garnered through terror and intimidation. "Peace" alone will not triumph over hatred like that which drives the Jihad. In fact, "peace" and hatred can coexist quite nicely. Today those who stand, almost alone, against the Jihadis are young American soldiers, sailors, airmen, Guardsmen, and Marines. We should thank God that they still volunteer to serve.

Left – In Dulab, Iraq, a Marine looks back while patroling a city street

Below – U.S. Marines escort captured enemy prisoners of war to a holding area in the desert of Iraq on 21 March 2003, during Operation Iraqi Freedom

U.S. Navy Hospital Corpsman Samuel L. Blanco with Iraqi children during a patrol with Marine Regimental Combat Team 5

NOT A RELIGIOUS WAR

Today no modern political leader dares describe the bloody contest being waged against the West as a "religious war." But even the most pragmatic among them should be able to comprehend the stark contrast between the temporal means and ends of radical Islam and the perspectives of Jews and Christians.

Radical Islam is propagated by teaching intolerance, hatred, and the efficacy of violence. The Judeo-Christian worldview starts with the knowledge that love conquers all—especially hate.

The New Testament defines love's aspects clearly: "Love is patient, love is kind. It does not envy, it does not boast, it is not proud. It is not rude, it is not self-seeking, it is not easily angered, it keeps no record of wrongs. Love does not delight in evil but rejoices with the truth. It always protects, always trusts, always hopes, always perseveres. Love never fails" (1 Corinthians 13:4–8a NIV).

There is nothing in the teachings, beliefs, or propaganda of radical Islam that even approximates such a description.

Interestingly, the U.S. Army's "seven core values" embody the very qualities contained in Paul's first letter to the church he had planted in Corinth: Leadership, Duty, Respect, Selfless Service, Honor, Integrity, and Personal Courage.

Though a warrior must often suppress other emotions on the battlefield, love is the exception—because embodied in that virtue are all the best qualities a human can possess.

For a radical Jihadist, this fight is all about dying the right way while killing an infidel. For us, it's all about living the right way because all the dying necessary was done for us two thousand years ago on a hill called Calvary.

★ ★ ★ ★ ★ ★ ★ ★ ★ ★ ★ ★ ★

2

COUNTER-ATTACK

"I believe in the meaning of honor and integrity. I am an action person who feels personally responsible for making any changes in this world that are in my power . . . because if I don't, no one else will." — MIKE SPANN, EXCERPT FROM HIS CIA APPLICATION

"The Bible says there is a time for peace and a time for war. Now is the time for war. I cannot wait to say it is now a time for peace." — MAJ JAMES BRISSON, CHAPLAIN, 1-160TH SOAR, 19 OCTOBER 2001, AFGHANISTAN

FIGHTING BACK

★ ★ ★ ★ ★ ★ ★ ★ ★ ★ ★ ★ ★

Within hours of the 9/11 attack, operations officers inside the Central Intelligence Agency headquarters in Langley, Virginia, and military planners at U.S. Central Command headquarters in Florida and at the heavily damaged Pentagon were working on how the U.S. could strike back against the perpetrators. Finding those responsible wasn't a problem.

Osama bin Laden's Al Qaeda terror organization proudly claimed "credit" for the vicious attack on several radical Islamic Web sites—and eventually in a videotaped interview. But getting at him proved to be a monumental task. When his "hosts," the brutal Taliban regime in Afghanistan, refused to hand him over, plans to remove the Taliban from power and dismantle Al Qaeda were put in motion.

Less than seventy-two hours after the attack, U.S. Navy carrier battle groups, amphibious task forces with embarked Marines, and attack submarines with Tomahawk cruise missiles were on the way to the Persian Gulf. U.S. Air Force B-1 and B-52 bombers, outfitted with the newest guided munitions, were dispatched to the U.S. base on the island of Diego Garcia in the Indian Ocean. But the greatest challenge remained: how to get adequate U.S. military force into land-locked Afghanistan.

It was never expected that the Iranians would help, but even American "allies" in the region refused any overt assistance. The Saudis, long supporters of the Taliban regime, denied the use of their air bases to U.S. combat aircraft, even though we had rushed to defend them in 1990 when Saddam invaded Kuwait. Pakistan was more helpful. Though Islamabad had also supported the neighboring Taliban regime, General Musharaff of Pakistan secretly agreed that U.S. forces could transit Pakistani territory to get into Afghanistan as long as U.S. forces were "invisible" and his government had "plausible deniability."

Others in the region were more forthcoming. U.S. diplomats and military officers quietly arranged overflight rights with Turkey, winning agreement for quietly establishing U.S. air and logistic support bases in the former Soviet republics of Uzbekistan and Tajikistan. In the Persian Gulf, Bahrain, Kuwait, and Oman granted permission for U.S. forces to overtly use their soil.

The plan adopted at U.S. Central Command—headquartered at McDill Air Force Base in Florida and endorsed by the Joint Chiefs of Staff and Defense Secretary Donald Rumsfeld—took all this into consideration. Less than a week after the 9/11 attack, President Bush approved the outline for an unconventional warfare operation to unseat the Taliban and destroy Al Qaeda. It would come to be called Operation Enduring Freedom.

An Air Force F-15E Strike Eagle over the mountains and high desert of Afghanistan

The regime that the U.S. targeted in Kabul was easily one of the most brutal on earth. From 1992 to 1996, the Taliban had waged a bitter civil war against the fractious Mujahadeen of the United Islamic Front (UIF) that had driven the Soviets out of Afghanistan. When they finally took power in the capital, Taliban theocrats, led by the eccentric Mullah Mohammed Omar, imposed absolute Islamic law over the Afghan population within their control and rewrote the rogue-state rule book on repression.

Universities and museums were closed. Girls were forbidden to go to school. Women were required to cover themselves completely with a burka and denied the right to work outside the home or even travel unless accompanied by their husband or a male relative. All music, television, dancing, and public entertainment were banned. Islamic courts enforced the law with public beatings, amputations, hangings, and beheadings—often carried out as public spectacles.

To some, the Taliban's worst offense was the destruction of the cliffside Buddhas in the Bamyan Valley. These were fifteen-hundred-year-old sculptures carved in sandstone. But in reality, the Taliban's greatest crime was to provide refuge and support to a radical Saudi multimillionaire, already well established as a radical Islamic terrorist: Osama bin Laden.

From 1996 to 2001, under the patronage and protection of the Taliban, bin Laden's Al Qaeda grew into a powerful global network of terrorists from every Islamic country on earth. In radical mosques, "cultural centers," charities, and madrassas—many of which he founded—bin Laden found willing recruits for his Jihad. The Taliban provided a safe place to train and direct them. By September of 2001, Al Qaeda "holy warriors" from Saudi Arabia, Egypt, the United Arab Emirates, Palestine, Lebanon, Chechnya, and Pakistan were serving as the Taliban's "palace guard." And Osama had already set in motion everything necessary for the 9/11 attacks. As we learned too late, it had all been plotted and planned from his Afghan sanctuary.

On 20 September President Bush, in a televised address to a joint session of Congress, demanded that the Taliban turn over bin Laden and all other Al Qaeda leaders, close the Afghan terror camps, release all foreign hostages, and allow U.S. inspections to ensure compliance. The Islamic radicals running Kabul rejected this ultimatum less than twenty-four hours later.

Over the course of the next two weeks, U.S. military Special Operations teams and CIA paramilitary officers were moved into position to support an offensive by the UIF, now dubbed the "Northern Alliance." Equipped with sophisticated satellite communications equipment, they reported to Central Command and CIA headquarters that, despite the assassination of one of its most effective leaders, the Northern Alliance was ready to move against the Taliban.

On 9 September, just two days before nineteen of bin Laden's radical Islamists hijacked four airliners in the U.S., three other Al Qaeda suicide terrorists posing as a TV crew detonated a bomb that severely wounded Ahmed Shah Massoud. He was the most effective, pro-Western leader in the anti-Taliban coalition. Massoud died of his injuries three days later, and Mohammed Fahim, a fellow Tajik, took over as the military leader of the Northern Alliance. Though less than certain of Fahim's ability to control this fractious anti-Taliban coalition, both the CIA and Special Operations Command officers on the ground sent a "good to go" signal back to Washington.

29 September 2001
President Bush:

"This war will be fought wherever terrorists hide or run or plan. Some victories will be won outside of public view, in tragedies avoided and threats eliminated. Other victories will be clear to all. Our weapons are military and diplomatic, financial and legal."

By the first week of October even Mullah Omar and the Taliban elite in Kabul were aware that their days could be numbered. Late on Saturday, 6 October, the Pakistani government informed Washington that the Taliban would be willing to put bin Laden on trial before one of their "Islamic courts" if the U.S. could provide "proof" of his complicity in the 9/11 attacks. President Bush immediately rejected this proposal as a delaying tactic and ordered the commencement of military operations.

A NEW KIND OF WAR

★ ★ ★ ★ ★ ★ ★ ★ ★ ★ ★ ★

Aviation ordnancemen load a two-thousand-pound joint direct attack munition (JDAM) bomb on an aircraft

The first strikes, on the night of 7 October 2001, were near-simultaneous raids on Taliban air defenses, command, control, and communications nodes and suspected Al Qaeda bases by sea-launched Tomahawk cruise missiles, B-1 and B-52 bombers from Diego Garcia, and U.S. Navy and Marine aircraft operating from carriers in the Arabian Sea and the Gulf of Oman. In just two nights of heavy precision bombing, the Taliban lost all their anti-aircraft radars and missile systems except for man-portable machine guns and surface-to-air missiles.

Within forty-eight hours of the start of hostilities, U.S. aircraft were roaming freely, day and night, over Afghanistan, dismantling the Taliban's military power with some of the most sophisticated weapons in the U.S. inventory. B-2 "Spirit" stealth bombers made scores of nonstop round trips from their bases in Missouri to drop precision guided munitions on Taliban and Al Qaeda positions. Armed Predator drones loitered over the landscape, sending "real time" streaming video to U.S. commanders searching for "high value" targets. And from bases in Uzbekistan, Kyrgyzstan, and Tajikistan, now protected by U.S. Army Rangers and elements of the 10th Mountain Division, intelligence officers "listened in" on Taliban and Al Qaeda satellite and cellular telephone communications.

Top – A B-2 Spirit stealth bomber Center – A B-1 bomber being refueled by a KC-135 Stratotanker
Bottom – An Air Force MQ-1B Predator goes out on patrol

On the ground, the Northern Alliance—bolstered by U.S. Special Forces teams equipped with night vision devices, laser target designators, and satellite communications equipment—moved to exploit the Taliban-Al Qaeda disarray. Afghans were awed by the ability of the U.S. to put "smart bombs" on target—more than two thousand of them—and

Army PVT Robert Sheppard, a heavy weapons specialist, scans the horizon while on patrol outside Kandahar Air Base, Afghanistan

by the visible presence of Americans in the fight. Thousands rallied to the Northern Alliance.

By 21 October, two weeks after the initiation of hostilities, Afghanis who had once fought for opposing "war lords" against one another were flocking to join the anti-Taliban cause. Many of them, particularly in the south, joined to help evict "the Arabs"—meaning Al Qaeda—from their country. Many in the media predicted that Afghanistan's fabled ethnic and tribal rivalries would prevent a cohesive campaign against the Taliban. But one member of the Special Operations forces summed it up this way: "You don't have to beat 'em if you can buy 'em."

On 9 November Northern Alliance forces, supported by U.S. Special Forces—some on horseback—drove the Taliban and their Al Qaeda allies out of their provincial stronghold at Mazar-i-Sharif. Three days later, Alliance troops were in Kabul, and the Taliban were in retreat to the southern city of Kandahar and the Afghan-Pakistan border with the Northern Alliance and their U.S. counterparts in hot pursuit.

Northern Alliance soldiers were essential in toppling the Taliban

As the Americans and their Alliance allies moved deeper into the country, the magnitude of what the Afghan people had been suffering for years became painfully evident. Tens of thousands of civilians were fleeing the fighting, and the onset of winter was just weeks away. To alleviate their suffering, President Bush ordered air drops of food, water, and

An Afghan man and his son transport hay for making bricks

relief supplies and established America's Fund for Afghan Children. In response to his appeal for each American child to donate a dollar, millions were raised. When the first shipment was sent to Afghanistan on 10 December 2001, it included 1,500 winter tents, 1,685 coats, and 10,000 packages containing hats, socks, toothbrushes, candy, and toys.

All of this was accomplished without the loss of a single American killed by the enemy. But that was about to change.

While bombs were still being dropped on Taliban and Al Qaeda holdouts, the U.S. government delivered more than $250 million in humanitarian aid to the people of Afghanistan. The Taliban responded by warning the refugees that the food was poisoned. Much of our mainstream media reaction was to point out that errant U.S. bombs had also killed civilians. Thus most of the cameras missed poignant stories such as that of Ashley, Aubrey, Alana, and Alyssa Welch. Their father, LTC Tracy Welch, had narrowly escaped the crash of American Airlines flight 77 into the west wall of the Pentagon on 9/11. When the girls attempted to donate blood, they were told that they were too young. So they organized four neighborhood car wash events and raised $10,000.

THE FIRST AMERICAN CASUALTY

★ ★ ★ ★ ★ ★ ★ ★ ★ ★ ★ ★ ★

American forces supporting the Northern Alliance troops included members of the CIA's ultrasecret Special Activities Division (SAD). Johnny "Mike" Spann was among them.

After rising to the rank of captain in the Marine Corps in 1999, Mike joined the CIA and became a member of the agency's paramilitary unit in the Directorate of Operations. Dozens of paramilitary officers—the actual number is still classified—were dispatched to Afghanistan to assist U.S. Special Operations forces in equipping, arming, training, and supporting the troops flooding into the Northern Alliance. After the attack on 9/11, Mike Spann was among the first in the SAD to volunteer for duty in Afghanistan.

During the last week of September, SAD operatives were deployed to establish a forward base for military Special Operations detachments which soon followed. Once on site, Mike and his teammates "vetted" Afghanis for duty with the Northern Alliance, organized intelligence collection and analysis cells for operations against the Taliban and Al Qaeda, and conducted counter-intelligence activities.

Northern Alliance soldiers

During the fight for Mazar-i-Sharif, more than three hundred Taliban fighters surrendered and were taken into custody by Northern Alliance forces and imprisoned in the city's nineteenth-century fortress. Because the detainees had potential intelligence value on the capabilities and whereabouts of key Taliban and Al Qaeda kingpins, SAD officers were assigned the task of interrogating them.

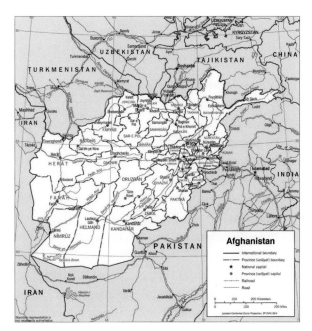

On 25 November, Mike Spann and his partner arrived at the prison and began to conduct interrogations. That's how they discovered that one of the detainees wasn't an Afghan at all. He was an American named John Walker Lindh. According to Lindh, he was a convert to Islam and had traveled first to Pakistan and then to Afghanistan with the intention of joining Al Qaeda.

Shortly after being interrogated by Spann, Lindh and his fellow prisoners overpowered their guards and murdered Mike Spann with two gunshots to the head, making him the first American casualty of the War on Terror.

Mike Spann was thirty-two years old when he died at the hands of a murderous countryman who had joined the Jihad. Mike left behind his widow, Shannon Spann, an infant son, and two young daughters.

Mike Spann's family at Arlington National Cemetery

THE MARINES ENTER THE FRAY

★ ★ ★ ★ ★ ★ ★ ★ ★ ★ ★ ★

The same day that Mike Spann was killed in the Mazar-i-Sharif prison uprising, the first U.S. "conventional forces"—the 15th Marine Expeditionary Unit (MEU)—landed in Afghanistan. Over the course of four days and nights, I was given the unique opportunity to document, firsthand, just how sensitive and difficult this entire operation was. A brief chronology of my journey reflects the extraordinary challenges in this campaign and how creative and courageous young Americans overcame them.

The concept of "embedding" correspondents with combat units had not yet been "re-invented" at the Pentagon. This meant that dozens of reporters and broadcast news crews were "stranded" in Bahrain waiting for clearances and credentials that would allow them "in-country." Some caught commercial flights to Pakistan and braved the dangerous overland drive across the border into Afghanistan. Not all of them made it.

Since my job was to document how Americans fight, FOX News dispatched me and Executive Producer Pam Browne to the headquarters of the U.S. Fifth Fleet. This was the naval component—made up of ships, sailors, and Marines—for the U.S. Central Command. As soon as we arrived in Bahrain, I called on an old friend and Naval Academy classmate, Vice Admiral Charles W. "Willie" Moore, the Fifth Fleet's commander. In a matter of minutes, he arranged for me to link up with U.S. forces heading into Afghanistan.

Before dawn we arrived at the Bahrain Naval Air Facility to catch a Navy C-2 "COD" for the three-hour flight to the USS *Theodore Roosevelt* (CVN-71) in the Arabian Sea. The twin-engine turbo-prop, packed with replacement personnel and critically needed equipment, was hastily offloaded when we reached the *Theodore Roosevelt*'s flight deck so strike aircraft could continue to launch and recover.

A Navy C-2 prepares for takeoff

For the entire twelve hours we were aboard the "Big Stick," the nuclear-powered carrier launched and recovered a near-continuous stream of bomb-laden F-14 Tomcats and F-18 Hornets for their six- to eight-hour-long missions over Afghanistan. Once on station, the aircraft would either carry out preplanned strikes on known Taliban-Al Qaeda targets or provide "on-call" air support for U.S. Forward Air Controllers accompanying Northern Alliance troops. To support every strike mission, the flight deck crews also launched aerial refueling tankers, airborne command and control aircraft, electronic warfare birds, and search-and-rescue helicopters. All of these had to be "recovered." Then the cycle would begin all over again—twenty-four hours a day, every day.

After a few hours of sleep—directly beneath the flight deck steam catapults—I was summoned to the air group ready room and told that a helicopter would be arriving shortly to take us to the USS *Bataan* (LHD-5), one of our Navy's newest amphibious assault ships for the next step closer to Afghanistan. Our FOX News crew would be allowed to accompany a team of Navy doctors and medical corpsmen, as long as we abided by certain guidelines:

- We could not reveal where we landed until such time as we were authorized to do so.

- We could not identify the unit that we were accompanying until allowed.

- No mention could be made of any future plans or operations.

We readily agreed to these conditions and packed up. Less than an hour later we were aboard a thirty-one-year-old CH-46 "Sea Knight" helicopter for the sixty-mile over-water flight to the *Bataan*.

USS *Bataan*

At 844 feet long, the USS *Bataan* is more than two hundred feet shorter than the *Teddy Roosevelt*, but no less busy. In the brief time we were aboard, the warship took on food, fuel, bombs, ammunition, and spare parts from the USS *Detroit*, launched and recovered AV-8 Harriers for strikes against targets in Afghanistan, and coordinated the movement of an entire Marine infantry battalion into Afghanistan.

As darkness began to close in over the Arabian Sea, a Navy lieutenant led me below deck, handed me three life vests, pointed to the two doctors from the medical team, and said, "I know this isn't your job, Colonel, but show the docs how to put these things on. They're probably great surgeons, but they've never been to sea before."

Fifteen minutes later we were aboard the *Bataan*'s two high-speed air cushion landing craft (LCACs) as they spun up their jet turbines for the forty-knot, thirty-minute trip to the venerable USS *Shreveport* (LPD-12), a ship that I had been aboard many times before.

When we arrived at the *Shreveport*'s darkened well deck, Marine and Navy embarkation personnel were ready with trucks already loaded with tons of weapons, ammunition, food, water, and equipment. They had everything the Marines would need for fifteen days without reinforcements or resupply at Forward Operating Base "Rhino," their code word for the air base outside Kandahar. As the vital equipment was being loaded aboard the two LCACs, a Marine gunnery sergeant took me aside, handed me a flak jacket and Kevlar helmet, and said, "Everybody has to wear one, sir." He then added, "I understand that the doctors with you have never done this before. Please make sure they put their 'flaks' over their life vests, just in case y'all go swimming."

I decided not to tell the two medical officers about the swimming part, but I did make sure their flak jackets were on top of their life jackets.

I need not have worried. Once all the equipment was loaded and it was totally dark, our LCAC pilot, a Navy chief, donned his night-vision goggles (NVGs) and we headed inland from over the horizon, flying at almost fifty knots without lights across the surface of the water.

When we arrived at "Red Beach," Navy and Marine shore party personnel leapt to the task of unloading all the supplies, personnel, and equipment; organized it all into a well-protected convoy; and trucked everything to a small but well-guarded airfield less than ten miles inland. Just moments after we arrived alongside the runway, in a remarkable demonstration of interservice coordination, a U.S. Air Force C-130 landed, hastily loaded the contents of the trucks into its cargo bay, and took off for Rhino. Though we couldn't say it at the time, Red Beach was on the coast of Pakistan.

Aviation ordnancemen transport laser-guided bomb unit-12 (GBU-12) and GPS-guided bomb unit-38 (GBU-38) to be placed in an F/A-18F Super Hornet aboard the Nimitz-class aircraft carrier USS *Dwight D. Eisenhower* (CVN 69) in the Arabian Sea

The flight deck of a U.S. aircraft carrier is a virtual ballet on a very dangerous stage. The various functions of the crew are defined by the colors they wear: red for ordnance handlers and crash/salvage teams, purple for those who fuel aircraft, green for catapult and arresting gear operators, blue for those who drive the tugs that move aircraft, brown for chock and chain handlers, and yellow for the officers and aircraft directors who choreograph the whole nonstop show. Visitors like me wear white. It's an extraordinary scene of activity. Every person has a vital task. One crusty old Navy chief put it this way: "The *T.R.* flight deck is the busiest American airport east of New York."

The Rhino airfield had initially been secured by a U.S. Army/U.S. Air Force Special Operations "pathfinder" team. They parachuted in and set up beacons to guide in USAF C-130s with the Marines aboard. The whole undertaking was a remarkable and little reported example of just how good our military has become at "joint" operations.

By dawn, there was no sign that tons of munitions and cargo and hundreds of U.S. military personnel had staged across Pakistan's Red Beach. No U.S. ships were visible offshore. And at a remote airstrip in Afghanistan, the Marines were unloading another planeload of vitally needed supplies and personnel. Less than forty-eight hours after they arrived, the doctors I first met aboard the USS *Bataan* were treating more than twenty casualties inflicted by an errant U.S. bomb.

C-130 Aircraft have been an indispensable part of U.S. operations for more than three decades and were among the first on the ground in Afghanistan

Enemy resistance began within twenty-four hours of the Marines' arrival. Though Taliban leaders were losing fighters at an astounding rate and watching critical cities fall to the Northern Alliance forces almost daily, they had stubbornly vowed to hold Kandahar. But on 6 December, just ten days after the first U.S. conventional forces arrived "in country," the city fell to a force of Pashtun fighters led by Hamid Karzai, the man who would become Afghanistan's first democratically elected president.

With the collapse of their defenses at Kandahar, most of the surviving Taliban and Al Qaeda fighters headed for the hills on the Afghan-Pakistan border. U.S. forces, bolstered by British, Australian, and French troops flowing into Rhino, Kabul, and new bases in the north, set up positions to cut off the enemy retreat toward the mountains. Over the next several weeks there were numerous harsh engagements with Taliban forces attempting to make a run for Pakistan. Though scores of Taliban and Al Qaeda fighters were killed, the Marines suffered no serious casualties. In fact, other than CIA officer Mike Spann, a former Marine captain, the Marine Corps would not lose a single man in combat in Afghanistan until April of 2004.

America's generals and admirals are often accused of preparing for the next war by refighting the last one. Whatever the validity of that charge in the past, it certainly wasn't the case in the opening phases of Operation Enduring Freedom. The campaign against Osama bin Laden's Al Qaeda terror network and the Taliban despots in Afghanistan was made up "on the fly" by soldiers, sailors, airmen, and Marines who rewrote military textbooks with one hand while they fought a new kind of war with the other.

From my firsthand observations for FOX News, it's evident that there were similarities to all other wars:

- massive numbers of ships, planes, men, materiel, and munitions;

- days and nights of back-breaking, sweat-drenched work being done by young Americans, thousands of miles from family and friends;

- countless hours of mind-numbing boredom punctuated by brief moments of stark terror; and

- loved ones at home, hoping and praying that a father, son, or brother—a mother, daughter, or sister—would return safely and soon.

But beyond these common connections to wars past, there was much about Operation Enduring Freedom that was different from anything our military had ever done before. Right from the start, this was a war for the record books:

- greatest number of aircraft hijacked in a single day: four;

- shortest time to build an international alliance to fight back: twenty-six days; and

- most journalists killed in a single week of war: eight.

And from 7 October 2001, when our counter-attack began, records continued to be set:

- The longest duration combat sorties in history: forty-eight straight hours (more than 14,000 miles by the B-2 bombers based at Whitman Air Force Base in Missouri).

- Longest close-air-support mission in aviation annals: eleven hours (by the U.S. Air Force 332nd Air Expeditionary Group).

- Highest number of close-air-support sorties flown in a single day in direct support of non-U.S. forces on the ground: seventy-one (by Navy, Marine, and Air Force F/A-18s, F-14s, F-15s, F-16s, and AV-8 Harriers).

- Deepest amphibious air assault ever conducted: 441 miles (by the 15th MEU).

- Longest resupply route to support a unit in hostile territory: 950 miles roundtrip (for the Marines at Forward Operating Base Rhino near Kandahar).

- Number of countries helping to win a war that do not want to be identified as "U.S. allies": seven.

That last entry in the record books is one reason why the war has been so challenging from the very start. U.S. commanders on scene, with whom I met, had to reconcile with the fact that the heads of state in the region didn't dare risk being seen as too close to the U.S.-led war effort. Afghanistan is a landlocked country, surrounded by nations where we had no U.S. military bases from which to launch offensive operations. This made the fight to finish the Taliban and Al Qaeda an extremely complex, very difficult, and very dangerous endeavor.

SIRKANKEL, AFGHANISTAN – Soldiers from the 1st Bn, 187th Infantry Regiment, 101st Airborne Division (Air Assault), scan a ridgeline for enemy forces during Operation Anaconda

INTO THE HINDU KUSH

★ ★ ★ ★ ★ ★ ★ ★ ★ ★ ★ ★

After the fall of Kandahar, Al Qaeda forces retreated to hideouts in and around the White Mountain region of Tora Bora in eastern Afghanistan along the border with Pakistan. There, they occupied a network of deep caves that had been used by the Mujahadeen during the war against the Soviets. When signals and human intelligence indicated that Osama bin Laden was likely hiding in the region, U.S. air strikes, guided by Americans accompanying Northern Alliance troops, pounded the entire region. But on 17 December, when the last of the cave and tunnel complex was overrun, there was no sign of bin Laden.

With the region now in the grip of a bitter Afghan winter, offensive operations ground to a near standstill.

If, as some suspected, bin Laden had fled into Pakistan, he would be difficult to find. The border region has long been notoriously lawless and beyond the reach of the government in either Kabul or Islamabad.

Pakistan's president, Pervez Musharraf, already the target of multiple assassination attempts by Islamic radicals, had quietly permitted the use of Pakistani air space and territory for U.S. forces to transit into Afghanistan. But he was adamant that Western troops would not be allowed to conduct military operations inside his country.

Musharraf had reason for concern. Though he maintains tight control over Pakistan's nuclear weapons, officials inside his own government—particularly the Pakistani intelligence and security services—were known to be sympathetic to the Taliban and Al Qaeda. Powerful Islamic radical imams routinely preached that the U.S.-led attack on Afghanistan was tantamount to waging war against Islam itself. On 28 October 2001, Islamist radicals burst into a church in Bahawalpur and blazed away for ten minutes with AK-47s, slaughtering sixteen Christian worshippers. And when *Wall Street Journal* correspondent Daniel Pearl was kidnapped in Karachi in January of 2002, Musharraf's police and security services proved unable to prevent the reporter's gruesome videotaped murder the following month.

During the winter of 2001–2002, remnants of the Taliban and Al Qaeda capitalized on the Pakistani president's precarious hold on power and the extraordinary difficulties of feeding and caring for hundreds of thousands of Afghan refugees to reestablish themselves in the largely lawless border regions of the two countries. By February of 2002, the U.S. Central Command had devised a plan to hunt down and strangle the terrorists hiding in the hills. They called it Operation Anaconda. They timed it to start in March in the still-snow-covered foothills of the Hindu Kush.

U.S. Navy SEALs discover caches of munitions and weapons in the mountains of Afghanistan

★ ★ ★ ★ ★ ★ ★ ★ ★ ★ ★ ★

OPERATION ANACONDA – U.S. soldiers pause to search for enemy movement during a patrol near Sirkankel, Afghanistan

The sound of an approaching chopper echoed through the inky, pre-dawn blanketing of Takur Ghar, a snow-covered, ten-thousand-foot peak in the remote reaches of northern Afghanistan.

Standing in the back of the MH-47E Chinook helicopter, a SEAL reconnaissance team clung to the red nylon webbing covering the walls of the aircraft. It wasn't easy to stay on their feet as they checked their gear one last time.

Petty Officer Neal Roberts prepared to be the first to exit the aircraft, positioning himself on the chopper's rear ramp. The snow flashing beyond the black opening glistened in the moonlight.

U.S. Central Command and the CIA had been monitoring a large pocket of Al Qaeda and Taliban forces in the area for some time. Operation Anaconda was designed to wipe them out. Part of the plan called for positioning recon and surveillance teams on hilltops to provide intelligence and to call in supporting fire.

This chopper held one such team.

As the Chinook approached the designated landing zone (LZ) in a small saddle just below the summit of Takur Ghar, the pilot spotted a scattering of goat skins and human footprints in the snow. The mountaintop was already occupied.

He called to the team commander. "Looks like our insertion may be compromised, sir."

"Do we have enemy contact?"

"No, sir, but there are definitely signs of recent activity here."

The Special Operations pilot flared the helicopter to slow it down, coming to a hover over their intended landing spot.

"Roger," replied the mission commander over the Chinook's intercom. "Abort mission."

Before the pilot could acknowledge the command, a rocket-propelled grenade (RPG) struck the helicopter like a small meteor, blazing through the aluminum skin, throwing flame and shrapnel around the cargo bay, puncturing hydraulic and fuel lines, and wounding one man. As the pilot struggled to maintain control of the bird, the helicopter pitched sideways. This tossed a crewman off the tail ramp just as a machine gun began peppering the aircraft like invisible fingers of death stabbing holes in the thin exterior, looking for flesh inside.

Tethered to the aircraft with a safety harness, the rear crewman dangled only a few feet below the ramp. Reacting quickly, PO1 Neal Roberts dropped to his belly and reached out to help the crewman inside. But it was clear the helicopter wouldn't stay in the air for long. The pilot jerked back on the controls to try to gain some altitude in the thin mountain atmosphere. The action nearly stood the chopper on its tail. With no safety harness to stop him, Roberts slid off the tail ramp. His teammates watched him fall about ten feet to the snowy outcropping below.

As the Chinook peeled away from the mountain, the rest of the team watched in horror and frustration as Roberts came under heavy enemy fire. The last they saw of him, he was shooting back, attacking a superior force all alone.

Among the American Special Ops troops on board was Petty Officer Stephen Toboz. Born in Lock Haven, Pennsylvania, Stephen is the son of Glenda and Steve Toboz, a special education assistant and a retired state trooper.

CH-47 Chinook helicopter

After he graduated from Lock Haven High School with his brother Shawn, Stephen attended Lock Haven University and then enlisted in the Navy in 1991. After basic training, he went to the Navy's "A" School, where he studied electronics before traveling to Coronado, California, for BUD/S (basic underwater demolition/SEAL) training. This is the most demanding training in the U.S. armed forces, both mentally and physically. Trainees endure six months of rigorous training broken into three stages—basic conditioning, diving, and land warfare. Phase one also includes the infamous "hell week" in which candidates must endure five and a half days of continuous training, with a maximum of four hours sleep total. It is the ultimate test of a person's physical and mental motivation.

Stephen received his Trident in May 1993, officially marking his membership in one of the most elite Special Forces units in the world. From there, he reported to Naval Amphibious Base Little Creek in Norfolk, Virginia, and for the next five years served as a member of SEAL Team 8. In 1998 he was assigned to the Naval Special Warfare Development Group at Dam Neck, Virginia—the most select of all SEAL teams. That's why he was on a Chinook helicopter being shot at in the middle of the night over the hills of Afghanistan in March of 2002.

Back on Takur Gar, the wounded helicopter limped about half a mile and made an emergency landing. Stephen and his comrades charged into the snowy darkness and immediately set out to rescue their fellow SEAL.

During the ensuing gunfight, the badly outnumbered Americans fought valiantly. Out of the nearly two dozen U.S. soldiers who set out to rescue PO1 Roberts, six were killed. Among the eleven more who were wounded was Stephen Toboz.

Ordered to pull back by his team leader, Stephen was hit by a Taliban bullet that tore a fist-sized hole in his right calf. The projectile then spiraled down his leg, shattering the bones in his ankle and foot. Hours later when he was finally evacuated off the frozen hilltop, "Tobo" was still shooting back at those who had tried to kill him.

The U.S. doctors in Afghanistan saved his life. The doctors in Germany and back home in the U.S. tried to save his leg. But after multiple surgeries, Stephen figured he would get better faster without it. He told his doctors to amputate the leg below the knee.

Remarkably, that didn't end his career in the Navy. After being fitted with an ultramodern prosthetic limb, Stephen Toboz rejoined his team in Afghanistan. He says he did it because "Neal Roberts was my closest friend" and because "my parents taught me patriotism, duty, and determination."

Today Stephen Toboz is retired, but he still trains SEALs as a civilian instructor. Since he no longer wears a uniform, unless his young students hear it from others who know the story, they might never know that Stephen Toboz has a metal leg and foot or that he was awarded our nation's third highest award for valor—the Silver Star.

The President of the United States takes pleasure in presenting the Silver Star Medal to Aviation Boatswain's Mate 1st Class (Sea, Air, and Land) Stephen Toboz, United States Navy, for service as set forth in the following CITATION: For conspicuous gallantry and intrepidity in action against the enemy while serving as a member of a special operations unit conducting combat operations against enemy forces in hostile territory from 3 to 4 March 2002. Petty Officer Toboz displayed extraordinary heroism, superb tactical performance, and inspiring perseverance as a member of a six-man team that flew back into an enemy stronghold atop a 10,000-foot mountain in order to rescue a captured teammate. Caught in automatic weapons crossfire upon insertion, PO1 Toboz immediately maneuvered against an enemy machine gun position, killing three enemies with accurate 5.56-millimeter fire. He continued to engage additional combatants until ordered to break contact by his team leader. While withdrawing, PO1 Toboz was hit by automatic weapons fire which shattered his lower leg ultimately resulting in amputation at a later date. Nonambulatory and nearly hypothermic, he pushed through exhaustion and intense pain to maneuver over one kilometer through icy and precipitous terrain, refusing morphine in order to preserve his security posture. PO1 Toboz' tactical expertise and courageous efforts significantly attrited the enemy fighters atop the mountain and contributed to their eventual defeat. By his outstanding display of immeasurable courage in the face of heavy enemy fire, untiring efforts, and selfless devotion to duty, PO1 Toboz reflected great credit upon himself and upheld the highest traditions of the United States Naval Service.

Navy SEAL Stephen Toboz back in Afghanistan

Sgt Jade Fry meets with local Afghan women in a voter registration center in Kandahar City. The presence of female soldiers displays America's resolve as a democracy to give equal rights to all its citizens.

KARZAI'S COURAGE

★ ★ ★ ★ ★ ★ ★ ★ ★ ★ ★ ★

In 2004, our FOX News team went back to Afghanistan to see how things had changed. Defying most of the critics in the so-called mainstream media, the people of what many considered to be an "impossible place to hold an election" had gone to the polls and chosen their first democratically elected leader.

For the first time in history, Afghan women went to the polls and cast ballots. They emerged triumphantly from the polling places with upraised purple index fingers or thumbs. In a live broadcast, I described it as the "indelible stain of democracy." Despite threats from Taliban propagandists and apologists that they would be killed for voting, people walked for miles—sometimes through minefields—just to cast their ballots.

The result was the selection of Hamid Karzai, a tall, ascetic man as the leader of their Loya Jirga, or legislative body.

Hamid Karzai

Hamid Karzai was living in Quetta, Pakistan, in 1999 when his father was gunned down in cold blood. The killers were agents of the Taliban government in Karzai's native Afghanistan. The killing was a warning to Karzai. He had been working to see the former king, Zahir Shah, reinstated in power.

The day his father was murdered was when Hamid Karzai dedicated his life to defeating the Taliban. And he didn't have to wait long to see his dream realized. Once the United States went to war in Afghanistan, Karzai emerged as a leader with the Northern Alliance forces, commanding a force of three thousand Pashtun fighters. With them, he helped wrest Kandahar from the Taliban and became the chairman of the transitional administration a month later when he met with other Afghan leaders in Bonn, Germany. Six months later, a council of tribal, civic, and religious leaders voted him the interim president of the country.

The road ahead promised to be rocky. He had his hands full trying to rebuild his nation, defeat the remnants of the Taliban, and dodge multiple assassination attempts. Two years later he won 55 percent of the vote for president in the first national election in Afghanistan's history. And all of this because American soldiers, sailors, airmen, and Marines were willing to fight back against those who had started a Jihad against us.

3

EXPANDING THE WAR

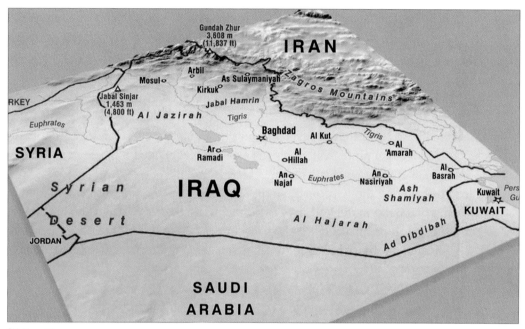

CIA Map of Iraq

THE CASE AGAINST SADDAM

After a U.S.-led coalition routed Saddam Hussein's army and drove them out of Kuwait in 1991, the United Nations slapped Iraq with an oil embargo and strong economic sanctions. These were designed to deny the defeated dictator the ability to rebuild his army and threaten his neighbors.

Almost immediately, complaints began to surface that the sanctions put an inordinate burden on the average Iraqi people. Critics claimed, without substantiation, that the trade restrictions were responsible for starving thousands of Iraqi children to death.

In 1995 the Clinton administration proposed a UN-administered "Oil for Food" program that would allow Saddam to sell limited amounts of Iraqi oil in exchange for approved humanitarian shipments of food and medicine that would go to the Iraqi people. In theory, the plan made sense. But as is often the case, especially when dealing with dictators and men whose morality can be bought, the plan was soon perverted. Even with hundreds of UN employees in Iraq as overseers, the oil-for-food program became rife with corruption.

The full extent of the fraud will never be known, but by January of 2002, U.S. and British investigators had uncovered evidence that Saddam's family and his Baath Party officials were pocketing billions in skimmed profits, smuggled oil revenues, and illegal kickbacks. Millions more in illicit funds were apparently being diverted to line the pockets of UN officials.

In Iraq, the effects of the corruption were far-reaching. Food and medicine purchased with oil-for-food funds were delivered to Iraqi government warehouses by Baath Party officials. From these "distribution centers" humanitarian supplies were doled out to supporters of Saddam's regime. A flourishing black market created a whole new revenue stream for the Iraqi dictator and his cronies.

Instead of bettering the lives of the Iraqi people, oil-for-food monies were diverted to buy weapons and build more than sixty extravagant palaces for Saddam and his family. In Baghdad and Tikrit, Saddam's hometown, he constructed luxurious walled citadels that I got to see firsthand in 2003 when U.S. forces first entered these cities.

Saddam Hussein built dozens of palaces around the country, such as the Al Faw Palace near Baghdad International Airport

Above – A mosque in Baghdad
Left – Saddam fancied himself a modern-day Nebuchadnezzar
Right – Saddam built this palace directly atop the ruins of
Nebuchadnezzar's ancient six-hundred-room palace in Babylon, to the
horror of archaeologists

Saddam's sons, Uday and Qusay, were put in charge of purchasing vast quantities of munitions and explosives to rebuild the Iraqi military in direct defiance of the terms of the 1991 armistice agreement. Skimmed funds were also sent to fill the coffers of European political elites who could help influence any vote in the UN for military action. By January 2002, intelligence reports and "defector" debriefs also indicated that some of the excess oil-for-food cash was being diverted to acquire weapons of mass destruction.

PREPARATION FOR PREEMPTION

★ ★ ★ ★ ★ ★ ★ ★ ★ ★ ★ ★

January 2002 State of the Union Address

On 29 January 2002, in his State of the Union Address, President Bush described Iran, Iraq, and North Korea as an "axis of evil." He announced to the world, "I will not wait on events while dangers gather. I will not stand idly by as peril draws closer and closer. The United States of America will not permit the world's most dangerous regimes to threaten us with the world's most destructive weapons." His statement made clear that the United States wasn't going to wait for a terror attack like 9/11 launched by the ayatollahs in Tehran, Saddam Hussein in Baghdad, or Kim Jung Il in Pyongyang. This was enough to drive the global left into paroxysms of angst.

In London, Hollywood director Robert Altman proclaimed, "When I see an American flag flying, it's a joke" and "this present government in America, I just find disgusting." This performance would soon be replicated thousands of times over by critics of the administration.

Sen. Tom Daschle (D-S.D.), then the majority leader of the U.S. Senate, initially gave the commander in chief high marks for his State of the Union Address. But on 11 February—the five-month anniversary of the terror attack that killed nearly three thousand Americans—he decided that it really wasn't nice to use labels like "evil." He told dozens of PBS viewers not watching the Olympics, "We've got to be very careful with rhetoric of that kind."

That same night at Brown University, AOL-Time Warner's Ted Turner took center stage in the "Blame America First" passion play. He told five hundred students attending the school that expelled him in 1960 that the nineteen terrorists who hijacked four airliners on 9/11 "were brave at the very least." He went on to deride President Bush for his "axis of evil" comment and baldly opined, "The reason the World Trade Center got hit is because there are a lot of people living in abject poverty out there who don't have any hope for a better life." The Ivy Leaguers applauded.

On 12 February former Vice President Al Gore joined the chorus of critics, contending that President Bush was showing "impatience and disdain" toward our "allies" in the campaign against terrorism. In remarks to the liberal Council on Foreign Relations, Gore claimed that terrorism is "today's manifestation of an anger welling up from deep layers of grievance shared by many millions of people." And what causes this anger? "Poverty, ignorance, disease and environmental disorder, corruption and political oppression." Mr. Gore' solution: Increased spending on foreign aid.

In late March of 2002, while American soldiers were dodging gunfire in the Afghan mountains near the Pakistani border, FOX News sent me to Normandy and London to complete two *War Stories* episodes. One covered the 1940 Battle of Britain and the other was about the June 6, 1944, Allied landings on the Normandy coast. In both France and the United Kingdom, I found extraordinary opposition to any military operations against Saddam.

In retrospect, it was naive of me to expect the French and British political classes to have anything but animosity for the United States and our worldwide fight against terrorism. And in fairness, those who actually work for a living—cab drivers, restaurateurs, and shopkeepers—expressed a fondness for Americans and respect for the Bush administration's goals. But in the press rooms, broadcast centers, and salons of the self-significant, there was an animosity toward the United States that I hadn't seen since the Vietnam War.

My first encounter was at a dinner in Paris after returning from Omaha Beach. In a room overlooking streets once patrolled by Hitler's storm troopers, members of the Parisian press and ex-government officials confronted me with a laundry list of grievances: "The treatment of the Afghan detainees in Guantanamo, Cuba, is inhumane." Another said, "There is no provocation for threatening Iraq." And yet another: "Don't expect us to help you make war against Moslems all around the world. George Bush is swashbuckling around the planet like President John Wayne."

I admit that my French is deplorable, and I can't confirm whether my inquisitor said "swashbuckling" or "buckswashling." But I'm fairly certain he was thinking of Ronald Reagan, not John Wayne.

In response, I politely reminded one antagonist that I had "just left the American cemetery at Colleville, overlooking Omaha Beach, where nearly ten thousand of my father's comrades in arms lie buried, and I don't want to hear anymore complaints about my country." Silenced, he shrugged and walked away.

Protestors rally near the European Union headquarters in Brussels

The next day, I learned that the timorous appeasement syndrome wasn't confined to Paris. In London, the criticism was almost identical, though easier to understand. A British newspaperman, staked out at my hotel, pointed to my Old Glory lapel pin and asked, "Here to show the American flag while your paratroopers are killing innocent Afghanis?" His follow-up was, "How many young British boys are going to have to die in the Hindu Kush before you Yanks are happy?"

British television filled the airwaves with members of Parliament castigating Prime Minister Tony Blair for supporting the United States' war on terror. On the morning I departed for home, the *Manchester Guardian* featured carping critics of Blair's own party. One whined that "any extension of the war to Iraq could bring about an intensification, and indeed a breach, of the anti-terrorist coalition." Another opined, "The American Air Force has probably killed more women and children than any other force in the world." Their refrains eerily resembled British Prime Minister Neville Chamberlain's 29 September 1938, promise of "peace for our time."

Had Chamberlain and the Europeans stood up to Hitler in 1938, rather than appeasing him, World War II might have been prevented and the death of 405,399 Americans might have been avoided.

American forces liberating France, 1944

The Euro-elites apparently forgot that the United States was attacked first and that, in many respects, the Jihad being waged against us is the consequence of Western tolerance for Islamic extremism. Mohammad Atta, Osama bin Laden's "unit commander" for the 9/11 attack, was a regular in Germany. Zacharias Moussaoui, eventually tried and convicted in Alexandria, Virginia, traveled freely in Europe on a French passport. Richard Reid, the infamous shoe bomber, wore his exploding sneakers aboard a U.S.-bound airliner from France.

By the summer of 2002, the most commonly heard refrain went something like this: "If Saddam Hussein's weapons of mass destruction were such a big threat, our European allies and friends in the region would be with us, and they are not. Therefore, we must not attack Iraq."

As American soldiers, sailors, airmen, and Marines prepared to fight Saddam's military, that's a pretty close paraphrase of what they were hearing from foreign capitals, retired officials of former administrations, and much of the media.

Europe's timid response to the prospect of military action against Iraq was easy to understand. By 2002, nearly every "NATO capital" was overrun with refugees from former colonies—many of them Islamic. The Europeans were beset with pervasive political, economic, and spiritual exhaustion, governments beset by internal European Union bickering, and fragile left-of-center political coalitions agreeing on little other than curbing U.S. influence.

Euro-business leaders were afraid of losing

Global Day of Protest against the Iraq War, 15 February 2003

their exclusive "axis of evil" cookie jar in Iraq where they could operate without American economic competition. "Nobody in Germany or continental Europe agrees with Bush," Holger Friedrich, a fund manager for Frankfurt-based Union Investment GmbH, said in August, as his firm purchased Iranian bonds to help fund the radical Islamic theocracy in Tehran. Even Britain's Aberdeen Asset Management Trust was invested in Iraqi and North Korean debt. "It's toxic stuff," admitted Colm McDonagh, an Aberdeen fund manager, "but when it moves, it really moves."

In 1997, Total SA, a French oil company with permanent suites at the Al-Rasheed Hotel in Baghdad, struck a two-billion-dollar natural gas contract with Iran. On the occasion, then-Premier Lionel Jospin applauded this triumph of French enterprise. "American laws apply in the United States," he sneered. "They do not apply in France." The French remained Saddam's principal European trading partners and financial supporters until the U.S.-led invasion in March of 2003.

The timorous grandchildren of those who tried to appease Hitler did not savor the prospect of U.S. intelligence teams roaming at will through the records of Saddam's "defense industries" and exposing Europe's complicity in building Iraq's arsenals. After the first Gulf War, Kenneth Timmerman chronicled in *The Death Lobby* Saddam's success in gaining the help of foreign corporations and governments in building his storehouse of ABCs—atomic, biological, and chemical weapons.

29 January 2002
State of the Union Address

European leaders—with the exception of British Prime Minister Tony Blair—apparently didn't believe President Bush when he said, "Some governments will be timid in the face of terror. (But) make no mistake about it; if they do not act, America will."

French engineers had helped build the Iraqi nuclear reactor at Osirak, which the Israelis destroyed in 1981. In 2002 the French were holding four billion dollars in unpaid Iraqi debts. German firms specialized in providing technologies for making poison gas and building missiles. W. Seth Carus, a senior research professor at the National Defense University, had noted in 1992, "Everything that showed up in Iraq—chemical, biological, nuclear—had a German element in it." And Saddam's "supergun," the long-range, nuclear-capable cannon that was nearly completed when Operation Desert Storm commenced, had been produced by companies from seven different European countries. Little of that had changed a decade later.

More ominous than Europe's craven reaction to Baghdad's aggressiveness was the stunning stance of Saddam's very vulnerable neighbors. The region's leaders had well-founded apprehension that they could all go the way of Anwar Sadat—in a hail of gunfire from radical Islamic extremists.

In Saudi Arabia, the House of Saud sought to prevent such an outcome by dancing with both the West and radical Islam. They devised an Arabian version of economic liberalism and political repression similar to that in communist China. The consequence of Riyadh's political polygamy was demonstrated on 9/11, when fifteen children of middle-class Saudis transformed themselves into suicide hijackers and mass murderers.

Regimes throughout the rest of the region, whether friendly or not to the United States, equate political freedom with instability. They are dominated by political systems typified by military coups, oil-saturated oligarchies, and events like Gen. Pervez Musharraf's seizure of control in Pakistan and his unilateral decision to revise the country's constitution.

The leaders of Iraq's neighboring governments had no great love for Saddam. But they had even less affection for the United States bringing about a democratic transition next door. After all, if "free and fair elections" work in Baghdad, they will also work in Tehran, Amman, Riyadh, Ramallah, Damascus, and Cairo.

By the autumn of 2002, our "allies"—the French, Germans, and most of "Old Europe"—were using every forum they could find to decry the Bush administration's "rush to war" in Iraq. Encouraged by massive anti-American protests on the streets of European capitals, President Jacques Chirac and Chancellor Gerhard Schroeder repeatedly urged the United States and Great Britain to delay plans for military action against Saddam until the UN's super-sleuth, Hans Blix, had "completed" his search for weapons of mass destruction (WMD) in Iraq.

U.S. chemical experts of the 101st Airborne Division examine a pod that may have been intended as a delivery system for a chemical-biological agent

WMD: THE CASUS BELLI

★ ★ ★ ★ ★ ★ ★ ★ ★ ★ ★ ★ ★

The search for nuclear, chemical, and biological WMDs in Iraq was significantly hindered by Saddam's response to UN-mandated inspections: deceit, denial, and deception. It was a stance that President Bush deemed to be simply unacceptable. That's what he told the United Nations General Assembly when he addressed the body on 12 September 2002, a year and a day after the 9/11 attacks. He asked the UN for a clear deadline for compliance. France and Russia refused to allow the resolution to pass the Security Council.

NORTHERN KUWAIT – Marines of Charlie Company, 1st Bn, 5th Marines, 5th Regimental Combat Team, take cover wearing MOPP level-4 gear

A week after the president noted that Saddam was defying over a dozen Security Council resolutions, Saddam invited UN weapons inspectors back to Iraq. Skeptics—and I was certainly one of them—pointed out that UN Security Council Resolution 687, passed in 1991, compelled Iraq to unconditionally accept weapons inspectors. Yet, since 1994, Iraqi authorities had

Monday, 2 December 2002

President Bush:

"The inspectors are not in Iraq to play hide-and-seek with Saddam Hussein."

consistently impeded UN access to its military and research facilities. UN inspectors in Iraq had been fired upon, assaulted, stripped of incriminating documents, and denied both air and vehicular access to "sensitive" areas. In 1997, Iraq even banned Americans from participating in UN inspections.

None of this background moved the Europeans to action, but it did convince a majority in Congress. On 10 October 2002, a bill authorizing the president to use military force against Iraq passed the House of Representatives by a vote of 296 to 133. The Senate voted for the measure 77 to 23. Still, the UN refused to "resolve" that the use of military force was necessary to bring Saddam into "compliance."

Instead, on 8 November the UN Security Council passed Resolution 1441, requiring Iraq to provide weapons inspectors with "immediate, unimpeded, unconditional, and unrestricted access" to suspected weapons sites. The resolution also created yet a new entity to determine whether Saddam was breaking the rules—the United Nations Monitoring, Verification, and Inspection Commission (UNMOVIC). By December the "weapons inspectors" were supposedly hard at work and declared that they had "earned the cooperation" of the Iraqi regime and had even gone "unannounced and unopposed" into one of Saddam's palaces.

Hans Blix

Heading the UNMOVIC "inspection teams" was Hans Blix, a Swedish diplomat and outspoken opponent of military action aimed at removing Saddam. The ever-so-courteous, always smiling Blix insisted on inspecting Iraq from his luxurious UN offices in New York City. It was, after all, holiday season in the Big Apple. And in Iraq, it was Ramadan, a tough time of the year to get a glass of wine and good cheese in a Muslim country.

But it wasn't just his penchant for the good life that raised concerns about Blix. He had earlier served as director general of the International Atomic Energy Agency during the very years that Iraq's blooming nuclear weapons program went undetected.

In his zeal to avoid offending the brutal regime in Baghdad, Blix referred to them as his "hosts." He minimized the involvement of experienced American and British inspectors with UNMOVIC because the Iraqis complained that they were "too aggressive in their disarmament searches." To replace U.S. and British experts on nuclear, biological, and chemical weapons, Blix launched an international affirmative action hiring program to recruit Chinese, Russian, and Chilean inspectors—but few with specialized expertise in the arcane sciences of "bugs, gas, and nukes."

One of the few Americans he did find attractive enough to put on his team had a two-year, community college degree in security management. His résumé included sadomasochistic sex groups, teaching courses on "sex slaves," and proficiency in "bondage" techniques. Given what we now know of Saddam's torture chambers, one wonders at the reaction of the Iraqi despot when he learned of this particular inspector's extracurricular activities.

There is considerable question as to whether the UNMOVIC "inspection team" would even have known what they were seeing if Saddam had left it all on display. Dr. Raymond Zilinskas, at the time director of the Chemical and Biological Weapons Nonproliferation Program at the Center for Nonproliferation Studies, told me, "If UNMOVIC lacks specialized scientific expertise in biochemistry, nuclear physics, microbiology, and 'weaponization' of biological and chemical agents, the inspectors might never know what the Iraqis have or don't have."

"Dr. Z" had been to Iraq before, as a bio-weapons expert with the UN Special Commission (UNSCOM). In 1994 he inspected sixty-one Iraqi biological research and production facilities and built a database on Iraq's "dual use" biological equipment. When I asked if his advice had been sought for UNMOVIC, he replied, "No."

On 5 February 2003, with tens of thousands of U.S. and British combat troops and aircraft already in Kuwait and more on the way, Secretary of State Colin Powell made a dramatic speech before the United Nations, laying out the case for military operations to remove Saddam Hussein. With George Tenant, director of the Central Intelligence Agency, seated behind him, Powell used satellite photos, diagrams of chemical and biological weapons facilities, and transcribed intercepts of Iraqi communications to describe the threat posed by an Iraqi despot armed with weapons of mass destruction.

Former Secretary of State Colin Powell makes his case before the U.S. Security Council, 5 February 2003

In his "bill of particulars" against Saddam's brutal regime, Powell emphasized that Saddam had already used these weapons against Iran and his own Kurdish population in northern Iraq. The intelligence on Saddam's chemical, biological, and nuclear weapons programs was ambiguous, as intelligence often is. But at its core, the case against Saddam rested on the need to prevent the Iraqi dictator from ever using these kinds of weapons again. This justification for military action would prove to be the first mistake of the campaign to bring down the "Butcher of Baghdad." It was also unnecessary because there were plenty of other reasons to remove this brutal regime.

By the time Colin Powell made his presentation, everyone knew that in 1993 Saddam had tried to assassinate former President George Bush and the emir of Kuwait. The UN and our Congress were aware that the Iraqi dictator had long provided material assistance to radical Islamic terrorist organizations such as the Palestine Liberation Front and the Abu Nidal organization and that he had granted refuge to Abul Abbas, the mastermind behind the hijacking of the cruise ship *Achille Lauro* and the murderer of Leon Klinghoffer. Saddam had publicly bragged that he was paying a $25,000 cash bounty to the families of Palestinian suicide terrorists.

The U.S. Congress and the UN both had a detailed British government report on crimes and human rights abuses in Iraq. The conclusions were horrific: "Torture is systematic. . . . Executions are carried out without due process of law. . . . Relatives are often prevented from burying the victims and have even been charged for the bullets used." An appendix chronicled some of the methods of torture, including rape, eye-gouging, piercing hands with an electric drill, acid baths, and electric shock.

When Operation Iraqi Freedom was finally launched on 20 March 2003, it was—in the words of one of the Marines I interviewed for FOX News—"the most telegraphed punch in military history." Saddam Hussein had been given more than seven months to destroy, remove, or hide anything he wanted before U.S. and British troops arrived on his doorstep.

After the shooting stopped, top U.S. weapons inspector David Kay reported that his investigators had uncovered widespread evidence of unreported biological and chemical weapons programs that had been concealed from UN inspectors. In the words of Dr. Kay: "Iraq's WMD programs spanned more than two decades, involved thousands of people, billions of dollars, and were elaborately shielded by security and deception operations that continued even beyond the end of Operation Iraqi Freedom."

The report stated that "over two dozen laboratories that were hidden in the Iraqi intelligence service . . . had prohibited equipment, and . . . at the minimum, kept alive Iraq's capability to produce both biological and chemical weapons." But Dr. Kay also noted that much of the evidence of WMD "was irretrievably lost" because prior to the war there was "deliberate dispersal and destruction of material and docu-mentation related to weapons programs."

Critics who complain that Iraq became "the central front in the war on terror" miss the gruesome point that it is much easier to kill and capture terrorists if there is a central front. In short, though it isn't politically correct to say it, it's better to battle terrorists in Baghdad than in Boston.

In 2002, Iraq had more than a dozen facilities capable of producing chemical weapons

PREPARING FOR THE ROAD TO BAGHDAD

★ ★ ★ ★ ★ ★ ★ ★ ★ ★ ★ ★

My "embed" orders from FOX News came in the form of an e-mail on 4 March 2003. Two days later I was in Kuwait joining a team of FOX News professionals who were already there. Griff Jenkins, my indomitable camera-man, field producer, and friend, had preceded me by several days. He met me at the airport. That night we were warmly greeted by Don Fair, the hard-nosed FOX bureau

On the flight line in Kuwait

chief in Kuwait. Don took us to the rooftop "studio" he had set up atop the Marriott Hotel.

Two other FOX News "embed teams"—Greg Kelly's and Rick Leventhal's—had been on site for almost two weeks. They were already getting used to the routine of nightly air-raid and chemical attack warnings as Saddam fired SCUD missiles into the country he had once occupied. After my first trip to the hotel's crowded basement "bomb shelter," I decided that the next time I heard the siren wail, I would go to a safer place—our far less crowded rooftop "studio"—instead of heading to the cellar. Eventually others caught on to my trick, and it got to be overcrowded on the roof. I took to sleeping in the bathtub with my gas mask at my side.

Several days were consumed with briefings by Central Command public affairs officers, medical officers, and military lawyers. More than seven hundred U.S. and foreign correspondents had applied for credentials to cover what everyone believed would be the imminent beginning of hostilities.

The assembled hoard of reporters, producers, and technicians were all offered inoculations against anthrax and smallpox, two of the diseases Saddam was believed to have in his "bugs" arsenal. Then we were all led outside and issued chemical protective suits and gas masks. Suddenly the otherwise jocular members of the media were deadly serious.

The possibility of being exposed to chemical weapons was only marginally worse than wearing these protective suits in temperatures above 100 degrees

On 11 March we were given the opportunity to go out into the Kuwaiti desert to visit the troops we would be covering. Griff and I headed out to Tactical Assembly Area (TAA) "Ripper," temporary home to one of the U.S. Marine regimental combat teams (RCTs) preparing for the assault into Iraq. Ripper was a dusty, dun–colored, tent city parked on a barren, flat, wind-blown plain, lacking vegetation and any recognizable terrain features.

The weeks of waiting for the invasion to start were used wisely— here soldiers of the 3rd ID train in the Kuwaiti desert

Without a global positioning system (GPS) receiver, it would be impossible to know where you were or where you were going. It was the temporary home of the fabled 7th Marine Regiment that was expected to be the "tip of the spear" for the First Marine Expeditionary Force (I MEF) in the upcoming attack.

The Marines in this arid southwest Asian desert were blissfully unaware of the political machinations at the United Nations that had held them there for more than a month, poised like a diver prepared for a plunge at the end of the board. And they couldn't have cared less about the protestations of the "Blame America First" crowd in San Francisco or various European cities. They did know that the French had "wimped out" once again. One Marine quipped to a visiting journalist, "The French have always been there when they needed us."

Despite the delay in getting done what they had come to do, it was apparent that these young warriors revered their commander in chief. And whether the nice folks at the UN or the critics in Europe or the anti-war activists in the U.S. liked it or not, they had a refreshing certainty about their mission—Saddam Hussein and the need to evict him from Iraq.

Contrary to how they were being depicted, these troops weren't "poor, uneducated, minorities," as some liberal politicians had alleged in propounding a reinstitution of conscription. The all-volunteer troops at TAA Ripper were predominantly white, middle-income Americans. Minorities were then—and still are—under-represented in these units, and nearly 100 percent are high school graduates.

Their "mission focus" wasn't because they had been "brainwashed" by their superiors. During a briefing by an intelligence officer, the troops asked penetrating questions and got honest answers about what they were about to face. Nor were they "bloodthirsty," as a foreign journalist described them to me. In fact, none of the soldiers, sailors, airmen, or Marines with whom I spoke told me they were "itching for a fight."

What many of the media elites covering the preparations for the gunfight in Iraq missed is that no one who has ever *really* been to a war ever wants to see another one. And a remarkable percentage of the young men at TAA Ripper already had combat experience. One commander estimated that more than half of his officers and senior noncommissioned officers (NCOs) had served under fire before—in the first Gulf War, the Balkans, or Afghanistan—and in some cases all three. They knew better than any correspondent, reporter, or politician the true nature of war—that it is the most terrible of human endeavors.

Yet, precisely because so many of them had so much combat experience, they were anxious to get on with the task at hand. They knew that the sooner it got started, the sooner it would be over. Many of them expressed frustration that what was supposed to be a "blitzkrieg" had become a "sitzkrieg."

Soldiers from the 3rd ID zero their battle sights in Kuwait before the invasion

And that wasn't the only problem with the delay. A "Recon Marine"—one of those whose job it was to penetrate deep inside enemy territory to scout out the routes, objectives, and enemy targets to be hit—said, "It's a new moon. We do our best work under conditions of marginal visibility. We don't like to operate when the moon is like a big light bulb in the night sky."

Another concern was expressed by an NBC officer, one of those responsible for ensuring that the Marines survived an attack from weapons of mass destruction. His comment: "The longer we wait, the longer Saddam has to plot and carry out a chemical, biological, or nuclear attack. And the hotter it's going to be wearing those protective suits and masks."

They weren't whining or complaining; their comments were just common sense. But even this was apparently misunderstood by some of those sent out to cover this high-risk venture. For reasons that escaped most Marines, the Pentagon provided press credentials to a significant number of foreign journalists. Unfortunately, many of the international media appeared to have an overt hostility toward the subjects they were sent to cover.

One female correspondent from a European news service was overheard asking—or was it telling?—one of the Marines that she had "never seen so much bravado, machismo, or arrogance" in her life. The young NCO listened and appeared to mull over her grievance before replying, "Yes ma'am, that's why they call themselves U.S. Marines."

FOX News cameraman Mal James became popular when he sent images of U.S. troops back home

EMBEDDED–FINALLY

★　★　★　★　★　★　★　★　★　★　★　★

On 13 March we were at last loaded on Kuwaiti civilian buses, surrounded by armed Kuwaiti Interior Ministry troops and police to protect us from rumored Iraqi terrorist attacks. Then we were driven out to the units with which we would be embedded for the opening phase of hostilities. I incorrectly assumed that since I had been a Marine infantry officer, I would be assigned to cover a Marine or Army ground combat unit. Instead, I was told that I would be embedded with a Marine Medium Helicopter Squadron—HMM-268, the "Red Dragons." It turned out to be a fortuitous assignment.

When Griff Jenkins and I arrived at HMM-268's forward operating base, we were immediately given a set of guidelines governing what we could and could not

Ready to begin the embed

report. As in all past wars, someone "up the chain of command" had decided what the media could or could not say, print, or show their readers and viewers. All of us, in the Fourth Estate accompanying the combat units being assembled on the Iraqi periphery, were admonished not to report exact unit troop strength figures, any future plans, or details of various weapons systems. In deference to Kuwaiti sensitivities, we were also directed not to specify our exact location—Ali al Salim Air Base—until we had "departed" for Iraq. Instead, we were "asked" to euphemistically describe the Kuwaiti air base as "in the vicinity of the Iraqi border."

Quite understandably, we were not permitted to report where we were going, or when. For some media people, these restrictions undermined what they considered the "freedom of the press." But most understood the rationale for these limitations and willingly complied. For those who found the burden of "self-censorship" too onerous, they could always "un-volunteer" and go home. That option, of course, didn't apply to another group of volunteers—the soldiers, sailors, airmen, and Marines, more than 200,000 strong—who were deployed in the trackless desert along the Iraqi border.

Two months before Griff and I joined them, the 250 Red Dragons of HMM-268 had been at Camp Pendleton, California, without any particular plans to travel. Then, on

10 January, the word came down: "Prepare your aircraft for immediate embarkation." Four days later the squadron's twelve CH-46 helicopters, their blades removed, were all packed and sealed, and on 15 January, the aging aircraft were lifted aboard a commercial ship in San Diego.

Mal James took this photo of me in a CH-46 over Iraq

Accompanying the "birds" was a detachment of a dozen HMM-268 Marines, led by a sergeant. "Now think of this," said 1st Lt. Ken Williamson, one of the squadron's pilots. "Here's a shipment worth more than sixty million dollars being signed for by a twenty-two-year-old Marine sergeant. Where else would you get that kind of responsibility at that age?" Where else indeed?

The rest of the squadron departed California at midnight on 9 February. For reasons still inexplicable to this old Leatherneck, the U.S. Marines never go anywhere in daylight. When they arrived "in country" on 11 February, the entire unit—officers and enlisted alike—pitched in to "build tents and fill sandbags, more than twenty thousand, that first week alone," said CWO Sean Wennes.

"Why so many sandbags?" asked one of the hoard of media that descended on this remote desert air base. "Because these tents don't even stop a sandstorm. They sure

won't stop a Scud," replied Cpl Phillip Sapio. "Sometimes a sandbag is all you have between us and them." By "them," of course, the Marine meant the Iraqis, who had denied having any of the long-range weapons capable of carrying conventional, chemical, or biological warheads into the heart of this desert base.

CH-46 helicopters from Marine Medium Helicopter Squadron 268

"Six hours after the helicopters arrived in port, they had been stripped of the weather-proof covers, had their rotor blades replaced, and were ready for flight," said Lt. Williamson. "Some people think that's extraordinary. And maybe for some organizations it would be, but for these Marines, it's what we do for a living," he added.

But picking up and moving isn't the only thing that Marines do for a living. They must also be prepared to fight when they get to where they are going. The Red Dragon helicopters had to be ready at a moment's notice to carry Marine infantry in a helicopter-borne assault, resupply units in contact, insert reconnaissance units deep into Iraq, and evacuate casualties. That meant their "Phrogs"—the nickname Marines gave these twin-rotor helicopters nearly forty years ago—must be constantly maintained, around the clock. In a sandstorm, that's hard to do.

On our second night with the squadron, a vicious sandstorm blew in from the northwest, carrying fine particles of sand all the way from the Saudi desert. This sudden sandstorm—the locals called it a *shamal*—was unlike any other kind of weather I've ever experienced. The wind literally blanketed the place with a fine dust that obscured and covered everything. It added an additional challenge for the troops who had to try to protect and clean the sophisticated computers, jet engines, and weapons that were coated with sand.

The howling wind, blowing across the dry, flat moonscape, flattened tents and filled the air with dust, making the thought of home even more attractive than usual. Life in this extreme climate and terrain prompted a longing for being anywhere without sand. One of the Marines received a rousing chorus of "Right on!" when he declared, "I don't think I'll go to the beach again for the rest of my life."

Marine maintenance technicians donned gas masks so they could work on aircraft in conditions that could only be politely described as "extreme." The dust storm filled the air with an orange haze that had the strange effect of turning daylight into dusk, blotting out the sun and changing the hue of every man and machine. Visibility was reduced to less than twenty yards. The wind, blowing steadily at twenty-five to thirty knots, howled like a banshee through the antenna guy wires.

A sandstorm approaches a U.S. air base

The "fog"—tiny particles of sand—got inhaled with every breath and swallowed with every mouthful of food. The fine dust whipped in beneath the sidewalls and portals of the tents. It jammed weapons. It seeped into every crevice and clogged the intakes of jet engines and the filters of the gas masks everyone carried everywhere, all the time.

Surveying the fury of the dust storm, one of the correspondents asked Lt. Williamson if the dust and dirt would affect the performance of his aircraft. The Marine veteran, tongue planted firmly in his cheek, replied, "Dust storms aren't allowed to affect us. It's contrary to Marine Corps policy."

GOOD TO GO

★ ★ ★ ★ ★ ★ ★ ★ ★ ★ ★ ★

The *shamal* lasted thirty-six hours. As soon as it passed, GySgt Dennis Pennington, a weapons and tactics instructor, took action. He arranged to fly all the helicopter gunners—the Marines who man the .50-caliber machine guns mounted on the left and right sides of the CH-46 helicopters—out to the Udari range so they could test-fire every weapon in the squadron armory. Griff and I videotaped the entire exercise as "Gunny" Pennington, a very experienced combat veteran, coached young Marines—who had never fired a shot in combat on rules of engagement—how to lead a target and the best way to protect a helicopter that has to land in a "hot" LZ. They came back sweaty, dirty, and tired but confident that they would be ready when the shooting started. Gunny Pennington's encouraging assessment: "They know what to do and they know how to do it."

On Sunday, 16 March, President Bush met in the Azores with Prime Minister Tony

Blair of the United Kingdom, President José Maria Aznar of Spain, and Prime Minister José Manuel Durao Barroso of Portugal. The four heads of state issued a communiqué, declaring that diplomatic efforts to convince Saddam to come clean on his weapons of mass destruction would end in twenty-four hours.

By Monday, 17 March, all the pilots and aircrews slated to fly into Iraq had been briefed by intelligence officers inside the Marine Air Group (MAG) 39 Air Operations Center. This was a partitioned area inside the steel building next to the squadron ready room tents. The Air Group S-3 then issued a detailed Operations Order and the Survival, Escape, Resistance, and Evasion (SERE) plan in the event an aircraft went down behind enemy lines. After all this, the Air Group S-1 had them all update their next-of-kin (NOK) information.

Sandstorms did what the enemy could not: put a stop to all sorties by U.S. helicopters

As the pilots and air crews departed the operations center, there was no back-slapping or joking around. Nothing focuses the mind of a Marine like a NOK form. It contains the details of who is to be informed, and how, when a Marine is killed, wounded, or missing in action.

That evening in Washington—it was 0300 in Iraq—dozens of Marines gathered around our little FOX News satellite transceiver to hear their commander in chief address the American people. When he said that the time had come for Saddam Hussein and his sons to leave Iraq and gave them forty-eight hours to do so, heads nodded in agreement, but nobody said a word. There was a similar reaction when the president said, "Their refusal to do so will result in military conflict, commenced at a time of our choosing." Nobody spoke when he added, "The tyrant will soon be gone."

No one in the hushed gathering commented on his statement that "the Iraqi regime has used diplomacy to gain time and advantage" and that "diplomacy can't go on forever in the face of a global threat." And when President Bush promised the Iraqi people, "The day of your liberation is near," I watched several of those who would have to make good on this commitment simply pat the back of the Marine nearest them.

As the president closed with his customary "May God continue to bless America," he looked grim. So did the Marines who had just heard him speak. Without so much as a word, the crowd broke up and went back to their duties or to sleep.

At 0800 on Tuesday, 18 March, Lt. Col. Jerry Driscoll, the Red Dragons commanding officer, summoned all the squadron pilots and air crews to a briefing in the squadron ready room. There, he assigned missions for the opening of hostilities. "When the order comes down," he said, "HMM-268 will be the lead air element carrying British Royal Marine Commandos into the attack on the Faw Peninsula." The squadron was also ordered to conduct inserts and extracts of reconnaissance units well inside Iraq and "cas-evac" missions—the evacuation of casualties from fire-swept "hot" LZs.

Driscoll told his pilots and air crews to go over their survival gear and get some rest in the hours ahead. He then ordered the maintenance crews to complete final checks on the Phrogs for any last-minute mechanical, hydraulic, electronic, or ordnance problems. The Red Dragon "wrench turners" and crew chiefs had been working around the clock, in fair weather and foul, looking after the aging birds.

By noon the desert sun was making bubbles on the flight-line tarmac and turning the skin of the aircraft into griddles that seared exposed flesh. That didn't stop the flight-line crews and mechanics from going over each aircraft with a fine-tooth comb.

Many of the Marines and Navy medical corpsmen took time to write to spouses, family members, and loved ones back home. Because of our satellite feed, the troops knew that back in the United States there were unfounded reports that the troops gathered on Iraq's borders were unprepared and ill equipped for the mission ahead. A bevy of "experts," including former generals and admirals, added fuel to this fire by claiming that our chemical protective suits wouldn't work, that there were insufficient troops, weapons, or equipment to take on Saddam's 480,000-man military.

Time spent in Kuwait before the invasion wasn't wasted; troops trained relentlessly to be ready when the order came to move

After weeks of waiting, U.S. troops were ready to get "boots on the ground" in Iraq

Some—including many who should have known better—suggested that it would take "at least three months" and "ten thousand or more U.S. casualties" to take Baghdad.

By Wednesday, 19 March 2003, the only information we were getting from the "outside world" was via our FOX News satellite transceiver. That's how we learned that the British Parliament, by a vote of 412 to 149, had approved the use of military force to disarm Iraq and oust its leader. It's

Marine air crews work to ready their CH-46 helicopters

also how we knew that British and American aircraft flying over Iraq were now dropping leaflets stating that war could start at any time and how we learned that UN Secretary General Kofi Annan, French President Jacques Chirac, and German Chancellor Gerhard Schroeder were all making last-ditch efforts to prevent military action against Saddam. Apparently the leaflets were more persuasive than the diplomats for some Iraqis. Late in the morning of the 19th, seventeen Iraqi soldiers surrendered to American troops deployed at a Kuwaiti border checkpoint.

Late that night we received a call, on our satellite phone from the FOX foreign desk, telling us that we should come up on our satellite link for an address to the nation by President Bush and to be prepared to provide "reaction" commentary.

As soon as we set up our satellite equipment, we were surrounded by Marines of all ranks, waiting to see their commander in chief address their countrymen about war. When President Bush said that the "opening stages of what will be a broad and concerted campaign" to liberate Iraq had begun, someone in the group muttered emphatically, "Finally!"

Calling in a report via satphone on the way to Baghdad

A U.S. Marine F/A-18 launches off the flight deck of a carrier in the Persian Gulf to strike at targets in Iraq

That was it. There was no cheering or back-slapping. When the president said, "The peace of a troubled world and the hopes of an oppressed people now depend on you," he was speaking directly to the pilots and air crews around me. The words themselves did not convey a particular sense of foreboding, but I did make time before dawn to take out the Bible I carry in my pack and read from it for a while. I did not know that within hours four of the men around me would be dead—the first American casualties of Operation Iraqi Freedom.

19 March 2003
President George W. Bush:

"The peace of a troubled world and the hopes of an oppressed people now depend on you."

CAMP DOHA, KUWAIT – Operators and planners worked around the clock at the Coalition Forces Land Component Command's Operations and Intelligence Center

4

HOSTILITIES HAVE COMMENCED

19 March 2003

Ali al-Salim Air Base, Kuwait

The president's announcement that the campaign to liberate Iraq was underway had little visible effect on the routine at Ali al-Salim Air Base. Bomb-laden British Tornado fighter-bombers continued to roar off the runway throughout the night and return empty. The Marines of HMM-268 were told that the ground offensive would commence after twenty-four hours of continuous bombing, and they simply continued their preparations. But in Iraq, the world had changed completely.

The first strike was carried out by two USAF F-117 Nighthawk stealth aircraft armed with two-thousand-pound, bunker-buster EGBU-27 guided bombs, steered to the precise location by GPS technology. The target was the Dora Command and Control Complex, underground concrete bunkers designed to protect Saddam's Baath Party

F-117 Nighthawk stealth aircraft

elites. An intelligence source claimed to have seen the Iraqi dictator and his sons Uday and Qusay entering the facility.

The F-117 raid was followed over the next thirty-six hours by waves of sea-launched Tomahawk cruise missiles, launched out of the Persian Gulf by the USS *McCain,* USS *Columbia,* USS *Providence,* USS *Milius,* USS *Donald Cook,* USS *Bunker Hill,* USS *Cowpens,* USS *Montpelier,* USS *Cheyenne,* and the Royal Navy's HMS *Splendid* and HMS *Turbulent.* The cruise missiles and precision strikes by guided bombs dropped from B-1s, B-2s, F/A-18s, and Tornados took out the entire Iraqi air defense system. Not a single aircraft from Saddam's air force got off the ground.

Above – U.S. warships launched Tomahawk Cruise missiles as part of the "Shock and Awe" campaign

Below – An F/A-18 Hornet returns from a combat mission over Iraq

Lt. Gen. James Conway

Shortly after the airstrikes began, Lt. Gen. James Conway, the commander of I MEF; Maj. Gen. James Amos, commanding the 3rd Marine Aircraft Wing (Reinforced); and Maj. Gen. Jim Mattis, commander of the 1st Marine Division (Reinforced), all issued guidance to those they were leading into battle. Copies of the 1st Marine Division commander's eloquent message were widely distributed to all hands:

"For decades, Saddam Hussein has tortured, imprisoned, raped, and murdered the Iraqi people; invaded neighboring countries without provocation; and threatened the world with weapons of mass destruction. The time has come to end his reign of terror. On your young shoulders rests the hope of mankind.

"When I give you the word, together we will cross the line of departure, close with those forces that choose to fight, and destroy them. Our fight is not with the Iraqi people, nor is it with members of the Iraqi army who choose to surrender. While we will move swiftly and aggressively against those who resist, we will treat all others with decency, demonstrating chivalry and soldierly compassion for people who have endured a lifetime under Saddam's oppression.

"Chemical attack, treachery, and use of the innocent as human shields can be expected, as can other unethical tactics. Be the hunter—not the hunted. Never be caught with your guard down. Use good judgment and act in the best interest of our nation.

"You are part of the world's most feared and trusted fighting force. Engage your brain before you engage your weapon. Share your courage with each other as we enter Iraq. Keep faith in your comrades to your left and right and in the Marine Air overhead . . . . For the mission's sake, for our country's sake, and the sake of the men who carried the division's colors in past battles—'who fought for life and never lost their nerve'—carry out your mission and keep your honor clean. Demonstrate to the world there is 'No Better Friend—No Worse Enemy' than a U.S. Marine."

—Major General James Mattis, Commanding General, 1st Marine Division, 20 March 2003

Strangely, the U.S. and British air attacks did not target the Baghdad electrical grid or the Iraqi Information Ministry. Al Jazeera, the Arabic-language satellite television network so supportive of Osama bin Laden, remained on the air, accusing U.S. and British bombs of killing innocent Iraqi civilians.

Baghdad Bob

Television signals beamed from Baghdad carried statements by the Iraqi minister of information, Mohammed Saeed al-Sahaf that, "the enemies of God committed the stupidity of aggression against our homeland and our people." "Baghdad Bob," as the troops referred to him, also broadcast calls for the Saddam *fedayeen*—paramilitary fighters from all over the Islamic world—to defend Iraq. These "holy warriors" were urged to be "ready to die as martyrs" while "destroying the American and British invaders."

Hearing this, one of the pilots who was huddled around our tiny FOX News satellite transceiver commented to no one in particular, "That's not good. We should have taken that guy off the air." At the time this pilot said it, we had no idea how right he was.

INTO THE FIGHT

★ ★ ★ ★ ★ ★ ★ ★ ★ ★ ★ ★

THURSDAY, 20 MARCH 2003

The sun was just setting as the eight CH-46s from HMM-268 landed at TAA Gibraltar, a British base just a few kilometers from the Iraqi border. Shortly after we touched down, dozens of other helicopters landed around us, until all that could be seen were helicopters—U.S. Marine CH-46s, CH-53s, UH-1Ns, heavily armed Cobras, British Pumas and CH-47s, all dispersed on the desert floor.

CH-46 Sea Knight helicopters prepare for a night mission

We flew to the remote outpost at 120 knots and less than fifty feet off the ground from Ali al-Salim Air Base. At such a low altitude we could see convoys of tanks, armored vehicles, artillery pieces, trucks, and Humvees all racing north toward the border with Iraq. As we approached our landing point, batteries of 155-mm howitzers were deploying in firing order. The war had been "on" for fourteen hours, and yet for us it had been a strangely surreal day.

At about 0930 local time, the "Great Giant Voice" announced that a missile raid was inbound and we ran for the shelters with our gas masks. Once again, Griff couldn't find his. About the time that the Patriot batteries opened fire on the incoming Iraqi missiles, he found it and came dashing into the bunker.

A U.S. Army armored phalanx headed for Baghdad

Right after the "all clear" from the SCUD attack, we loaded all our cameras, satellite broadcast equipment, and personal gear aboard two of the squadron's CH-46s. HMM-268 had been given the mission of carrying Royal Marine commandos in a helicopter-borne assault to seize the Faw Peninsula before Saddam's forces could cut oil flow to Basra. Lt. Col. Jerry Driscoll, the squadron commander, assigned himself the responsibility of flying lead for two, four-plane divisions full of troops. With Driscoll's concurrence, I was given a space on his helicopter and Griff was put aboard Dash Three, the third helicopter in the flight of eight.

By nightfall, there were more than fifty U.S. and British helicopters on the ground at TAA Gibraltar. As crew chiefs and gunners made final checks on their "birds," the pilots assembled for a final briefing. While the Royal Marines going on the mission rested on their rucksacks, I crawled up on one of the helicopter's stub wings to eat an MRE (meal, ready to eat), drink some water, and say a quiet prayer. Long ago I learned that it's wise to eat, drink, pray, and sleep when you can; once the shooting starts you may not have time to do any of these things.

The following accounts are from dispatches I filed as the units with which I was embedded entered Iraq and fought their way to Baghdad and beyond.

HELICOPTER DOWN!

★ ★ ★ ★ ★ ★ ★ ★ ★ ★ ★ ★

FRIDAY, 21 MARCH 2003

It is nearly midnight, and the silence here on the desert floor is being punctuated by the thunder of 155-mm artillery and multiple rocket launchers, firing off in the distance to the north. With darkness settled in around us, the flash of the guns and occasionally the arc of rocket-assisted projectiles (RAP rounds) can be seen on the horizon. Lying or sitting on the ground, one can feel the concussions. These prompted one of the British Royal Marines to comment, "Pity the poor bloke who's on the receiving end of that."

One of his less experienced mates asks no one in particular, "Is that ours or theirs?"

When no one responds I reply, "It's ours. That's the 11th Marines, firing a Regimental TOT (Time on Target) on Safwan Hill, clearing the way for the 5th and 7th Marines to cross the berm into Iraq."

Safwan Hill is a pile of sandstone that dominates the terrain just north of the Iraq-Kuwait border. It appears on the aviation chart I'm carrying simply as "466," but it is believed to be an Iraqi observation post. From the hill, just west of the Iraqi border town of Safwan, the Iraqi army can undoubtedly observe and bring fire to bear on any of the

1st Marine Division's twenty-two thousand troops and several thousand combat vehicles as they break through the berm along the demilitarized zone on the attack north.

According to the scuttlebutt among the troops, Maj. Gen. Mattis, the division commander, has ordered that the hill be "a foot shorter" before the 1st Marines cross into Iraq. The 11th Marines' artillery and strike aircraft from Navy carriers in the Persian Gulf and Ahmed Al Jaber Air Base in Kuwait are trying to comply by dumping tons of high explosives on the target.

U.S. Army engineers use bulldozers to create a breach in the berm built by the Iraqis on the border of Kuwait

At the MAG-39 Forward Operations Center, set up beside a UH-1N helicopter about 150 yards behind our helicopter, one of the communicators confirms that all is going according to the modified plan, even though the H-hour for the ground attack had to be advanced twelve hours because of the unscheduled "decapitation" strike on the Dora Command Center. Until 19 March, General Franks's plan of attack had called for a simultaneous air and ground strike, designed to deceive the Iraqis who were anticipating another prolonged air assault like the thirty-eight-day bombardment that had preceded the ground attack during Operation Desert Storm in 1991. Officers at Central Command had taken to talking openly about the "shock and awe" of an air campaign as though it would go on for days before any ground troops crossed the border.

Instead, Franks had agreed that coincident air and ground attacks would take place just before dawn on 21 March. But once Baghdad had been hit, waiting longer for the ground attack seemed to the Marines like an invitation for Saddam loyalists to start destroying the country's oil infrastructure. So at 2030 hours local, on 20 March, RCT-5 and RCT-7 were given the order to blast through the berm west of Safwan and head north, making them the first ground combat unit to put "boots on the ground" inside Iraq. It wasn't, however, the first contact with the enemy. Earlier in the afternoon, at about 1600 hours local, elements of the 3rd Light Armored Reconnaissance (LAR) Bn, serving as a screening force for RCT-7, had engaged several Iraqi APCs (armored personnel carriers) south of the Iraq-Kuwait border. FOX News correspondent Rick Leventhal, embedded with the 3rd LAR, reported that the Marine Light Armored Vehicle (LAV) 25s had promptly dispatched the enemy vehicles using TOW anti-tank missiles and the 25-mm chain guns mounted on the LAVs.

After a two-hour barrage, the big guns have fallen silent. In the darkness, all but invisible from less than three kilometers away, we can hear hundreds of armored vehicles and trucks, moving without lights, echoing across the desert as RCT-7 moves up for the attack. The first mission for RCT-5 and RCT-7 is to drive straight past Safwan and north to seize the vital Rumaylah oil fields, GOSPs (gas-oil separation plants), and pumping stations near Az Zubayr before the Iraqis can destroy them.

A slight wind has come up, blowing a light cloud of dust and smoke our way as the word comes down to "saddle up" and launch. While the Royal Marines gather their gear and start boarding their assigned helicopters, Griff and I shake hands and give each other a silent hug. Then we each head to our respective aircraft to grab our cameras so we can start recording this first assault deep into Iraq.

After discussing the matter with Lt. Col. Driscoll and Maj. Chris Charleville, the HMM-268 operations officer, we have agreed that Griff and I will fly on different helicopters. By doing so, we'll minimize interference with ground combat element load plans and spread out the weight and space requirements for our satellite equipment and camera gear. But there is another reason for splitting up our two-man team that no one mentions: if a helicopter goes down, we can be reasonably sure that half of our videotape and one of us will survive to tell the story.

Embedded journalists faced the same dangers as the troops

Marines rearm and refuel an AH-64 Cobra helicopter at a forward arming and refueling point (FARP) on the way to Baghdad

Ten commandos, including the Royal Marine battalion commander, all carrying heavy packs and weapons, cram themselves into my aircraft. Many of these Brits have seen action before—some of them in the Falklands back in 1981, others in Northern Ireland, Gulf War I, Bosnia, and Kosovo—and some of the oldest have served in all of these difficult and dangerous places. But tonight's mission may well be their toughest. If all goes as planned, this lightly armed infantry battalion will disembark north of Basra, Iraq's second largest city, and establish a blocking position. Their goal: to keep enemy reinforcements from reaching the Basra garrison—believed to be elements of the Iraqi 51st Mechanized Division and a Republican Guard regiment.

Other elements of the British 3rd Commando Brigade and the American 15th MEU are to capture the oil port at Umm Qasr, just across the Kuwaiti border about thirty miles south of Basra, while Navy SEALs, Royal Marines, and British Special Operations units coming in from the Persian Gulf seize the oil terminals at Ma'amir and Al Faw. This complicated, high-speed operation is aimed at preventing the destruction of Iraq's oil wells and infrastructure and the kind of catastrophe that Saddam wreaked on Kuwait and the waters of the Persian Gulf back in 1991.

GySgt Dennis Pennington, Lt. Col. Driscoll's crew chief, checks the troops to make sure they are all strapped in. I climb through the forward personnel door, grab my tiny digital camera with its night-vision lens, and fasten a gunner's belt around my flak jacket, high on my chest. With the gunner's belt tethered to a tie-down on the deck of the helicopter,

Side gunners use .50-caliber machine guns to protect their choppers from ground fire

I can move about inside the troop compartment and still step forward into the cockpit between the pilot and copilot or even lean out the right side personnel door hatch, just forward of the .50-caliber mount. To ensure that I can hear and record radio and intercom communications, Pennington has rigged up a "cranial" helmet for me and hooked it into the aircraft communications system.

Lt. Col. Jerry Driscoll is in the cockpit with Capt. Aaron Eckerberg, his copilot, running down the preflight checklist just as though we were about to take a training flight at Camp Pendleton. I hear the electronic ping of the Singars encryption system as each of the other birds in our flight "checks in" with Driscoll, confirming that they are "ready to turn"—prepared to start their engines and lift off for Iraq. I hear a helicopter in our flight—I don't catch which one—call in to inform us that Griff, using his newly-acquired nickname "Mailbag," is aboard with his gear. All is ready.

Then, before the engines are started, another call comes over the radio: U.S. Navy SEALs and British Special Boat Service operators in the vicinity of our insert LZ are in contact with enemy troops. An AC-130 gunship and USAF A-10s are being called in to "soften up" the zone and take out nearby enemy anti-aircraft batteries. And so we wait. After about thirty minutes I notice that despite the tension, Pennington is following my rule of "sleep when you can." Sitting on the floor, leaning back against a case of .50-caliber ammunition, he's the picture of absolute confidence—fast asleep.

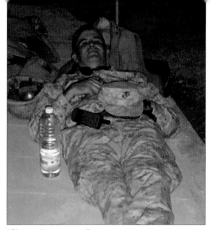
"Sleep when you can"

Finally, shortly after 0200, the terse message comes over the radio from Col. Rich Spencer, the MAG-39 commanding officer: "We're good to go. Godspeed, gentlemen." The largest night helicopter-borne assault in history is now underway.

The whine of the APUs (auxiliary power units) on the rear of the birds is soon overwhelmed by the sound of more than a hundred engines and rotors turning. In front of us, total darkness. As we lift off, out the side of the bird my camera catches the plume of dust as we rise into the darkness. Inside, the Royal Marines insert magazines into their weapons and fire a round. Pennington and Cpl Nathan Kendall, the left-side .50-caliber gunner, lock and load their machine guns with belts of ammo as we head for the border at more than one hundred knots (about 115 mph) and less than fifty feet above the ground.

My videotape of the assault lift shows that, initially, visibility is fairly clear as we proceed northeast toward Iraq, though there are increasing amounts of dust in the air, and occasionally I have to flip my NVGs up because the fires from several burning oil wells cause them to "flare" and temporarily blind me. I can clearly see the other three birds, flying close behind us, no more than five or ten rotor widths away. All four helicopters are supposed to land in the same zone to disgorge their passengers. The next four birds, trailing a mile or so behind us, will land in the assault LZ after we take off. As I aim the camera back into our troop compartment, only the eyes of the Royal Marines' camouflage-painted faces show clearly through my night-vision lens.

Seconds later, when I turn to "shoot" again out the open hatch, the sky has suddenly turned hazy. The ground below, whipping by at more than one hundred knots, is still visible through my NVGs, but out in front of us a local sandstorm—a miniature *sharqi*—has reduced visibility to just a few yards. The windblown dust, perhaps created by the firing on Safwan Hill or the movement of thousands of our armored vehicles off to our northwest, has mixed with the smoke from a handful of burning oil wells, obliterating the sky. Through my NVGs the air around us appears to be filled with "pixie dust," as though we were looking through the frosted glass inside a light bulb.

As we approach the border, the highway that was built in more peaceful times to connect Basra with Kuwait City is just visible below us. I'm musing about seeing a car drive beneath us when I hear Driscoll say over the intercom, "Power lines ahead. We're pulling up to go over. Gunny, give me a 'clear' when we're past."

I step back inside as we pull up so Pennington can stick his head out the open hatch. When we pass over the lines, I hear him yell "Clear!" over the noise. And then, as the bird starts to descend again, there is an urgent call over the secure radio: "Dash Three, Dash Four! Pull up! Pull up!"

Suddenly, there is a blinding flash on the left side and slightly below our helicopter. Though our bird never wavers on its course, up in the cockpit, Lt. Col. Driscoll is instantly on the intercom and the radio: "What was that?"

Pennington responds first, his voice flat, coming through the lip mike: "Dash Three has gone down, sir."

There is a moment of silence while the magnitude of what has just happened sinks in. My camera, pointed over the port side .50-caliber machine gun, captures the terrible fireball. I know the answer even before Driscoll comes on the radio and asks, "Any survivors?"

"Dash One, this is Dash Four. Negative. No way."

Flying at 120 knots, one hundred feet off the ground is difficult in daylight . . . much more so at night

Driscoll calls out on the secure search and rescue net anyway, "Helicopter Down," and then the grid coordinates from his GPS. "Request you launch the TRAP (tactical recovery of aircraft and pilot) mission to that location."

Within seconds of the crash, everyone on our helicopter has figured out what happened, though no one knows what brought Dash Three down. I can sense the stunned reaction, even though it is impossible to hear anything over the roar of the engines and rotors other than what comes through my earphones.

The Royal Marine battalion commander unfastens his seat belt, comes forward, and sticks his head into the cockpit. He and Driscoll confer for a few moments, and then he backs out and stands upright, a tiny flashlight in his hand. Standing right next to me, he flips through the pages of a small notebook until he finds the list of those who were on Dash Three. He shakes his head and says, just loud enough for me to hear, "War's bloody awful. Those poor lads." And then, looking back toward his Marines, he shouts, "We're pressing on!"

But we can't. In just a matter of a few miles and a few minutes, the weather and visibility deteriorate considerably. The AC-130 working over our insert LZ reports heavy anti-aircraft fire and that the approach to our zone is obscured by ground fog, dust, and smoke from the oil fires. All this is being monitored by I MEF headquarters and the MAG-39 Air Operations Center. After several minutes of radio chatter, the command, "Abort the mission," is broadcast to all the aircraft over the secure voice channel. The decision has been made well up the chain of command to wait until after first light and to try again when the weather and visibility are better.

Now, with more than fifty helicopters in the air, the challenge becomes getting them all safely back to where we started without bumping into one another in the haze.

Driscoll calls the battalion commander back up into the cockpit to inform him of the decision that has just come down. As the Royal Marine lieutenant colonel backs out and heads back to his seat, he is clearly agitated.

Our route back to the pickup zone in Kuwait takes us back over the still-burning wreckage of Dash Three. As all aboard crane their necks to see what they can through the portholes, a thought suddenly comes to me: *Was Griff on Dash Two or Dash Three?*

By the time we make it back to our landing point, it's nearly 0400 and I have all but convinced myself that Griff had boarded Dash Two—the helicopter that had been parked about twenty meters to our right side when we took off for the assault. As soon as the commandos disembark and our bird shuts down, I run over to the helicopter parked to our right and ask the crew chief if Griff is aboard.

The forty-year-old CH-46 Sea Knight helicopters – known as Phrogs – are the workhorses of the Marine Corps

When he replies, "No, sir," adrenaline surges through my gut, and I have immediate remorse. *How am I going to tell his lovely wife Kathleen and daughter Madeline that Griff has been killed?*

Overwhelmed with dread, I run over to several other birds as they land, but there is still no sign of Griff. He's been my producer for more than six years, and I'm sick at the thought that he is lying dead in the wreckage of Dash Three. Wearing my NVGs, I make my way back to my helicopter, but the pilots are gone, summoned to a briefing with the MAG-39 commanding officer. Pennington is on top of our bird, checking things out with a small flashlight held in his teeth. When he climbs down and puts his NVGs back down, I ask him, "Do we know yet who was aboard the bird that went down?"

"Yes, but you can't report it until we notify next of kin," he replies. And then he continues, "Maj. Aubin and I came to 268 from MAWTS (Marine Aviation Weapons and Tactics Squadron). He and Capt. Beaupre were two of the best pilots I know. And SSgt Waters-Bey and Cpl Kennedy both really knew their stuff. They were all really good men. You know that, you've flown with all of 'em."

"What about the passenger list?" I ask, not wanting to say Griff's name.

"There seems to be some kind of mix-up on the manifest," he responds. "Apparently the troop list only shows seven PAX [military shorthand for 'passengers'], but before take-off, Maj. Aubin reported 'twelve souls on board.' That means there were eight in back, in addition to the crew. The Brits are checking."

This confirms my worst suspicions and I say, "Oh Lord, then Griff must have been the eighth person aboard. How can I get out to where the bird went down?"

"I'll check," he replies and then adds, "I'm sorry, Colonel."

As I'm boarding our bird to await word on how I can get to the wreckage, and silently praying, *Dear Lord, please let Griff be alive*, my satellite pager goes off. It's the FOX News foreign desk in New York. I dial the number in Manhattan on my Iridium satellite phone, identify myself, and am informed that CBS has just run a story that there has been a helicopter crash with sixteen American and British casualties—and do I know anything about it.

I reply, "Yes. I saw it happen and I have it on tape, but there is uncertainty about how many were aboard. My field producer Griff Jenkins may be among them. Please don't make any announcements about this until I can get confirmation. I'll call you as soon as I have more."

As I put the phone back in my flak jacket pocket, a civilian pickup truck, driven by Capt. Frank Laemmle, one of the HMM-268 squadron pilots, pulls up next to our bird. He asks if the MAG-39 Operations officers can look at my videotape to see if it might help them figure out what happened to Dash Three.

We ride together in the cab of the truck to where the pilots have gathered next to Col. Spencer's UH-1N, and I play the tape for them to see. One of the assistant operations officers asks if they can have a copy of the tape to take back to Ali al-Salim Air Base for use in the investigation of what brought Dash Three down. I have no way of transmitting what's on the cassette to New York from out here. And what's in my camera can't air until the next of kin of all the casualties are notified. So I agree to make a duplicate when we return to base. But I knew that doing so without Griff's assistance and camera would be difficult.

As I turn to reboard the truck for a ride back to my bird, I see Gunny Pennington

Griff Jenkins, combat cameraman and field producer extraordinaire

walking up. He says, "Look who I found!" and steps aside to reveal Griff Jenkins.

To the surprise of everyone except Pennington, I yell, "Thank God!" and grab Griff around the neck, giving him a big hug. Clearly confused by my embrace, he gives me one in return. "When we came back after turning around," he explains, there was too much dust, so Dash Two had to land way on the other side of the zone rather than next to you, where we belonged."

Instead of riding in the truck, we walk back to the helicopter where my gear is stowed. I'm immensely glad to see him and tell him about my up-and-down emotional uncertainty about whether he had been aboard Dash Three.

When we arrive back at the bird, I call New York and tell the FOX News foreign desk duty officer with great relief that I've found Griff alive. I also tell him that I've been asked to make a copy of our tape and not to air what's on it until the NOK notification is complete. I then tell him that four U.S. Marines are confirmed dead and seven British commandos are believed to have been killed when Dash Three went down.

It is nearly dawn. Without sleep for more than twenty-four hours, I'm consumed with several overwhelming emotions: great joy that Griff is safe but a feeling of sadness and guilt that I was grateful that he had survived while others had not, and a sense of profound

Weapons maintenance comes before rest. This Humvee gunner cleans his machine gun at sunset

sorrow that I experience every time I see Marines lose their lives. War truly is the most horrible of human endeavors.

With first light, the weather over the Basra LZs improves considerably, allowing the helicopter assault that had been aborted the night before to be carried out. But by then the seven remaining HMM-268 helicopters have returned to base, replaced by British Pumas and CH-47s. The MAG-39 officials have already prepared the usual terse official casualty report for release after the Marine Corps had personally notified the families of those killed:

On 21 March at approximately 0200 local, Maj. Jay Thomas Aubin, 36, of Waterville, Maine; Capt. Ryan Anthony Beaupre, 30, from St. Anne, Illinois; SSgt Kendall Damon Waters-Bey, 29, of Baltimore, Maryland; and Cpl Brian Matthew Kennedy, 25, from Houston, Texas, were killed when their CH-46 helicopter crashed in Kuwait while carrying out combat operations in Operation Iraqi Freedom.

The British Marines, already heavily engaged north of Basra, are unable to confirm who was aboard the ill-fated helicopter for more than forty-eight hours. When they do, Central Command adds the names of the British commandos killed in the crash:

Maj. Jason Ward, Capt. Philip Stuart Guy, WO Mark Stratford, Color Sgt John Cecil, Operations Mechanic 2nd Class Ian Seymour, Lance Bombardier Llewelyn Karl Evans, and Marine Sholto Hedenskog.

CAS-EVAC!

★ ★ ★ ★ ★ ★ ★ ★ ★ ★ ★ ★

By 1000 an investigation into the cause of the crash is already underway. After a few hours of rest, Lt. Col. Driscoll summons his pilots and then his air crews to brief them on the crash. He rallies them for the day's missions: four aircraft assigned as cas-evac for 5th Marines, four more birds on ready alert for other emergency missions, and the remaining three into maintenance.

A few minutes before 1100, the "Great Giant Voice" sounds the alarm and everyone heads for the bunkers. For the Marines, donning a gas mask, pulling on the chemical protective suit, and finding a seat inside the sandbag-covered concrete is now getting to be old hat. When the Patriot battery to our west opens fire with two loud concussions, nobody even flinches. Near the entrance, two Marine NCOs are playing cards. Several others are reading paperback books through the "bug-eye" lenses of their gas masks. Even Griff is getting the hang of this now. He's not only better about keeping his gas mask with him, but I notice that when the "All Clear" is finally sounded, he's fast asleep.

While I'm on the air a few minutes past noon—it's 0505 in the eastern U.S.—the squadron receives a "tasking" from the Direct Air Support Center (DASC). It is directed to position two helicopters forward because both 5th and 7th Marines are in heavy contact with elements of the Iraqi 51st Mechanized Division, with casualties expected.

Griff and I break down our gear and head to the flight line with Maj. John Graham, the Squadron Executive Officer. Lt. Col. Driscoll had intended to fly the mission, but his MAG-39 and 3rd MAW (Marine Aircraft Wing) superiors wanted him to remain in Kuwait to be available for NOK notifications and the investigation into last night's crash.

Just before Griff and I depart for the flight line, I find Jerry Driscoll alone in the rear of the ready room tent, drafting the most difficult correspondence anyone ever has to write: letters from a commander to the relatives of his dead Marines. Having had to write such missives myself, I know exactly how he feels. The burden of command is never heavier than at a time like this.

The flight north to where the 5th Marines are engaged is unremarkable. Flying a CH-46 at thirty to fifty feet over the desert at better than one hundred knots is certainly challenging to the pilot and copilot. At that altitude and speed, the ground—and therefore death—is less than a half second away. On the heels of last night's fiery crash, no one needs to say "be careful" to the two pilots up front. Yet, for those of us in the back of the aircraft, the flight into Iraq is monotonous—reminding me of the old adage that "war is 95 percent boredom and 5 percent stark terror."

As we whip over the trackless desert that is southern Iraq, we can see large herds of camels, an occasional dried-up irrigation ditch, the heat rising in ripples out in front of us, and little else. There is not a tree, bush, shrub, or oasis of any kind in sight. I'm glad I packed my GPS and topped off my water before we left.

After half an hour or so, the smoke and flame from three of the seven oil well heads that Saddam loyalists succeeded in blowing up become visible. And then the call from the 5th Marines air officer—call sign "Fingers." They have casualties: two emergency and one priority. He transmits the grid coordinates over the secure radio. After Maj. Graham enters them into the helicopter's GPS navigation system, we change our course to make the pickup.

As we make our approach, I can see up ahead what appears to be several small houses and an oil installation inside a chain-link fence. It's one of the outposts that were the initial D-day objectives for the 5th and 7th Marines.

A radio call to the unit on the ground confirms that we're at the right place, but the voice on the ground informs us that "the zone isn't hot, but it isn't cold either." Leaning out the hatch with my camera running, I see a green smoke grenade go off to mark the landing point and show the wind direction. The officer or noncommissioned officer running this zone knows what he's doing.

The LZ is surrounded by several LVTs (landing vehicle, tracked) and armed Humvees. When we get closer, I notice that there is no one up and walking around. The Marines are all lying down or crouched while manning the .50-caliber, Golf 240 machine guns, or TOW missiles on the Humvees. The "up guns"—coaxial-mounted .40-mm grenade launchers atop the LAV turrets—are all aimed outside the little perimeter.

As the two helicopters touch down on the dirt roadway, Marines rush toward us carrying three litters. Two are loaded aboard our helicopter; one is placed aboard Griff's bird behind us. Following instructions not to broadcast the identity of wounded or dead combatants from either side, I allow my camera lens to catch only the faces of the litter bearers as they run on and off the bird.

They are nearly all very young. Wearing their chemical protective suits, flak jackets, and Kevlar helmets, they are sweating profusely. As the litters holding the casualties are strapped in, Maj. Graham tells Cpl Morales, our crew chief, to give the litter bearers several boxes of our water bottles to take back with them.

Our two shock-trauma medical corpsmen start treating the wounded even before we take off. It's only then that one of the docs notices that one of the two casualties isn't a Marine; it's a severely burned eleven- or twelve-year-old Iraqi girl. Her devastating injuries appear to be several days old.

A radio call to the unit on the ground confirms that the child was brought to the Marines by a relative and that she had been burned in a cooking fuel accident before the war even started. The girl's parents had begged the Marine unit in the area for help. They decided to load her on our bird with their wounded because there was nothing more that could be done for her in the field.

Unfortunately, there is little that the docs aboard our helicopter can do for her either. Kuwait refuses to allow any Iraqi prisoners or wounded—civilian or military—into their territory. Maj. Graham makes a command decision to take the burned girl to the hospital ship USS *Comfort* out in the Persian Gulf, and he files a flight plan to do so.

But as we head southeast for the Gulf, we get a call asking if the two helicopters have life rafts aboard. They don't. Everything that's not essential to our mission has been stripped to make them lighter. We weren't supposed to be operating anywhere near water, so we don't even have life vests aboard.

Maj. Graham is now faced with a terrible dilemma: return the child to where we picked her up or take her and the other casualties out to sea in hopes that she can be saved. He asks over the intercom how we in the back feel about flying over water without flotation gear. Everyone agrees: "Go for it."

A half hour later we're aboard the USS *Tarawa*, an amphibious assault ship that I have been on many times before. She has a full hospital aboard and all that's needed to treat the wounded.

While the birds refuel, Griff is given a tour of the ship. The crew gives us as much cold water and fresh-baked cookies as we can carry. Just before dark we return to the flight line at Ali al-Salim Air Base.

USS *Tarawa*

Navy and Marine Corps flight deck crewman await the landing of a CH-53 Super Stallion helicopter on board amphibious assault ship USS *Tarawa* (LHA 1)

The pilots all head to the MAG-39 intelligence section for a mandatory debriefing. As the crew chiefs and maintenance personnel swarm over the helicopters, Griff and I head back to the HMM-268 ready room to set up our satellite transceiver and feed our tape to FOX News in New York. That's how we find out what's happening in the rest of the war.

Central Command headquarters in Qatar reports that the Iraqi 51st Mechanized Division has collapsed, yielding more than eight thousand enemy prisoners of war. For the first time an Iraqi division commander and his deputy have personally surrendered. On the far right, the British 7th Armored Division is already on the outskirts of Basra. The U.S. Marines' RCT-7 has captured all of the crucial oil infrastructure targets in the vicinity of Az Zubayr, and the 3rd Bn, 7th Marines, along with a company from 1st Tank Bn have subdued Safwan. Farther west, RCT-5 has seized all of their objectives intact, including the six major GOSPs and the Ar Rumaylah oil fields. And on the far-left flank of the I MEF advance, RCT-1 has raced more than fifty kilometers across the desert and is already just south of Jalibah.

As before, dozens of Marines of all ranks gather around us to watch huge explosions rock the enemy capital on our tiny TV. When FOX newsman David Asman, whose son is serving with Task Force Tarawa, informs us that the Army's 3rd ID has advanced sixty miles into Iraq, there are cheers. The only bad news: Two more U.S. Marines—a second lieutenant with the 1st Bn, 5th Marines, and a corporal from the 2nd Bn, 1st Marines—have been killed in action. And there is one other unpleasant item: Saddam is still alive and has been seen on Iraqi TV.

★ ★ ★ ★ ★ ★ ★ ★ ★ ★ ★ ★ ★ ★

5

TO THE BANKS OF THE EUPHRATES

"[T]he fighting is fierce and we have inflicted many damages. The stupid enemy, the Americans and British, failed completely. They're not making any penetration."
— MOHAMMED SAEED AL-SAHAF, IRAQI MINISTER OF INFORMATION, 23 MARCH 2003

Huey and Cobra lifting off from a FARP on the way to Baghdad

SATURDAY, 22 MARCH 2003

We're encamped beside two haze-gray helicopters parked behind the 5th Marines Regimental Team mobile command post, just north of the captured Iraqi air base at Jalibah, southeast of An Nasiriyah. On my map I can see that we're not far from Ur, once home to Abraham and Sarah before they began their long walk to Canaan around 2000 BC.

Off to our west, the 3rd ID has been racing through the desert—spearheading the main attack for the U.S. Army's V Corps. Supported from the air by nearly every plane in the USAF arsenal and their own Apache attack helicopters, the 3rd ID is aiming straight for the southern approaches to Baghdad and pressing hard against Saddam's Republican Guard Medina division.

SSG Scott Maynard mans his .50-caliber machine gun during the fight for Baghdad

As soon as the Jalibah air base was secured, the 3rd MAW established a forward arming and refueling point (FARP) on the roadside runways and began cycling in cargo aircraft loaded with fuel, ordnance, and equipment. Nearby, an Army shock-trauma hospital was erected in a matter of hours to provide immediate life-saving surgery for the severely wounded.

Just before nightfall I flew on an "armed recon" up Route 1. The mission was to reconnoiter out along the flanks of the two columns and look for signs of enemy activity. As my camera rolled on the Cobra gunships escorting our flight, below us tens of thousands of coalition troops, weapons, and vehicles were on the move in a two-pronged attack to the north toward Baghdad.

The breath-taking array of tanks, LAVs, trucks, amphibious assault vehicles (AAVs), Humvees, artillery pieces, rocket launchers, portable bridging, and engineer equipment went on as far as the eye could see. But other than a handful of wrecked Iraqi tanks and armored vehicles and a few trenches filled with flaming oil that sent plumes of black smoke into the sky, there were few signs of the enemy.

Shortly after dark an Iraqi general surrendered to some Marines in an AAV. The general's Shia and Kurdish conscripts had vanished and the Iraqi division simply ceased to exist—thus explaining the absence of enemy activity in the immediate area.

Iraqi forces who chose to fight took heavy losses

After Griff and I wolfed down an MRE, we set up our equipment in the dark, preparing for our nightly report on *Hannity & Colmes*. As usual, once the tiny video transceiver locked into New York's signal, those wanting to catch up on the war news surrounded us.

Watching from Iraq, there was a telling difference between the news coming from embedded journalists in Iraq and the armchair admirals pontificating about the war from the safety of the states. By and large, the journalists traveling with coalition forces

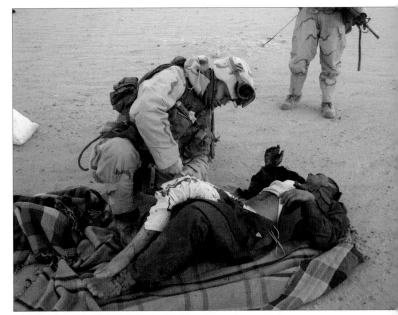

Compassion doesn't take sides– here a 3rd ID medic treats a wounded enemy soldier

gave a straightforward account—though many seemed amazed at how good the American soldiers, sailors, and Marines were at the work of war. Many expressed surprise at the humanity and compassion of coalition troops—young men going out of their way, often at great personal risk—to care for Iraqi civilians, enemy prisoners, and wounded combatants.

Reports from Baghdad were completely different. For the troops who gathered around our miniature TV screen, the best entertainment in Iraq became the regular press briefings proffered by the Iraqi information minister, Mohammed Saeed al-Sahaf (Baghdad Bob). As Saddam's official spokesman, he somehow held a straight face while claiming that Iraqi forces had "destroyed" the Army's 3rd ID and "halted" the Marine advance. What made it all more frustrating than funny was the fact that so many reporters in Baghdad appeared to take him seriously.

Today, Baghdad Bob reported that 207 civilians were killed in allied raids on the city during the previous night. He also says that Iraqi soldiers have driven American and British troops back from Basra after killing hundreds, perhaps thousands, of them. The Marines find all this to be highly amusing.

But as funny as Baghdad Bob has become to the troops fighting here in Iraq, they are clearly wary of the media and concerned about how they are being presented to the American people.

AN NASIRIYAH, THE BLOODY GAUNTLET

★ ★ ★ ★ ★ ★ ★ ★ ★ ★ ★ ★ ★

Marines evacuate a wounded comrade during the initial push toward Baghdad in April of 2003

SUNDAY, 23 MARCH 2003

Shortly after we finished our 0100 broadcast—6:00 p.m. Eastern Standard Time—a messenger from the RCT-5 command post raced up to our helicopter with information that a U.S. Army convoy had been ambushed inside the city of An Nasiriyah. Our four pilots hustled inside the command post, where they were told to prepare an emergency cas-evac. Gesturing to a large map with a grease pencil, one of the RCT-5 air officers pointed out locations of friendly and enemy units as radio operators logged fresh information coming in over the radio nets.

The Shiite city of An Nasiriyah is bounded on the north by the Saddam Canal and on the south by the Euphrates River. In 1991 Saddam had brutally repressed an uprising there. This led our military intelligence to presume that most of the city's 400,000 residents were less-than-loyal to the regime. Marine engineers and U.S. Naval Construction Battalion "Seabee" specialists judged that the city's four bridges—two to the south over the river and the pair to the north over the canal—were capable of holding the seventy-two-ton weight of an M-1

Abrams tank if the spans could be captured before Saddam's troops seriously damaged or destroyed them. The coalition battle plan called for the rapid capture of all four bridges.

Task Force Tarawa and RCT-1 were given the mission of seizing the four bridges just after first light on 23 March. The plan called for Task Force Tarawa to seize the southern spans and open the route through An Nasiriyah so that RCT-1 could race through the city and grab the northern bridges before the Iraqis knew what hit them.

But now, just hours before the attack to seize the bridges was scheduled to begin, an Army convoy of the 507th Maintenance Company, trying to close up on the 3rd ID, had taken a wrong turn and been ambushed near one of An Nasiriyah's southern bridges. Though the 507th wasn't supposed to be a frontline combat unit, these soldiers suddenly found that in this war, everywhere is the front line. Concerned that the small group of clerks and technicians would be wiped out, Task Force Tarawa was given the mission of rescuing the surrounded survivors.

At 0300, Task Force Tarawa moved out with a company of tanks leading a battalion of Marines in seven-ton trucks and AAVs. But shortly after dawn, Iraqis along the railway bridge south of An Nasiriyah ambushed the lead elements of this heavily armed column. The combat-hardened Marines responded with overwhelming firepower that not only repelled the ambush but destroyed ten Iraqi tanks.

By noon, most of 2nd Marine Regiment was engaged in and around An Nasiriyah. Hoping to get some footage of the action, I jumped on a HMLA-267 armed Huey and flew to the recently captured Tallil Air Base, where an Army shock-trauma hospital had been set up to process casualties. When I got there, wounded soldiers and Marines were arriving at the hospital in a steady stream, and the doctors, nurses, and medics were hard-pressed to keep up.

A destroyed bridge over a canal north of An Nasiriyah

Cobra pilots returning to rearm and refuel describe Marines fighting from their vehicles as regular Iraqi army units and civilian-clad fedayeen pummeled them with small-arms fire and RPGs from one- and two-story buildings lining "the gauntlet"—the main highway through An Nasiriyah. The foreign fighters are said to be from Syria, Saudi Arabia, Jordan, Lebanon, and Iran. One of the pilots says that these so-called fedayeen are entering the city from the north, riding in buses, private autos, even motorcycles—all spoiling for a fight.

Despite the mounting Marine casualties, there is some good news: 1st Bn, 2nd Marines, has rescued a half dozen or more wounded soldiers of the 507th who had been hiding out in the outskirts of An Nasiriyah since the ambush of their ill-fated convoy.

Mid-afternoon, I jump on a CH-46 cas-evac helicopter. As we approach the pickup zone north of An Nasiriyah, it is obvious that this has been the scene of a terrible fight. Blasted and smoldering American vehicles are intermingled with wrecked Iraqi tanks and civilian vehicles. Just north of the bridge, a Marine LVT, apparently torn apart by an RPG or an anti-tank rocket, still has the bodies of dead Marines inside.

The driver of this car was killed before he could detonate his vehicle in the midst of a U.S. convoy

As the wounded are loaded, I can see RPGs and gunfire raining down from the buildings a few hundred meters away. Cobra gunships are raking the rooftops and alleys of nearby buildings with rockets, TOW missiles, Hellfire missiles, and bursts of fire from their 20-mm Gatling guns. Farther to the south, 155-mm artillery rounds are obliterating structures and city streets. The din of rifle and machine-gun fire from the Marines on the LVTs deployed around the zone—and from dismounted infantry in ditches beside the road—can be heard over the helicopter engines and rotors. Every time an Iraqi or fedayeen fighter shows himself, the Marines respond with a fusillade of fire from their G-240 machine guns, rifles, and grenade launchers. As the up-guns of the LVTs lob rounds with good effect into second-story windows, litter bearers, hunched down to reduce their target profile, race for the helicopters, carrying their wounded comrades.

The helicopter returned immediately to the field hospital where Army doctors, nurses, and medics stabilized the wounded before sending them back to Kuwait for more advanced care. There, the most grievously injured are loaded aboard Air Force C-17 "Nightingale" transports and evacuated to the big U.S. military hospital in Landstuhl, Germany—a facility offering treatment as good or better than any stateside hospital.

In order to get back north to RCT-5, where I had left Griff and my gear, I hitched a ride on a Marine resupply convoy that was forming up at the FARP. Unlike the ill-fated 507th Maintenance convoy the night before, this one had tanks, LAVs, and hardened Humvees interspersed among the supply vehicles, all bristling with weapons and grim-faced Marines.

This convoy, more than a hundred men and tens of millions in military hardware, was being commanded by a young Marine Reserve lieutenant. The mission, as he explained it, was to safely deliver critically needed ammo, food, water, and fuel to RCT-5, approximately twenty-five kilometers up Highway 1. Speed was of the essence, and he assigned missions to every vehicle team on what to do in every contingency, including how to handle casualties and what to do if a vehicle became disabled. He finished his orders with a terse command: "Nobody gets left behind."

We drove through the night completely blacked out, every driver using NVGs. With foreign fedayeen fighters known to be in the area, the tension was heavy, but we arrived at RCT-5 without incident.

Col. Dunford's mobile command post was just off the hard-surface road. Fifty meters behind it I could see four CH-46 helicopters, parked in a field. That's where I found Griff, surrounded by the four air crews—Lt. Col. Jerry Driscoll, the squadron commanding officer—among them. They were clustered around our little satellite transceiver watching FOX News—and to a man, they were fighting mad.

Iraqi state television and Al Jazeera had been broadcasting gory videotape and pictures of dead American soldiers killed in the 507th Maintenance Company ambush. Even worse than the gruesome sight of American dead were shots of five American soldiers from the 507th—now prisoners.

In the dark, one of the Marines said, "This reminds me of Somalia." He was referring to the notorious 1993 incident in Mogadishu when a U.S. Army Delta Force and Ranger Task Force suffered eighteen killed and more than seventy wounded in an event made famous in the book and movie, *Black Hawk Down*.

The similarities in how dead Americans are defiled by radical Islamic extremists is certainly valid, but that's about the only parallel between the gunfight in An Nasiriyah and what had happened in "The Mog" (Mogadishu). Back in 1993, the Rangers and Delta Force operators had no armor, artillery, or fixed-wing air support. A Pakistani general under UN control commanded the quick reaction force (QRF) that came to their "rescue" eighteen hours later.

In An Nasiriyah, the ambush of thin-skinned vehicles manned by inexperienced support troops of the 507th was a disaster, no doubt. But unlike the situation in Somalia, Task Force Tarawa was able to quickly bring to bear enormous coordinated, disciplined firepower in their rescue of the beleaguered logistics convoy. For the soldiers in Mogadishu there was no such back-up.

The mood among the men brightened consider-ably when President Bush came on TV to say,

As they appeared on Iraqi television, soldiers of the 507th Maintenance Bn who were captured after taking a wrong turn in Nasiriyah during the initial push

"Saddam Hussein is losing control of his country." He also pointed out that the U.S.-led coalition forces were achieving their objectives, and he warned the Iraqis, "The people who mistreat U.S. prisoners of war will be treated as war criminals." One of those prisoners we knew to be a female. Only later did we learn her name: PFC Jessica Lynch, a twenty-year-old supply clerk from the 507th Maintenance Company.

PFC Jessica Lynch

WITH HMM-268 & RCT-5

★ ★ ★ ★ ★ ★ ★ ★ ★ ★ ★ ★

1800 Hours, Local; Monday, 24 March 2003

We've been on the move since dawn. Despite continued resistance from bands of Baathists and fedayeen inside An Nasiriyah, Gen. James Mattis, the 1st Marine Division commander, has decided to proceed with his original plan for a two-pronged attack north toward Baghdad. He's sending two RCTs north, continuing the attack up Route 1 to Ad Diwaniyah. To our east, Task Force Tarawa has been given the mission of securing An Nasiriyah and its bridges so that RCT-1 can pass through and attack the city of Al Kut and its airfield on the north bank of the Tigris—scene of the great British defeat at the hands of the Turks in 1916.

By sunrise, Marine engineers and Seabees, working through the night without lights, had put down a pontoon span over the Euphrates next to the Route 1 highway bridge in an effort to ease the congestion for units crossing the river and heading north toward Ad Diwaniyah. Even though the 5th Marines seized the concrete-and-steel highway bridge intact before the Iraqis could destroy it, only one M-1 tank at a time is being allowed to cross over the Euphrates.

As Col. Joe Dunford's RCT-5 continued to press the attack north, Griff and I accompanied them, sometimes moving in a Humvee but more often via the HMM-268 helicopters. Each time we landed, Griff and I would race out of our respective birds to set up our broadcast equipment—usually three times before noon. By then, our satellite connection with FOX News in New York had become the best source of information about what was happening in An Nasiriyah and elsewhere in the campaign. Unfortunately, the news wasn't good.

Marine casualties in An Nasiriyah continued to mount, and the RCT-1 Task Force Tarawa advance toward Al Kut had stalled. We heard reports of fedayeen irregulars in civilian clothes waving white flags as if to surrender, only to fire on our troops when they approached. Others described foreign fighters using human shields and ambulances full of explosives to kill coalition troops. In Baghdad, Saddam was said to be unfazed by a round-the-clock rain of precision air strikes—more than one thousand per day. Al Jazeera continued to parrot Iraqi regime claims of massive civilian casualties inflicted by coalition forces—something that left the Marines around us shaking

their heads in disgust. All this was apparently sufficient to drive most of the chattering class of retired generals and admirals on U.S. television into deep depression—a sentiment they passed on to the American people.

Meanwhile, there were intelligence reports that hundreds, if not thousands, of Muslim males were flooding into Iraq in buses, cars, pick-up trucks, even motorcycles. To some, it seemed as though the invasion of Iraq was sucking every angry, disillusioned Arab male in the Middle East to join the Jihad against the coalition.

A 3rd ID soldier gives water to an Iraqi detainee

Whatever the motivation for these foreign fighters, American forces now have another enemy to face here in Iraq. And because U.S. casualties from the engagement are so high—twenty killed in action and more than ninety wounded in action—many of the troops who fought to open "the gauntlet" through An Nasiriyah are now referring to 23 March as "Bloody Sunday."

Interestingly, despite the negative news from home—and increasing evidence of foreign fighters that the soldiers and Marines could see for themselves—most of the warriors around us were undismayed. The common sentiment became a refrain: "It's better to fight them *here* than at home."

After four days of furious movement, grinding fatigue, and heavy combat, the morale of the troops remained remarkably high. Little did we know that yet another adversary was about to join the fight—the weather.

A massive sandstorm cloud about to envelop a U.S. military base in Iraq, just before sunset

★ ★ ★ ★ ★ ★ ★ ★ ★ ★ ★ ★

6

MOTHER OF ALL SANDSTORMS

"It was MOASS—the Mother of All Sand Storms! If you were a tank commander, you couldn't see your front slope. If you were a driver, you couldn't see your ground guide."
—GySgt Erik Benitez, USMC, battalion master gunner, 1st Tank Bn, I MEF

24–26 March,
North of An Nasiriyah

FOX's Greg Kelly talks via satellite phone as a sandstorm moves in

It began shortly after dark on Monday, 24 March, with a low-pitched moaning wind that lashed into the helicopter, whipping dirt around inside the bird. The temperature dropped as the wind rose. Though we were all wearing our chemical protective suits, we had to wrap up in poncho liners to stay warm enough to sleep.

Griff and I stayed with the air crews, shivering inside the helicopters, listening to the wind howl outside. Fine particles of grit swirled around inside the cabin, finding their way into every crevice—weapons, engines, instruments—even our broadcast gear.

By 0400, when we dragged ourselves outside to prepare for a "hit" on *Hannity & Colmes*, the satellite antenna we carried would have been blown away by the force of the wind had we not anchored it with a sandbag. The blowing sand had the appearance of fine driven snow through the green night lens of the camera.

Iraqi sandstorms can take on biblical proportions . . .

These tiny airborne particles were a nuisance during our broadcast. But their effect on the pilots and drivers was far more profound. Even on the hard surface roadway, the never-ceasing stream of armored vehicles, trucks, and tanks moving north slowed to a crawl because the drivers couldn't see the vehicle in front of them. And the helicopter air crews didn't relish the idea of flying in weather like this. Nobody wants the stress of flying blind at fifty feet above the ground.

Dawn came late—made so by the unearthly haze of wind-whipped sand. When the sun did rise, only the colors shifted. The powdery "moon dust" turned everything—earth, sky, vehicles, even the haze-gray helicopters—the color of rust. It lined our nostrils, caked on our skin, and stung the eyes. But these were mere distractions compared to the real danger posed by the fact that the Marines couldn't see the enemy—or anything else beyond a few meters.

. . . and reduce visibility to zero in only minutes . . .

But on the plus side, everything moved slower inside the storm, so many Marines took advantage of the lull to catch up on sleep and fine-tune their planning inside the command post. Someone handed me a cup of hot coffee, and I listened in as two CIA paramilitary officers debated about whether the storm could be properly described as a *sharqi* or a *shamal*. They finally asked two Kuwaiti officers accompanying RCT-5 as interpreters. Unfortunately, the Kuwaitis couldn't resolve the issue either, prompting one of the Americans to observe with a shrug, "It's been that way over here for thousands of years—the people in this part of the world can't even agree about the weather. Let's just say that this is a sandstorm of biblical proportions." They got no disagreement from me.

The command post for RCT-5 had once been a school, then later an arsenal for Saddam's Baath Party. I trudged up the stairs of the one-story building to get a look around, but the blowing sand made the effort futile. On the roof, four Marines were pulling security, one on each corner. In addition to their helmets, body armor, and chemical suits and dust goggles, their faces were wrapped Bedouin-style with the dark green slings from their first-aid kits. The frigid wind was downright fierce. I asked the fire team leader, a corporal, if they'd seen anything.

The look I got from the Marine NCO had "stupid question" written all over it. "The entire Iraqi army could be out there, and we wouldn't know it until they were knocking on the front door."

Fortunately, though the troops on the ground couldn't see any farther than we could spit, they had friends in high places with a much better view. Well above the storm, JSTARS aircraft were still identifying targets and passing them along to the artillery, as evidenced by the "crump, crump, crump" of the 11th Marines' 155-mm howitzers firing over our heads.

The Iraqi artillery was firing too. Emboldened by the concealment offered by the blowing sand, they started hammering our front lines with mortar and rocket fire. American counter-battery radar could still see in the gloom. So even before the enemy rounds landed, entire battalions of American artillery zeroed in on the enemy positions and returned the fire.

The sandstorm grounded the Marines' close air support (CAS) fixed-wing aircraft—the F-18s and AV-8 Harriers. This became immediately obvious to the Iraqis who took the opportunity to try to move troops and equipment under cover of the dust. What they didn't know was that the sensors and automated target-plotting systems aboard U-2, JSTARS, and EP-3 aircraft flying above the red clouds were still able to track them and send GPS-guided munitions in for the kill. Within minutes of detecting an Iraqi convoy or radio emission, one or more of a wide variety of missiles, rockets, or artillery would come streaking out of the sky to ruin the enemy's day.

. . . shutting down nearly all operations until they pass

While standing on the roof of the school-turned-Baath-ordnance-depot-turned-U.S.-Marine-command-post, we could hear some of these high-altitude aircraft, and a moment later we felt a large explosion off to the north. Some unsuspecting Iraqi who thought he couldn't be seen had just learned otherwise—prompting a predictable response from the Marines: "Yeah, man! Get some!"

Griff Jenkins appeared out of the orange mist a few moments later and shouted over the wind, "We have a cas-evac. Let's go." As I hustled down stairs for the mission brief, I wondered if the blast we heard might have caused "friendly" casualties. Inside, I learned from Lt. Col. Jerry Driscoll that this wasn't the case.

Two RCT-5 Marines had been seriously wounded by an RPG during a skirmish with an Iraqi infantry patrol. I watched Driscoll and his wingman, Capt. Aaron "Fester" Eckerberg, plot the grid of the pickup zone and the en route checkpoints on their charts. They jotted down the frequency of the unit waiting for them on the ground, then we all hurried outside to the helicopters. The weather was still deteriorating, but neither pilot showed any sign of hesitation. No questions. No complaints. They were going to get one of their own and bring him to safety.

We stumbled through the gathering gloom to the aircraft where we were joined by two Navy shock-trauma medical corpsmen. As we lifted off, I heard Gunny Pennington, the crew chief, say over the intercom, "Nice day for flying, eh, Colonel?"

Driscoll's deadpan voice came back, "Ah yes. Red Dragons . . . real players." I stuck my head out the right side hatch with my camera, noticing that Capt. Eckerberg's CH-46, though only seventy-five feet away, was nearly invisible in the dusty haze. The ground was indiscernible as well, about the same distance below. Driscoll's instruments showed we were doing less than half our normal speed of 120 knots, which is good since there was no horizon and everyone aboard was straining their eyes for power lines, radio towers, light poles, and highway overpasses—hoping to see them before we hit them. By the time we got near our objective, forty minutes had passed.

The rifle platoon commander who had called for the cas-evac does a good job directing us to his location, about 1,500 meters east of the highway. Though we can't see him and he can't see us in the soup, he succeeds in bringing us in by the sound of our rotors.

For a few moments, the sandstorm works to our advantage. We have flown past the Marine position. Over the radio, the platoon commander tells us to turn back to the south. But in so doing we fly directly over the enemy force that attacked his platoon an hour ago. As we make our approach, I hear the distinctive "crack" of AK-47s firing in our direction. But the Iraqis or fedayeen can't see us and are firing wildly. I thank God once again that these guys don't know how to shoot.

Driscoll finds the zone and we land to find that one of the two casualties—the platoon's Navy medical corpsman, hit by the full force of an RPG—has died without regaining consciousness. The Marines who race aboard our CH-46 gently lower the litter holding his body to the floor of the helicopter and run back out again. There is no time for sadness, but the other corpsmen in the aircraft are clearly affected by the loss of one of their own.

The other casualty, a Marine corporal, has multiple fragment wounds—one of which is a life-threatening piece of shrapnel in his abdomen from an RPG. Driscoll orders the wounded corporal to be loaded aboard Eckerberg's aircraft, and we launch immediately for the Army shock-trauma hospital some fifty miles to our southeast.

Dust is a constant enemy, causing problems with electronics, weapons, and vehicles

But now the full effects of this *sharqi* or *shamal*—or whatever the sandstorm was called—descended upon us. Unable to see the ground from fifty feet, Driscoll brought us down to twenty-five feet and reduced air speed to less than thirty knots. We virtually air-taxied back down Route 1—the wheels just off the ground, the rotor tips barely visible in front of us. Col. Driscoll's voice came over the intercom, as calm as if he were out for a Sunday afternoon drive, "Gunny, keep a sharp eye out. I sure don't want to bump into someone coming this way in our lane."

We crept along this way for half an hour. The conditions were a pilot's nightmare. We edged up to overpasses, skirted power lines, and prayed for protection. Before long, Capt. Eckerberg radioed that his bird was having engine problems. Driscoll told him to set it down on the roadway. We followed suit, waiting with engines running in the gloom.

Thirty minutes passed before Eckerberg's crew was able to patch things up so we could continue our harrowing low-speed, low-altitude, low-visibility flight. But after another half hour or so of skimming along a few feet above the road, Eckerberg reported that he was about to lose his left engine. We landed on the roadway once again, this time shutting down to avoid sucking any more sand into the engine.

On Driscoll's orders, Gunny Pennington went out to look for the other helicopter. I tagged along, figuring Eckerberg and crew were, at most, a couple of hundred yards behind us. For security, we each grabbed an M-16 and some ammo magazines. I took my GPS and Camelback water bladder, and then we headed back down the highway.

U.S. Army soldiers from the 82nd Airborne Division evacuate wounded soldiers during a sandstorm

But the other chopper wasn't there. We kept walking and calling on the radio, but the static-charged dust swirling about rendered it useless. Even my GPS signal was intermittent. When we'd traveled over a mile back down the highway and found nothing, we decided it wouldn't do for us to end up as captives being paraded before the Al Jazeera and Iraqi state-run television cameras. We turned around and hurried back the way we'd come.

Aboard Griff's bird, two Navy shock-trauma medical corpsmen, Chief Tom Barry and PO Jason Comeaux, had started treating the wounded Marine corporal as soon as he was brought aboard. There was little they could do to treat the shrapnel wound in his gut. The docs feared he was in danger of internal bleeding and going into shock, so they started an IV and wrapped him in blankets.

Medical corpsmen are tough, brave, yet amazingly gentle men. Chief Barry had seen combat before. When our aircraft were forced to land, he announced, "We've only got hours here; we don't have days to get someone with a gut wound into surgery."

We've been here for hours, huddled in the belly of the darkened aircraft, alone in the center of the deserted highway. Over the noise of the wind we can hear the sound of gunfire and mortar or RPG impacts about a kilometer off to our north. From the volume of fire it sounds like a really intense engagement, and it seems to be getting closer. To make matters worse, we have no idea where the nearest "friendlies" are. For all we know, the next thing we might see is a group of Iraqis or fedayeen on "technicals"—those pick-up trucks with a .50-cal mounted on the back—roaring down the road behind us. Magazines and ammo have been distributed to all, and we are prepared for the worst.

Inside the chase bird, Chief Barry and "Doc" Comeaux had Griff playing the role of "nurse" for the badly wounded corporal. While one of the "docs" stood guard, he helped the other corpsman change the blood-soaked battle dressings, switch IV bags, and pat his lips with a moistened gauze pad to relieve his thirst.

By dark, the young Marine's temperature was rising, his pulse and blood pressure were growing steadily weaker, and there was blood in his urine. Chief Barry sat up with him for the entire night in the shuddering CH-46 as the wind howled outside.

Just after dawn on Tuesday, 25 March, a Marine Humvee with a big American flag fastened to its side came creeping down the road. We were fortunate that it wasn't an Iraqi or fedayeen vehicle because we couldn't hear or see it until it almost hit the back of the helicopter. The driver, a Marine lieutenant colonel named Stroehman, was out reconnoitering a location for a FARP just south of our position when the sandstorm hit. He and his men had spent the miserable night in the open along Route 1.

It was Stroehman who came up with an ingenious solution for getting the disabled helicopter to a safer location. Using a strap from a large cargo net and his Humvee, he towed the CH-46 to his defensive perimeter like an oversized camping trailer. Once that was done, they considered loading the wounded man on Stroehman's Humvee and trying to crawl down Route 1 to the field hospital at Tallil. But they decided against it since they didn't know if enemy units were between them and the FARP, and darkness was already settling in again.

Through the second night, the wounded Marine suffered terribly. Dust caked around his nostrils, mouth, and eyes. The doctors administered small amounts of morphine to ease his pain and antibiotics through the IVs in hopes of reducing the infection from his stomach wounds. Each time the wind buffeted the CH-46 he gritted his teeth as he, along with the rest of us, was pummeled like a load of laundry in an unbalanced washing machine.

On the morning of the 26th the wind changed to a strong but steady breeze. We could finally see the glow of the sun—still overcast, but the storm was obviously blowing itself out. As the ceiling lifted and the visibility improved slightly, a Marine Corps Huey helicopter came hovering slowly down the road, looking for fuel. Lt. Col. Stroehman directed the bird to land next to one of his fuel trucks and told the pilot, Maj. Tim Kolb, about the plight of the wounded corporal. Maj. Kolb agreed instantly to take him to the hospital at the Tallil FARP.

Finally, as the weather cleared at dawn on the 27th, we were able to evacuate the body of our deceased Navy corpsman, HM3 Michael Johnson. A CH-46 from HMM-268 took his remains back to Kuwait. His family in Little Rock, Arkansas, was informed of their terrible loss. A year later a new medical clinic at the Marine Corps recruit depot in San Diego was named in his honor—a reminder to all new recruits that Marines love their corpsmen.

U.S. Marines pay their final respects during a memorial service for three fallen comrades

★ ★ ★ ★ ★ ★ ★ ★ ★ ★ ★ ★

7

TO THE GATES OF BAGHDAD

Iraqi armor was no match for the U.S. M-1 Abrams tank

THURSDAY, 27 MARCH 2003

Dawn this morning is the first time we've seen the sun rise in five days. Joe Dunford's reinforced regiment, with RCT-7 in trace, is on the move up Route 1 toward the Tigris River and Baghdad. Off to our east, despite continued harsh engagements with small groups of foreign fedayeen, Task Force Tarawa and RCT-1 have succeeded in forcing the passage through An Nasiriyah and have reopened the offensive up Route 7 toward Al Kut. Farther south, the British have surrounded Basra, secured Iraq's southern oil infrastructure, and liberated the towns along the Shatt al Arab waterway so that it can be swept for mines. Off to the west, the main attack by the Army's V Corps, spearheaded by MG Buford Blount's 3rd ID, has beaten the Medina division of the Republican Guard and is now resupplying its armored columns north of Najaf.

From our satellite hookup with FOX News in New York we learned that during the night, as the dust storm blew itself out, more than nine hundred paratroopers of the 173rd Airborne Brigade had parachuted onto an airfield north of Mosul. This set the stage for the northern offensive that had been derailed when NATO ally Turkey refused to allow the 4th ID to enter Iraq from Turkish territory. With the air clear of sand for the first time in five days, the sky filled with Marine Cobras, AV-8 Harriers, and F-18 strike fighters, flying close air support (CAS) missions for the lead elements of RCT-5 as they closed in on Ad Diwaniyah.

During the sandstorm, deep strikes directed by high-flying USAF JSTARS aircraft and Navy P-3s continued. But close-in missions controlled by Marine forward air controllers—Marine pilots assigned to ground combat units—all but ceased while we were enveloped in orange dust. Once the air cleared they returned with a vengeance, firing TOW and Hellfire missiles from the Cobras and dropping laser-guided bombs on enemy armor and emplacements in front of the Marine column.

Only seven days into Operation Iraqi Freedom, almost half the country and nearly all of its resources were in coalition hands. The vaunted 485,000-man Iraqi army was mauled in every confrontation with American and British forces. More than eight thousand Iraqi soldiers were already prisoners and tens of thousands more decided not to die for Saddam and simply walked away from their defensive positions.

Some Iraqi units, like those at Najaf and An Nasiriyah, fought fiercely and surrendered ground reluctantly when confronted with overwhelming U.S. firepower. But many others engaged for a while, then slipped into civilian clothes and joined the local population. It became common for soldiers and Marines sweeping

It's hard to tell who the enemy is if he's not shooting at you

through a trench line from which they had just taken fire to find the position littered with green uniforms, helmets, gas masks, empty magazine pouches, and black boots. And then, just moments later they would come upon dozens of beardless young men with short, military-style haircuts, garbed in Arab dress, just standing around with no apparent place to go.

Everyone knew that just minutes or hours before, these "civilians" had been wearing the discarded uniforms. Yet stopping to detain them would have delayed the movement north. This would have aggravated an already strained logistics system if trucks had been diverted from resupply runs to haul enemy prisoners south to prisoner-of-war camps.

Third ID soldiers accept the surrender of Iraqi forces

Some of my embedded "colleagues" in the press expressed surprise that on the drive toward Baghdad there were few civilian casualties. In fact, there were times—most notably during the close fighting in An Nasiriyah—when several carloads of civilians ignored orders to stop at a Marine roadblock and were fired upon. That there were relatively few such incidents is a tribute to the exceptional discipline and the leadership of the junior officers and noncommissioned officers—corporals, sergeants, staff sergeants, and gunnery sergeants, the people who make the difference in a firefight.

After crossing the Euphrates River and leaving the trackless southern desert behind, we passed by or through increasing numbers of small villages, palm groves, harvested fields, and cultivated farms. Each time the attack halted, the Marines sent patrols off to the flanks of the column, which stretched from just south of Ad Diwaniyah all the way back to the Euphrates River. Often, civil affairs units, human exploitation teams, and medical personnel accompanied these patrols to win some "hearts and minds" by providing limited emergency medical help, humanitarian rations, water, and even small amounts of fuel for tractors and irrigation pumps.

A U.S. Army medic examines a wounded Iraqi soldier

And these gestures were having the desired effect. Iraqi civilians began coming to us and bringing their sick and injured, along with information about the enemy. A few even admitted to being former Iraqi soldiers who actually believed that removing Saddam was a noble and worthy cause. If more of them had felt that way, perhaps this war could have been avoided.

THEY ALL FALL DOWN

★ ★ ★ ★ ★ ★ ★ ★ ★ ★ ★ ★

THURSDAY, 27 MARCH 2003
AD DIWANIYAH TO HANTUSH, IRAQ

On the afternoon of the 27th, Maj. John Ashby, the executive officer of the HMLA-267 helicopter unit, asked if I wanted to ride along as he and his wingman flew Brig. Gen. John Kelly, the assistant commander of the 1st Marine Division, to Qal' at Sukkar, about 110 kilometers east on Route 7. Gen. Kelly was making a quick trip to brief the commanders of Task Force Tarawa and RCT-1 whose lead elements were already less than fifty miles from Al Kut and ready to attack north across the Tigris River.

The flight east was uneventful. The two Huey helicopters were escorted by two heavily armed Cobra gunships. We stayed well south of the villages along Route 17, the east-west highway connecting the two prongs of the 1st Marine Division attack.

While we were on the ground, the two Cobras—one of them piloted by Allen Grinalds, the son of one of my dearest friends—were scrambled to support a Marine unit in contact. They were still out on that mission when Gen. Kelly returned to the LZ. He decided not to wait for the Cobras to return, rearm, and refuel, so the two Hueys lifted off into the setting sun without escorts.

Both UH-1N helicopters had door-mounted, .50-caliber XM2 machine guns. The bird I was in also had a pod loaded with 2.75-inch rockets and a six-barreled, GAU-17 mini-gun hanging out the right side.

We flew west following Route 17, at fifty to seventy-five feet, clipping along at ninety to one hundred knots, trailing the lead helicopter by fifty to one hundred meters. I was sitting on a troop seat in the center of the bird, following our course on my map and had just marked our location, "Al Budayr," when I heard through my headphones, "We're taking fire!"

I look up from the chart to see the lead bird veering left and right as green tracers just miss the left side of the helicopter. The VIP bird with Gen. Kelly aboard rolls left as its machine gun unleashes a burst almost straight down at the weapon on the ground that had just fired at and barely missed their helicopter.

I grab my camera and hold it over Maj. Ashby's head, aiming it forward through the wind screen. Five or six men wearing what look like black pajamas are running out of a two-story building carrying AK-47s. They appear transfixed by the lead helicopter as it screams directly over their heads.

As the lead helicopter swoops hard left out of our line of fire, Ashby says over the intercom, "Arming rockets. Stand by." His voice is cool as ice, flat, unexcited, like he's ordering lunch over the phone as he flicks a red switch on the console. Through my viewfinder, I can see several of the Iraqis kneel down and fire at the lead bird as it passes over them. They still haven't seen us. But then, just as Ashby tilts our UH-1N into a shallow dive from 150 feet, one of the black-clad shooters spots us. As he wheels to aim at our helicopter, I hear Ashby say calmly, "Firing rockets."

There is a roar as three of the rockets ripple out of the pod on the left side of our helicopter. Although I don't recall being startled by the sound, the tape later shows that my camera jerks and then quickly focuses back on the trajectory of the three deadly missiles. They are fleschette rounds. Each warhead contains thousands of tiny metal darts set to detonate twenty feet from the target. They perform as advertised, and puffs of red smoke from all three missiles erupt over the Iraqis. They are cut down in an instant by a shower of steel.

Ashby pulls up and hard left, the G-force pushing me back in my seat. The camera points off at a crazy angle, and Ashby's voice comes over the intercom: "And they all fall down." No euphoria, no joy, no sadness—simply a statement of fact.

The view from a UH-1N armed Huey helicopter in flight

QUAGMIRE

★ ★ ★ ★ ★ ★ ★ ★ ★ ★ ★ ★

A resupply convoy headed for the front lines

At 0300, Griff and I set up our satellite gear for our regular report on the *Hannity & Colmes* show. We were surprised to find out from FOX News that the U.S. Central Command had ordered an "operational pause." This was so supplies of food, water, fuel, and ammunition could catch up with the ground forces before the final push on Baghdad. The Marines gathered around us were stunned by the information, since there had been no serious shortages of anything but sleep and showers. In the eight days since the war started, the logisticians had been doing an amazing job of pushing forward all necessary supplies—plus spare parts and the myriad items of equipment needed to keep a military force of this size and complexity on the move day and night.

I made my way to the RCT-5 canteen to scrounge a cup of hot coffee and found a tired and exasperated Col. Joe Dunford. He cautioned me that we could not air the information because it involved current and future military operations. Then he told me he had just received orders to turn around and move back south because CENTCOM (U.S. Central Command) was concerned that we were inside the "red zone" for chemical attack. The Marine columns advancing on Baghdad from the east on hard-surface roads were in reasonably good shape logistically. But the Army's V Corps pushing up through the western desert was in need of fuel and ammunition after their heavy engagements at Najaf.

As ordered, his five thousand Marines turned around and rolled back down the road to the Route 1/Route 8 interchange.

Back in the United States, the second-guessing of the Pentagon was well under way. Much of the so-called mainstream media said that Operation Iraqi Freedom had run afoul of bad planning. Once again, retired generals took to the airwaves with dire predictions about how many months it would take to capture Baghdad. The word "quagmire" was used as if coalition forces were bogged down in a swamp.

This created consternation for those who gathered around our tiny TV set to watch what was being said about the "pause" and the move to the rear. They heard the "talking heads" saying that the Marines had to stop because they had outrun their supplies. This was being said even while four-engine Marine C-130s landed on the nearby highway to disgorge tons of supplies and pump thousands of gallons of fuel into waiting tank trucks and fuel bladders.

One afternoon after we had pulled back, we were preparing to go live on our network morning show, *Fox & Friends.* The producer called me on my satellite phone to say that the *New York Times,* the *Washington Post,* and several other newspapers were beating the drum about the Marines being out of food, water, and ammo. I told him it just wasn't true and that I would be glad to put some Marines on live to tell the American people how things really were.

The producers in New York said, "Great, let's go now!"

Standing in front of the camera, I asked a nearby Marine gunnery sergeant if he had anyone available to go live on FOX News. In an instant, Sgt Jason Witt was on my left and a young lance corporal was on my right.

Without time to brief the young Marines on what was happening, I could hear Steve, Edie, and Brian, the hosts, talking to me through my earpiece. Their first question was about the Marines having outrun their supplies.

I turn to Sgt Witt and ask: "Have you guys been hungry out here?"

"No, sir," he replies. "We've been well taken care of."

"And how about thirsty?"

"No, sir . . . we're good."

"And ammo?"

The sergeant grins and answers, "Good on ammo, and morale is good, sir."

I turn to the lance corporal, "The New York Times *says the Marines are out of food, water, and ammo. Are you hungry?"*

"No, sir."

"Are you thirsty?"

"No, sir."

"Are you short on ammo?"

"No, sir."

"Well, what do you need?" I persist.

Without a moment's hesitation, the young Marine replies, "Just send more enemy, sir."

To some, these two Leathernecks probably sounded as if they were spouting macho Marine bravado. But they had all been told before they left Kuwait that they were going into the attack "light" on supplies. All the Marines had been informed that they would receive two MRE rations per day, a total of five thousand calories. They were also told, "Potable water will be delivered in bottles, so don't waste it on bathing. Ammunition and fuel are the number one priorities for resupply, so don't waste them either. When you can, shut off your engine. And if you find uncontaminated Iraqi diesel fuel, use it."

Marines who have been in the service for more than a few years joke that the official motto of the Marine Corps may be *Semper Fidelis*, but the real slogan is, "The Marines have done so much with so little for so long that we now can do anything with nothing forever." For them, this was "business as usual."

"The Marines have done so much, with so little, for so long that we now can do anything, with nothing, forever."

MAKE READY TO MOVE OUT

★ ★ ★ ★ ★ ★ ★ ★ ★ ★ ★ ★

MONDAY, 31 MARCH 2003

During the "operational pause," 3rd Bn, 4th Marines, part of RCT-7, cleared Route 17 of fedayeen like those who had shot at our Huey helicopters over Al Budayr on 27 March. There were gunfights every day, most of them against bands of foreign fedayeen and roving Iraqi irregulars.

Because these "irregulars" were all but invisible to high-flying surveillance aircraft, the Army and Marines

Unmanned aerial vehicles became indispensable as the war went on

made increasing use of unmanned reconnaissance aircraft—UAVs or RPVs. One of these units set up on a nearby roadside airstrip. Griff and I were allowed to videotape the takeoff and recovery of several Pioneer UAVs, the less expensive predecessor to the now-famous, sleek new Predators. We filed this report:

Pioneer UAV ready for takeoff

Hurled into the sky from an elevated launch rail by compressed air, and recovered on a highway, the boom-tailed Pioneers have a GPS tracking system, cameras, emission detectors, and electronic sensors jammed into their fuselage. And even though each one costs nearly a million dollars, they are all flown under remote control by young enlisted Marines. When an RPV spots an enemy force, emplacement, or equipment, fixed wing, rotary wing, or artillery fire can be brought to bear on the target in a matter of minutes. The VMU-2 control van also has the ability to transmit the image of what the RPV is seeing in real time to ground combat unit commanders or to print out aerial photos of the area over which the RPV has flown.

When one of these Pioneer UAVs spots a group of Iraqi soldiers or fedayeen massing, the area is first hit with artillery fire and then Cobras are called in to follow up. These attacks are so devastating that the survivors often surrender, some of them waving white flags at the low-flying RPVs.

Leaving its launch rail

After one such event, Griff and I became participants in a surreal scene like something out of a movie. As we were setting up our camera and satellite transceiver for a live shot back to New York, two young military-age Iraqi males carrying white flags walked up behind Griff and surrendered to him. We quickly summoned MAJ Sara Cope, the commanding officer of the Military Police detachment, and she had them taken into custody. She later told us that they had given themselves up because they were hungry and thirsty. This somewhat deflated Griff's claim that they had done so because he looked so tough in his FOX News baseball cap.

DRIVE NORTH

★　★　★　★　★　★　★　★　★　★　★　★

Thankfully, Iraqi indirect fire was usually inaccurate

On 1 April, the "operational pause" ended with a vengeance. By midnight, three reinforced battalions of "Fighting Joe" Dunford's RCT-5 were on the move, back up Route 1 under a dramatic display of artillery fire. Throughout the night, bright orange RAP rounds arced over our heads, pounding enemy positions that had been reoccupied when the Marines were told to reverse course for the "pause."

Though I've spent a quarter of a century in the Marine Corps, I was still amazed at the speed with which the Marine columns raced north toward Baghdad. With the exception of contingents in Afghanistan and small detachments deployed with Marine expeditionary units elsewhere around the world, the Marine Corps had committed all of its tank and LAV battalions, over half its infantry and artillery, two-thirds of its engineers, all of its bridging equipment, over half of its helicopter assets, and nearly the same proportion of its AV-8 and F-18 fixed-wing aircraft to Operation Iraqi Freedom. In all, more than sixty thousand Marines, more than one-third of the entire Marine Corps, were in this fight. And so, when I MEF gave the order to "get up and go" after the "tactical pause," the Marines were determined and ready.

Beside us on the highway there is a steady rumble as Dunford's one thousand tracked and wheeled vehicles move north up Route 27 headed for the Tigris River. Behind us at Ad Diwaniyah, RCT-7 is in a series of running gunfights with fedayeen and Iraqi irregulars. Over the last twenty-four hours, the Iraqis have been lobbing 122-millimeter rockets at the Marines from within the city. Several of these Soviet-era BM-21 rockets have hit in the vicinity of the RCT-5 command post, causing us to scramble for cover. On two occasions we were ordered to "mask up" for fear that they might be firing chemical warheads. Though these rockets are wildly inaccurate, each one is packed with 140 pounds of high explosives—and no one wants an Iraqi rocketeer to get lucky.

Enemy resistance as we moved up the highway was sporadic, nothing like the sustained fighting that Task Force Tarawa endured at An Nasiriyah. There, dismounted infantry battled from block to block and house to house against fedayeen, who had the advantage of sheltering themselves among the civilian population.

RCT-7 dispatched 3rd Bn, 4th Marines, reinforced by a company of tanks, to enter Ad Diwaniyah and root out the fedayeen and Baathists loyal to Saddam. The smart ones surrendered; those who didn't died. By early afternoon, enemy resistance inside Ad Diwaniyah had ceased. So had the rocket fire.

By nightfall on 1 April, 1st Bn, 5th Marines, succeeded in smashing through a dug-in Iraqi infantry company that had been defending the bridge over the twenty-meter-wide Saddam Canal—the last obstacle before reaching the Tigris River at An Numaniyah. Off to the west, the Army's 3rd ID, with Greg Kelly embedded, was battling their way toward the Karbala Gap southwest of Baghdad. But neither of these were big news. Instead, the "scoop of the day" was from CENTCOM headquarters in Qatar, which had handed out a terse news release that left more questions unanswered than it explained:

> **1 April 2003**
>
> **FOR IMMEDIATE RELEASE**
>
> **U.S. ARMY POW RESCUED—OPERATION IRAQI FREEDOM:**
>
> Coalition forces have conducted a successful rescue mission of a U.S. Army prisoner of war held captive in Iraq. The soldier has been returned to a Coalition-controlled area. More details will be released as soon as possible.

While we were preoccupied with the realities around us, all kinds of speculation had floated around about the engagement in which eighteen vehicles of the 507th Maintenance Company from Fort Bliss, Texas, had become separated from the rest of their convoy and fallen prey to a fedayeen ambush.

According to those I interviewed who were on the rescue, the operation was put together very hurriedly on 31 March. An Iraqi civilian in An Nasiriyah had told a Marine sergeant that an American female soldier was being treated for severe injuries in the city's Saddam Hussein General Military Hospital. The information was passed up the line. Before long Task Force 20 (TF-20)—a secret unit comprised of CIA paramilitary personnel, Delta Force operators, and Navy SEALs—was given the job of getting her out.

The wounded POW information could have been a ruse to lure U.S. troops into a trap. Many Iraqi schools and hospitals had been converted into arsenals by the fedayeen. So Special Ops command put together a "raid plan" by the end of daylight on 31 March. The mission required the Marines to create a diversion several blocks from the hospital while an Army Ranger security cordon was established around the medical facility. Then Task Force-20 operators would swoop in by helicopter to take down the hospital, rescue any American POWs, and extract them before the Iraqis could react.

According to the eyewitnesses I talked to, the plan went flawlessly. At precisely 0100 hours local on 1 April, the Marines kicked off an impressive display of firepower with troops, tanks, and artillery as the Task Force-20 operators flew in aboard TF-160 Nightstalker helicopters to seize the hospital, with AC-130 gunships providing cover.

The lights went out in the hospital as planned. The Iraqis—disoriented by the Marine fire on the other side of town, the noise of the helicopters, and stun grenades—offered little or no resistance. The rescue team, using NVGs, was able to search the buildings and grounds for other Americans. They apparently found Army PFC Jessica Lynch exactly where the source said she was, an unarmed Iraqi male nurse standing beside her bed.

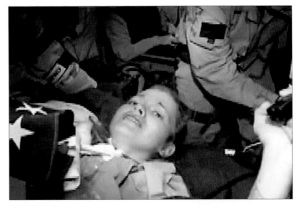

As it turned out, several Iraqi doctors, fearful that she might die, had intended to turn her over to the Americans but were afraid to do so because of the fedayeen. During the raid, one of the hospital staff members led the commandos to the morgue where the bodies of two deceased Americans were located and pointed out where nine more bodies were buried outside. After evacuating PFC Lynch by helicopter, the Rangers retrieved the bodies of the other American dead. There has been a lot of speculation about the mission in the years since. But according to my storyteller, at the time it was a "perfect operation. No American casualties. No Iraqi casualties. Mission accomplished."

Above – Captured when her convoy was ambushed in An Nasiriyah, Lynch was rescued by U.S. Army and Marine units
Below – PFC Jessica Lynch en route home

ACROSS THE TIGRIS

★ ★ ★ ★ ★ ★ ★ ★ ★ ★ ★ ★

The U.S. M-1 Abrams tank is the most accurate armor platform ever built

By dawn on 2 April, the 2nd Bn, 5th Marines, and 2nd Tank Bn had battled their way through An Numaniyah—a city of about seventy-five thousand people—and were firing at Iraqi armor across the Tigris. The Iraqis, caught completely by surprise at the Marine advance up Route 27, had failed to destroy the heavy span over the Tigris at An Numaniyah.

I walked into the RCT-5 command post and found Joe Dunford patiently talking to his tank battalion commander on the radio as if chatting on the phone with an old friend. No bravado. No tough talk. Just two warriors who respected each other, knowing the lives of their men hung in the balance if they made the wrong decision.

As the sun crests the horizon on his right, Lt. Col. Mike Oehle, the commanding officer of 2nd Tank Bn, can see the Iraqis on the far side of the Tigris through the thermal sights of his M-1 tank. The enemy has a handful of T-72s, some BMPs, and dug-in infantry with RPGs. Oehle's unit has already taken some RPG hits coming through the city, but his command is intact, and so is the massive concrete-and-steel span across the muddy Tigris. Incredible as it seems, the Iraqis still have not blown the bridge.

Crossing the Tigris on the concrete bridge at An Numaniyah is a terrible risk. The threat of being cut off by a superior force on the other side is very real. So too is the possibility that the Iraqis might have the bridge registered by artillery, rigged with high explosives or even chemical weapons. Dunford asks Mike Oehle if he thinks the bridge can be taken. Oehle says, "We can do it."

After a brief but furious fight supported by Cobra gunships, the bridge was in American hands and the lead elements of 2nd Tank Bn crossed the Tigris. That night, they used the cover of darkness to rearm, repair, and refuel, in preparation for the run to Baghdad.

PRESS ON TO THE CAPITAL

★ ★ ★ ★ ★ ★ ★ ★ ★ ★ ★ ★

Lt. Gen. Jim Conway and Maj. Gen. James Mattis decide to "Go heavy kinetic all the way to Baghdad"

The order came down by radio during the early hours of 3 April, and Dunford wasted no time carrying it out. Before dawn, Lt. Col. Sam Mundy's 3rd Bn, 5th Marines, supported by a company of LAVs and a company of tanks, kicked off up Route 6 beneath a barrage of artillery. With the first hint of dawn, the Cobras went to work, buzzing up and down the highway over Mundy's column like pairs of angry wasps, looking for targets. As they closed in on Al Aziziyah there was plenty to shoot at.

The first call for a cas-evac came in a little after 0700 hours. Less than three minutes later we were in the air, flying up Route 6 at 50 feet and 120 knots, en route to pick up three of Mundy's Marines who had been wounded by Iraqi mortar fire.

As we fly up the highway, "fire trenches" burning bright orange are sending plumes of black smoke billowing into the sky. The roadside is littered with wrecked Iraqi trucks and armor, some of it still burning. The troops, with their penchant for pithy vernacular, have taken to referring to the wrecked enemy equipment as "roadkill."

As the CH-46s land on the green smoke that marks the pickup zone just outside Al Aziziyah, my camera catches a platoon of dismounted Marines, all prone and pointing outward. Directly on the nose of Driscoll's bird is an M-1 tank, buttoned up, its turret traversing back and forth as the gunner trolls for targets. Smoke is rising from several multistory structures in the city. While the litters with the wounded are loaded in the back, an F/A-18 rolls in low and drops an MK-81 one thousand-pound bomb. By the time the sound of the concussion reaches us, the jet is already out of sight in the blue sky above and we are airborne with the casualties aboard.

It went like this for the rest of the day. In Al Aziziyah, 3rd Bn, 5th Marines, encountered both fedayeen and elements of the Republican Guard Al Nida division. As casualties increased, so did the calls for Red Dragon cas-evac helicopters. Lt. Col. Driscoll and his aircrews were constantly in the air—and getting shot at.

As we approach the pickup zone, a smoke grenade pops just as Driscoll lifts the nose of the CH-46 to flare for landing. I'm leaning out the right side door of the helicopter with my video camera when I see an RPG whizzing toward us from a grove of trees. I'm not supposed to, but instinct takes over and I yell, "RPG, three o'clock, incoming!" into the intercom mike on my helmet.

The engines screech and the rotor blades sound as if they might break as Driscoll pulls up, momentarily arresting the helicopter's descent. The RPG passes beneath us and detonates against the berm beside the roadway to our left.

The Marines below us, having seen where the RPG came from, open fire in a furious fusillade. Directly below us there is a swirling sandstorm generated by our rotor wash. Leaning out the door, GySgt Pennington calmly says over the intercom, "Straight down, twenty feet, sir." Trusting the judgment of his crew chief, Driscoll lowers the twelve-ton helicopter straight down and drops the ramp. The armored assault vehicles and the dismounted troops keep the enemy in the tree line pinned down. The litter bearers, running hunched over, bring the three wounded up the ramp and snap the litters into the straps on the left side of the bird. The two corpsmen, Docs Newsome and Comeaux, are already evaluating them and starting IVs to reduce shock as we lift off. The whole process—from landing to takeoff—has taken less than four minutes.

By late afternoon the 2nd Tank Bn had broken through the Iraqi defenses at Al Aziziyah and Mundy's infantry was clearing Iraqi defenders from the streets and alleys. Mundy's last task, accomplished just before nightfall, was to push a rifle company across a small bridge over the Tigris River. By the time his Marines won the sharp, pitched battle at the bridge, RCT-5 had captured three crossing points over the waterway.

After dark, Dunford moved his command post forward, beyond the town Mundy had just secured. Griff and I rode with them up Route 6 in a Humvee. Through our NVGs we could see dozens of shattered Iraqi tanks and other vehicles littering the edges of the highway. It was clear that the Iraqis meant to hold Al Aziziyah—but had failed. A good number of the Iraqi tanks had been destroyed, not while facing the oncoming Marines but while heading northwest in retreat toward Baghdad.

After a few hours of sleep, Griff and I dragged our broadcast gear out of the Humvee and plugged in to file our report. When we came up on the satellite link, Greg Kelly, embedded with 3rd ID, was reporting on the furious day-long battle to capture Saddam International Airport. The videotape he and Mal James shot and fed over a satellite dish back to Fox News Center in New York was some of the most dramatic combat footage I've ever seen.

When we went live on *Hannity & Colmes* at 0330, the star-lit sky was once again full of RAP rounds as the 11th Marines' artillery softened up Iraqi defenses around the Tigris River town of Tuwayhah, less than thirty-five kilometers from Saddam's capital. I concluded my report by stating the obvious:

"The U.S. Army in the west and the Marines in the east are literally knocking on the gates of Baghdad."

★ ★ ★ ★ ★ ★ ★ ★ ★ ★ ★ ★ ★

8

INTO BAGHDAD AND BEYOND

"There are no American infidels in Baghdad. Never!"
— BAGHDAD BOB

"I got on FOX News and said, 'I know where he is, tell him to stay there for 15 minutes and I'll come get him' because we were right outside the Ministry of Information."
— LTC ERIC SCHWARTZ, COMMANDER, TASK FORCE 1-64, 2ND BN COMBAT TEAM,
PRESIDENTIAL PALACE, BAGHDAD

★ ★ ★ ★ ★ ★ ★ ★ ★ ★ ★ ★ ★

FRIDAY, 4 APRIL 2003

The final push into Saddam's capital became a grueling operation for the soldiers closing in from the west and the Marines battling in from the east. In the pre-dawn hours of 3–4 April, the Army's 3rd ID was heavily engaged at the Saddam International Airport. Greg Kelly and his FOX News field producer/cameraman, Mal James, covered the withering gunfight and actually broadcast some of it live, via their satellite dish.

Kelly and James had been embedded with the 3rd ID all the way from Kuwait and had already covered the fight at An Najaf and

Mal James en route to Baghdad

the breakthrough at the Karbala Gap against the Medina division of the Republican Guard. Both of them had narrowly avoided serious injury or death when the armored column in which they were embedded came under fire.

Greg Kelly with the 3rd ID

Late on 3 April, a company-sized unit from 3rd ID, consisting of fewer than twenty Abrams tanks and Bradley fighting vehicles, conducted a "reconnaissance in force" action west of the airport and seized two intersections on a key approach. Told to "hold in place," they did so against overwhelming odds throughout the night. By dawn on 4 April, the small unit had withstood over a dozen assaults by Republican Guard armor and dismounted fedayeen.

By late afternoon on 4 April GEN Blount's 1st, 3rd, and 4th Brigade Combat Teams of the 3rd ID had seized the airport and were defending it against determined Iraqi counter-attacks. T-72 and T-55 tanks attempted to retake the airport, supported by armored vehicles and truckloads of suicidal fedayeen. It was during these fierce engagements that SFC Paul Ray Smith of B Company, 11th Engineer Bn, saved the lives of scores of U.S. soldiers.

A 3rd ID Bradley enters Baghdad

MEDAL OF HONOR CITATION

For conspicuous gallantry and intrepidity at the risk of his life above and beyond the call of duty:

Sergeant First Class Paul R. Smith distinguished himself by acts of gallantry and intrepidity above and beyond the call of duty in action with an armed enemy near Baghdad International Airport, Baghdad, Iraq, on 4 April 2003. On that day, SFC Smith was engaged in the construction of a prisoner of war holding area when his Task Force was violently attacked by a company-sized enemy force. Realizing the vulnerability of more than one hundred soldiers, SFC Smith quickly organized a hasty defense consisting of two platoons of soldiers, one Bradley fighting vehicle, and three APCs. As the fight developed, SFC Smith braved hostile enemy fire to personally engage the enemy with hand and anti-tank weapons and organized the evacuation of three wounded soldiers from an APC struck by a RPG and a 60-mm mortar round. Fearing the enemy would overrun their defenses, SFC Smith moved under withering enemy fire to man a .50-caliber machine gun mounted on a damaged APC. In total disregard for his own life, he maintained his exposed position in order to engage the attacking enemy force. During this action, he was mortally wounded. His courageous actions helped defeat the enemy attack and resulted in as many as fifty enemy soldiers being killed, while allowing the safe withdrawal of numerous wounded soldiers. SFC Smith's extraordinary heroism and uncommon valor are in keeping with the highest traditions of the military service and reflect great credit upon himself, the 3rd Infantry Division "Rock of the Marne," and the United States Army.

On 5 April 2005, two years and a day after he was killed, SFC Smith's eleven-year-old son David received the decoration from President Bush, making his dad the first recipient of America's highest award in the war on Islamic terror.

The 1st Marine Division was closing in on Saddam's capital from the east. Keeping the ever-lengthening supply lines open fell to Task Force Tarawa—a task that was becoming more challenging by the hour.

Griff and I spent most of the 4th and 5th of April with the HMM-268 Red Dragons, flying cas-evac missions for Joe Dunford's RCT-5 as it led the Marine advance. The closer we got to Baghdad, the "hotter" the zones became. When a Marine M-1 tank was hit by an ATGM (anti-tank guided missile)—either a Russian-supplied Sagger or one provided by our NATO allies, the French—Driscoll led a flight of two CH-46s "downtown" in Al Aziziyah. It was a hair-raising trip.

Gunny Pennington and Cpl Kendall are crouched down behind their locked and loaded .50 caliber machine guns. Driscoll is making radio calls to the unit on the ground with the casualties. A Marine on the ground advises that they have "popped a smoke" and that the zone is "tight" and "hot." Driscoll's response is a laconic, "Roger, one Phrog inbound."

We sweep down a city street, just clearing the utility poles and rooftops. As Driscoll slows to a hover, a black-clad figure leans out a second-story window and points an AK-47 at us. Pennington sees him and says without preamble, "Firing the right side fifty."

The noise of the gun opening up just two feet in front of my camera is deafening as the black-clad shooter disappears amid chunks of flying brick and mortar. Somehow Driscoll manages to put the CH-46 down in the middle of an intersection. His wingman lands about twenty-five meters behind us. As the rear ramp drops down, there are power lines all around us. Marines, dismounted from their vehicles, are firing into the buildings in every direction. An M-1 tank's main gun booms above the din.

As the dust from our landing clears, Marines and Corpsmen carrying litters start running in a low crouch for the back of our helicopter.

As the casualties are being loaded aboard, an RPG passes in front of the helicopter, exploding in the dirt about fifteen meters beyond us, prompting Driscoll to call over the radio, "How much longer, folks? This is a pretty sporty zone."

While I'm considering this description of the hottest LZ I've ever been in, three Humvees race up from the left, machine guns blazing from their rooftop turrets. It's

the mobile command post for "Grizzly Six," Col. Joe Dunford, the commanding officer of RCT-5.

With the fedayeen pinned down by heavy fire from the Humvees, eleven casualties aboard our helicopter and ten on the bird behind us, the two heavily loaded helicopters lift a few feet off the ground. With power lines just inches away from the blade tips, they rotate 180 degrees so they can head out over "friendlies."

Driscoll's helicopters performed like this for forty-eight hours, carrying water and ammo to the troops in the field and evacuating wounded Marines on the return trip.

On one mission, our bird was hit by machine gun fire, severing a fuel line. Marine ingenuity took over. Within minutes the crew chief had it fixed, using only his Leatherman tool.

By the end of the day, HMM-268 had evacuated more than three dozen critically wounded Marine casualties. One of them was a staff sergeant who had walked aboard the helicopter while helping to carry one of his wounded comrades on a litter.

We've been admonished not to show the faces of U.S. casualties, so my camera catches only his right hand, wrapped in a blood-soaked battle dressing, as he sits down in one of the troop seats.

On the way to the Army shock-trauma hospital, I run out of videotape. We arrive at the hospital, and I help unload the litters so the most seriously injured will be treated first. The corpsmen tell the "walking wounded" seated in the troop seats to wait. After the last litter case is off the bird, I turn to help the staff sergeant with the wounded hand and notice that he is nearly unconscious. As he tries to stand, I see he has been sitting in a pool of his own blood. I yell for one of the docs, who runs up and opens the staff sergeant's flak jacket. He's been gut shot—his intestines are bulging out through the wound. The doc yells, "Keep him awake!" and runs to get a litter team.

As we gently load him on the stretcher, I ask him, "Why didn't you say something?"

He says, "The other guys were hurt worse than I am."

As darkness fell on 5 April, the Marines were ready to cross the Diyala River and more than twenty-five hundred Republican Guard had surrendered to Task Force Tarawa. Iraqi officers were deserting their troops, and friendly intelligence reported that the fedayeen were executing Iraqi deserters.

★　★　★　★　★　★　★　★　★　★　★　★

THE "THUNDER RUNS"

Early in the morning, COL Dave Perkins, commanding the 3rd ID's 2nd Brigade Combat Team, put together what he dubbed Task Force 1-64—a column of M-1 tanks and Bradley fighting vehicles—and charged into the heart of Baghdad in a show of force, in order to further demoralize the enemy. Supported by low-flying A-10s and 3rd ID artillery, the armored column took the Iraqis completely by surprise.

Ironically, as COL Perkins's Task Force 1-64 was blasting their way into the heart of Baghdad, the Iraqi information minister, Mohammed Saeed al-Sahaf, appeared on Iraqi and Arab TV to announce that Americans were nowhere near Baghdad. As he was speaking, FOX News put up a split screen showing U.S. Army tanks parked on the lawn of one of Saddam's downtown palaces. Though enemy fire hit every vehicle in Task Force 1-64, only one Abrams tank was lost. The crew was safely recovered, and there were no U.S. casualties.

Hundreds of Syrian, Jordanian, Saudi, Egyptian, and Yemeni fighters had come to Iraq as fedayeen, intent on becoming martyrs while fighting Americans. Soldiers and Marines grimly obliged. The regular Iraqi Army and even the Republican Guard may have tried to flee or be taken prisoners, but I saw only two of the fedayeen taken alive. Both were badly wounded.

★ ★ ★ ★ ★ ★ ★ ★ ★ ★ ★ ★

SUNDAY, 6 APRIL

A beautiful chapel service provided a brief respite from the war. Sam Mundy's sergeant major had put together a little choir of Marines for the chaplain. Griff's camera recorded the manliest rendition of "Amazing Grace" I'd ever seen—to the accompaniment of artillery.

The respite didn't last long. A few minutes after the chapel service, Capt. Shawn Hughes, one of the Huey pilots from HMLA-267, asked if I'd like to go along on a reconnaissance mission. I quickly agreed. Since there was only one seat available, Griff stayed behind.

A "field expedient" chapel service on the way to Baghdad

We flew north to the Diyala River, marking possible crossing points on the cockpit GPS. About half an hour into the mission, Capt. Hughes received a call over the radio asking him to do a BDA (battle damage assessment) on a nearby Iraqi air base that supposedly had been hit by a coalition air strike.

My map showed the base, and below the name was the notation "abandoned." But as we approached the air field at about seventy-five feet and one hundred knots, the place was anything but. Russian-built MI-8 helicopters on the tarmac told us that if it was targeted by an air strike, they missed.

None of the hangars seemed to have been damaged, either. As the two Hueys wheeled around the far end of the field, men in green uniforms ran from a building, uncovered wheel-mounted anti-aircraft machine guns and started blasting away. Others were already taking a bead on us with AK-47s.

The GAU-17 Minigun can fire several thousand rounds per minute

Over the radio I hear the flight leader say, "We're taking fire." As Hughes veers the bird to make it harder to hit, my camera mike catches the roar of the mini-gun beside me as SSG Compton tries to hold his bursts on target.

As we whip over a truck loaded with troops, they all open fire, and the lead bird runs into the hail of bullets. Through my camera lens the fuel spewing from the Huey's belly looks like something out of one of those old World War II movies, with planes falling out of the sky, trailing streams of smoke as they go down. If one of his anti-aircraft flares goes off right now, or if the bird is hit with a tracer round, it will disappear in a fireball.

I hear over the headphones, "I'm losing fuel pressure and power. I'm going to try to make it across the Diyala." Hughes responds with a terse "Roger."

Both birds have been hit, and there is no time to find the perfect LZ. As the two damaged helicopters settle in on a farmer's field next to an irrigation ditch, Hughes is calling out a distress signal.

The TRAP call is heard by an AV-8 Harrier flying several miles south of us. Hughes tells him that both aircraft have sustained battle damage, but that we have no casualties, yet. He passes on the grid coordinates of trucks we saw loading up with Iraqi troops. The AV-8 heads off to hunt after passing our coordinates to Highlander—the LAVs of 1st LAR Bn. They are several miles south and headed our way fast.

SSG Compton does a quick inventory of our defensive weapons: eight Beretta 9mm pistols, three M-16s, a 240-Golf machine gun, two .50-caliber machine guns—one of them jammed—and a Sony video camera.

The whole scene—downed U.S. aircraft in enemy territory, the irrigation ditch—reminds me of the final scene in the movie The Bridges at Toko-Ri. *In the film, based on James Michener's novel, William Holden and Mickey Rooney are gunned down by Chinese communist troops, and they take refuge in an irrigation ditch.*

I volunteer to fix the jammed .50-caliber, telling the Marines, "I've seen the end of this movie and it's not pretty." No one knows what movie I'm talking about.

As it turned out, we didn't need any of the hardware. By the time the AV-8 Harrier and a couple of F-18 jets had expended all their ammunition, there were no Iraqis left to come after us.

When I finally got back to RCT-5 and HMM-268, Griff and the air crews were asleep in the CH-46s. But as I climbed into a litter for a brief nap, Lt. Col. Driscoll looked up and whispered, "You OK?"

"Yes," I replied.

"Good. You're grounded."

An AV-8 Harrier aircraft such as this one came to our rescue when we were shot down north of Baghdad

The second "Thunder Run" into Baghdad began shortly after sunrise with a terrible roar. COL Dave Perkins's 2nd Battalion Combat Team had just begun moving toward the so-called "regime district"—a complex of Baath party offices, palaces, and parks on the west side of the Tigris River—when an Iraqi rocket landed in the midst of his mobile command post. The high-explosive warhead wrecked a dozen vehicles, killed five soldiers, and wounded thirty more. Yet, in less than an hour, Perkins reconstituted his Task Force 1-64 command group and joined the seventy M-1 tanks and sixty Bradleys in the two-pronged attack into the power center of Saddam's regime.

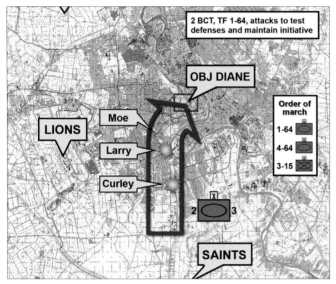

For the next two hours, Perkins's armor engaged in a series of running gunfights to blast their way through Iraqi and fedayeen roadblocks. By noon, 2nd Bn Combat Team had established a perimeter around the presidential palace, convention center, and the Al Rasheed Hotel. The hotel was home to dozens of journalists and foreign supporters of Saddam's regime. But the fighting had just begun.

In order for Perkins's armor to hold the ground they had seized, they had to be resupplied. To ensure that fuel and ammunition could get through, GEN Blount ordered that Task Force 3-15, commanded by LTC Steven Twitty, seize and hold three key intersections on the highway into western Baghdad. Though these strong points were designated "Larry," "Moe" and "Curly" on the battle maps, holding them turned out to be anything but funny.

By mid-afternoon hundreds of fedayeen—intent on becoming "martyrs"—were attacking all three perimeters. The foreign fighters arrived on foot, in commandeered trucks, stolen taxi-cabs, and cars packed with explosives. Volleys of mortar rounds and RPGs rained down on the soldiers, usually followed by human wave suicide assaults. U.S. casualties mounted, among them CSM Robert Gallagher, a grizzled veteran Army Ranger, previously wounded in 1993 in Somalia. Shot through the calf on strongpoint "Curly," he continued to fight, even as a medic applied a field dressing to his wound.

Command Sergeant Major Robert Gallagher

In 1993, CSM Gallagher was part of Task Force Ranger (75th Ranger Regiment), which attempted to capture Somali warlords in Mogadishu. During the fierce fighting on 3–4 October, he was severely wounded. Ten years later, in Iraq, the reporters traveling with his unit, Task Force 3-15 IN, jokingly nicknamed him "Black Hawk Bob." The name stuck. The sergeant major cultivated a hearty, gruff persona with his troops, and they affectionately called him by his nickname, although never to his face.

Gallagher's years of experience with 75th Ranger Regiment (Gallagher and Chuck Holton served four years together in the same battalion) served Task Force 3-15 IN well. He brought that elite force's training and combat techniques to his new unit. He instituted focused training when the soldiers reached Kuwait. The soldiers completed an exhausting but confidence-building regimen. The support soldiers trained alongside the infantrymen, learning to clear trenches, destroy bunkers, and engage targets from any position. Drivers and assistant drivers went through ambush training using live ammunition. Even the fuel handlers attached to the task force completed a live-fire exercise. This paid huge dividends later.

Derived from interview with CSM Robert Gallagher, 19 May 2003, as reported in "On Point—The United States Army in Operation Iraqi Freedom" by the Center for Army Lessons Learned (call.army.mil)

CSM Gallagher with his crew

Though bloodied, the strong points held. At dusk, a resupply convoy of twenty armored vehicles and fifteen trucks led by Army CPT Ronny Johnson ran the fedayeen gauntlet to resupply Perkins's soldiers camped on the grounds of Saddam's west Baghdad palace.

The previous tenant was nowhere to be found.

★ ★ ★ ★ ★ ★ ★ ★ ★ ★ ★ ★

TUESDAY, 8 APRIL

By dawn on 8 April, Saddam Hussein's regime had all but collapsed, but the fighting wasn't over. Fierce battles ensued as the 1st Marine Division took two badly damaged bridges leading into the city.

Late in the afternoon, Griff and I rolled across the Diyala River with the 3rd Bn, 5th Marines, and linked up with the Army's 3rd ID.

To enter the city center, our column had to traverse "Saddam City." More than a million displaced Shiites lived there in a group of crumbling, multistory, Soviet-style apartments without running water or functioning sewage systems.

It's worse than anything I've ever seen in Calcutta, Haiti, or Bangladesh—teeming with naked children, their stomachs distended from malnutrition, raw sewage running in the streets, and piles of trash. Some of it is smoldering with a stench that is enough to make even the troops we're with—who haven't bathed in weeks—smell good.

Despite the conditions, or maybe because of them, the streets were lined with thousands of waving and cheering Iraqis. Ragged children splashed barefoot through puddles of stinking effluent, chasing our convoy. Within a mile or so, the Marines gave away every morsel of food in our vehicle.

As the sun set, we were finally allowed to remove the baggy chemical-biological protective suits that we had been wearing since leaving Kuwait. The Iraqis were unlikely to use such weapons in their capital—we hoped.

We kept the suits nearby, just in case.

★ ★ ★ ★ ★ ★ ★ ★ ★ ★ ★ ★

The streets were lined with cheering Iraqis as Lt. Col. Brian McCoy pushed his dismounted 3rd Bn, 4th Marines infantry, followed by dozens of tanks and other vehicles. The parade ended in downtown Baghdad. When they reached Firdus Square, they found a large crowd taking out their pent-up fury on a forty-foot, black metal statue of Saddam Hussein. After pelting the sculpture with stones and garbage, the Iraqis enlisted the support of the Marines in removing this eyesore.

With the cameras of the international press recording it all, Cpl Edward Chin climbed the King Kong-sized statue of Saddam and draped an American flag over its head. The Stars and Stripes covered Saddam's head for a brief moment. Then, after replacing Old Glory with an Iraqi flag, Cpl Chin secured a chain around Saddam's neck and hooked the other end to the winch cable on an M-88 tank retriever.

As the statue pitched forward on its pedestal, the crowd roared its approval and began to clamor over the fallen idol, attacking it with hammers, stones, and—in an Arab insult—with their shoes. When Saddam's huge head was detached, the cameras caught children jubilantly beating on it. The symbolism was inescapable: Saddam Hussein had been toppled. Strangely absent from the U.S. broadcasts were the retired generals and admirals who just days before had prognosticated that it would take months of heavy combat and thousands of U.S. casualties to take Baghdad.

A Marine watches as the statue of Saddam topples

★ ★ ★ ★ ★ ★ ★ ★ ★ ★ ★ ★

Though Saddam's regime was finished, the fighting in Baghdad wasn't over. Intelligence indicated that a special Republican Guard unit and numerous fedayeen had taken refuge inside the presidential palace complex on the east side of the Tigris River.

Dunford chose Lt. Col. Fred Padilla's 1st Bn, 5th Marines, reinforced by armor, CIA specialists, and a contingent of Delta Force operators, to seize the complex.

In order to take advantage of his troops' NVGs and thermal sights, Lt. Col. Padilla's column—more than seventy tanks, AAVs (armored assault vehicles), LAVs, and Humvees—started rolling through Baghdad's streets well before dawn. But as his lead tanks reached the Jamhuriyah Bridge, the column was hit with a barrage of RPGs and automatic weapons fire from the Al Khulafa Mosque.

With the length of his column under attack and suffering casualties, Padilla made a bold decision. He was uncertain about when the rest of his battalion could close up on the palace complex, his battalion's primary objective. So he ordered his lead element, supported by four tanks and a platoon of AAVs, to smash their way into the palace grounds. It was during this protracted engagement, while trying to evacuate a wounded Marine from Alpha Company, that GySgt Jeffrey Bohr was felled by AK-47 fire from a nearby building (see citation on p. 149).

Once inside the walls surrounding the palace complex, Padilla's Marines seized enough open space to bring in helicopters to evacuate their casualties. I jumped aboard a CH-46 flown by Maj. Don Presto for the flight into the "Palace Zone."

Lt. Col. Jerry Driscoll, CO of HMM-268, briefs his pilots and aircrews before launching for the "Palace LZ"

Each trip out of the Palace LZ leaves the back of our CH-46 looking like a charnel house. Blood-soaked battle dressings, IV bags, latex gloves, pieces of Marine battle gear, and puddles of blood are all over the deck. Each troop seat along the right side of the bird has a pool of blood in it. I suddenly wonder, after all these years, if this is why the nylon webbing is dyed red.

On our third trip into the zone, a Marine captain with battle dressings on his legs and arms hobbles aboard with the litter bearers. He has dirt and blood all over his face and hands, and his flak jacket is shredded. The wounded Marine taps me on the shoulder and hands me a piece of cardboard—torn from an MRE case—on which he'd scrawled a note to his commander: "Send more ammo of all types."

I take the piece of cardboard and tuck it into my flak jacket and then try to help him into a troop seat, but he waves me off and says, "I'm not going. I have work to do."

Suddenly he stops, looks at me again, and shouts over the roar of the helicopter and the gunfire, "Ollie North? What are you doing here?"

I point to the FOX News patch on my jacket and shout back in jest, "Making a war movie."

Without another word, he whips a little disposable camera out of his cargo pocket, wraps an arm around my shoulders, holds the camera out in front of us with his other bloody paw and yells "Smile!"

It's one of those weird moments in the midst of horror that make the inhumanity of war just a little bit more humane. Before I can force the photographer into a seat, he turns and limps off the helicopter. On the back of his flak jacket is stenciled his name: "Basco."

I delivered the "need more ammo" note to the RCT-5 Bravo Command command post when we stopped there between missions. One of the other birds evacuated Capt. Basco after he collapsed from loss of blood.

RCT-5 came in hard on Saddam's palace

The gunfights at the mosque and the palace complex were the last major battles in the capital, and one of my most memorable moments in the campaign.

On one of the early cas-evac flights, we had taken aboard a young lance corporal named Mejia whose forearm had been smashed by a bullet. Despite his wound, he had helped carry another litter-borne casualty. When we arrived at the aid station, I helped Mejia down the helicopter ramp. He insisted that I place him next to the litter he had helped carry aboard the helicopter.

The young Marine then sat down between the handles of the stretcher and cradled the bloody head of his comrade. The wounded Marine had an IV in his arm, the bag of saline fluid suspended from an M-16 jammed into the ground. I asked the lance corporal if I could get him some water but when he looked up at me, tears were running down his face. He said simply, "He's dying, isn't he, sir?"

I choked. "I think he's already gone, son."

Mejia brushed some dirt off the dead man's face and after a moment, looked back at me. Then, through his tears, the young lance corporal said, "He was my gunny, sir. He was a really good man. He was my hero—not just for the way he died, but for the way he lived."

There are people with gray in their temples who don't understand what that young warrior knew. A hero isn't something you are; it's something you do.

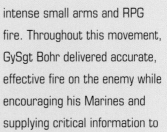

The President of the United States takes pride in presenting the Silver Star Medal (Posthumously) to Jeffrey E. Bohr Jr., Gunnery Sergeant, U.S. Marine Corps, for conspicuous gallantry and intrepidity in action against the enemy while serving as Company GySgt, Company A, 1st Bn, 5th Marine Regiment, RCT-5, 1st Marine Division, I MEF, in support of Operation IRAQI FREEDOM on 10 April 2003. With his company assigned the dangerous mission of seizing a presidential palace in Baghdad and concerned that logistical re-supply might be slow in reaching his comrades once they reached the objective, GySgt Bohr selflessly volunteered to move in his two soft-skinned vehicles with the company's main armored convoy. While moving through narrow streets toward the objective, the convoy took intense small arms and RPG fire. Throughout this movement, GySgt Bohr delivered accurate, effective fire on the enemy while encouraging his Marines and supplying critical information to his company commander. When the lead vehicles of the convoy reached a dead end and were subjected to enemy fire, GySgt Bohr continued to boldly engage the enemy while calmly maneuvering his Marines to safety. Upon learning of a wounded Marine in a forward vehicle, GySgt Bohr immediately coordinated medical treatment and evacuation. Moving to the position of the injured Marine, GySgt Bohr continued to lay down a high volume of suppressive fire, while simultaneously guiding the medical evacuation vehicle, until he was mortally wounded by enemy fire. By his bold leadership, wise judgment, and complete dedication to duty, GySgt Bohr reflected great credit upon himself and upheld the highest traditions of the Marine Corps and the United States Naval Service.

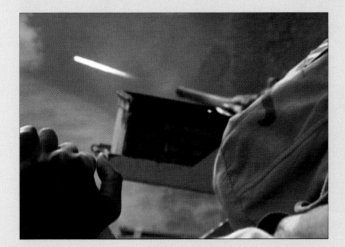

FRIDAY, 11 APRIL

It was the first day since the 20th of March that Griff and I hadn't heard the sound of nearby gunfire. Actually, the most memorable part of the day was our report on *Fox & Friends.* Somehow they had found the wounded Marine who had taken my photo—Capt. Basco—and I got to interview him from his hospital bed in Landstuhl, Germany. As amazing as it was to be talking from Iraq with a man in Germany over a satellite connection to New York, I was most impressed by the top-notch level of care our wounded warriors were receiving.

☆ ☆ ☆ ☆ ☆ ☆ ☆ ☆ ☆ ☆ ☆

SUNDAY, 13 APRIL

After spending Saturday flying around and not seeing much, Palm Sunday services were a welcome respite. It was standing-room-only for the Marines. I've been to hundreds of these chaplain-led worship services. They are ad-hoc affairs held on the hangar deck of an assault landing ship, a bomb crater at Khe Sanh, an artillery revetment at Con Thien, a jungle-covered hillside in Central America, a bunker in Beirut, a sweltering tent in Kuwait, and countless other "field expedients." But none of those venues were more memorable than that gathering of 250 bone-weary, grimy young men clad in their battle gear, standing, sitting, and kneeling in the dusty courtyard of a bombed-out Republican Guard barracks in Baghdad.

The chaplain's words were inspiring and almost prophetic. He used the Gospel text about Christ entering Jerusalem a week before His terrible death as a lesson for the young Marines gathered for worship. "The crowd's cheers turned to jeers. Jesus didn't live up to their expectations," he said. "Most of the people didn't understand His purpose in being there and turned on Him."

"Marine" Chaplain Carey Cash, USN

In a way, the same thing was happening to these Marines. Most of the people in Iraq welcomed them, showering them with flowers, handing them little hand-made American flags, and loving them for having ended Saddam's reign of terror. But back home, it seemed as though their victorious entry into Baghdad, like Christ's entry into Jerusalem on Palm Sunday, was widely misunderstood. Complaints in the U.S. press about "failures to prevent Iraqi looting," the destruction of "cultural sites," the "inability to get water and electricity flowing" seemed grievously unfair to these boys-turned-men who had fought so hard and sacrificed so much to get this far.

★ ★ ★ ★ ★ ★ ★ ★ ★ ★ ★ ★

WEDNESDAY, 16 APRIL

The night had been remarkably quiet. Most of the organized fighting had stopped except for a handful of armed clashes and sniping incidents in Baghdad and Mosul. Most of the gunfire seemed to be the work of irregulars, the fedayeen, or the tens of thousands of criminals that Saddam released from prisons just before the start of the war.

Shortly after dawn on Wednesday, I was sitting on the ramp of an AAV (armored assault vehicle) washing my feet and changing my socks—one of those pleasant, solitary rituals that infantrymen try to practice daily but often cannot—when Griff came running up to me with the Iridium satellite phone. "CENTCOM says that the Marines down south have captured 'Abul somebody' you were looking for," he exclaimed.

"Abul who?" I asked, somewhat irritated that my solitary time was being interrupted.

"I don't know," Griff replied. "Here," he said, handing me the phone, "talk to New York."

The foreign desk had the story right. The name was Abul Abbas, and he'd been captured Tuesday night by Task Force 20 operators during a raid on the outskirts of Baghdad. Abbas, a

Abul Abbas

Palestinian terrorist, had masterminded the October 1985 hijacking of the Italian *Achille Lauro* cruise ship while I was on Ronald Reagan's National Security Council staff. He had been wanted by the U.S. government for nearly twenty years.

The terrorist faction led by Abbas had been a conduit for the money Saddam provided to the families of Palestinian suicide bombers. President George W. Bush named him in a speech in 2002 as part of his argument for removing Saddam Hussein from power. "Iraq has . . . provided safe haven to Abul Abbas," he said, then added, "And we know that Iraq is continuing to finance terror and gives assistance to groups that use terrorism to undermine Middle East peace."

It took longer than anyone wanted, but capturing Abbas confirmed what Ronald Reagan had said back in 1985: "You can run, but you can't hide."

Griff and I finally arrived in Tikrit with a column of armor from the 4th ID

Shortly before noon, while I was interviewing Dunford, Driscoll, and Mundy for our documentary archive, I received another call on my satellite phone from the FOX foreign desk.

"How far is Camp Pennsylvania from where you are?" asked the duty officer in New York.

"About five hundred miles," I replied. "It's in Kuwait. I'm just south of Tikrit. Why?" I asked with a twinge of uncertainty.

"Well, that's where the 4th ID is forming up," he answered. "Someone at the Pentagon has asked for you to be embedded with them as they move into Iraq."

"Yeah, well, tell 'em I smell real bad and maybe they'll take someone else," I said, hoping that maybe Greg Kelly or Rick Leventhal might have been cleaned up by now.

"Can't," he replied. "They asked for you by name. Besides, the other teams are on the way home."

"Well, that's a stunner," was all I could say, knowing that this wasn't going to go down well with Griff, who had a new baby at home who hadn't seen her dad in a couple of months. "How long?" I asked, hoping for an answer of days rather than weeks.

"Couple of weeks," he said and then hastily added, "There is some thought that they might find Saddam."

"OK," I said, "a couple of weeks, but if I'm not home for my daughter's wedding in June you might as well leave me here because I'll be safer in Baghdad than in my own kitchen."

That night, Griff and I joined the U.S. Army's 4th ID, five hundred miles south, in Kuwait. On Easter Sunday we finally got to Tikrit.

* * * * * * * * * * * *

9

LIBERATION LOSES ITS LUSTER

With LTC Pepper Jackson in Bayji, Iraq

TIKRIT, IRAQ

* * * * * * * * * * * *

EASTER MONDAY, 21 APRIL 2003

We "celebrated" the resurrection on the road in a Humvee. Just before dark on Easter Sunday we arrived at the outskirts of Tikrit with LTC Larry "Pepper" Jackson's 3rd Bn of the 66th Armored Regiment, part of the 4th ID out of Fort Hood, Texas. When his armored column halted for the night, Griff and I rode forward with SFC Terrigino, the senior NCO in the battalion's reconnaissance platoon, as they scouted the route into Saddam's hometown. The only evidence that this had once been the dictator's stronghold were the burned-out hulks of Iraqi tanks, trucks, and armored vehicles on the shoulders of the road.

One of Saddam's many palaces in Tikrit became the 4th ID headquarters

Early on Monday we accompanied LTC Jackson into the city and went directly to the deposed despot's opulent palace perched on a bluff overlooking the Tigris River. This was the third of Saddam's many palaces I'd been in at that point, but it was the only one not damaged by coalition bombs. MG Ray Odierno, the 4th ID commanding general, had decided to use it as his headquarters.

Like all of Saddam's residences, this one overlooked some of the most beautiful scenery in all of Iraq. It was encircled by irrigated orchards of fig and eucalyptus trees. An enormous swimming pool graced the south side of the ornate, three-story building. Carefully manicured gardens were terraced into the hillside to the east and south. On the west side, there was a six-car garage, complete with an armored Mercedes limousine.

Yet just out of sight in the surrounding neighborhood, there were thousands of homes without electricity, running water, or sewage systems. Saddam had to have been totally oblivious to the suffering of his people as he turned the country's oil profits into his own personal fortune—or he just didn't care.

Not surprisingly, all of the Iraqi dictator's staff had fled as the Marines of Task Force Tripoli closed in on Tikrit a week earlier. In the days after 4th ID replaced the Marines, Army patrols had managed to capture and detain several of the Iraqi dictator's relatives and high-ranking Baath Party officials before they could flee to Syria. Before I departed the castle, COL Don Campbell, the commander of the 1st Bn Combat Team, told FOX News: "Our missions are to find Saddam, his two sons, and his henchmen and establish a civil government here in this province . . . and we're going to do just that."

As it turned out, the first parts of the mission would be easier to accomplish than the last.

BAYJI, IRAQ

★ ★ ★ ★ ★ ★ ★ ★ ★ ★ ★ ★ ★

FRIDAY, 25 APRIL

We moved with Pepper Jackson's 3rd Bn, 66th Armor, to Bayji, out in the desert northwest of Tikrit. Though U.S. Special Operators had infiltrated the city during the early phase of the campaign, Jackson's troops were the first to take up positions in the area. His soldiers found the local oil refinery, pipelines, and pumping facilities intact and immediately secured them. But in the desert just outside the city, they also found one of the largest ordnance storage facilities in Iraq. They quickly determined that it was completely unsecured.

Saddam had constructed the ammunition depot and nearby railroad switching yards during the 1980–88 Iran-Iraq war because the site was beyond the range of Iran's missiles and air force. The Iraqi army unit responsible for securing the place had simply walked away from their guard posts when Baghdad fell on 9 April. With no one there to stop them, local Iraqis removed nearly twenty kilometers of chain-link perimeter fence and began systematically looting the hundreds of bunkers and warehouses.

Saddam stored 300 million tons of ordnance at the Bayji munitions depot

The depot was far too large to be secured by a single battalion, so Jackson ordered his companies to outpost the facility and set ambushes on the avenues of approach to the ammo dump. His instructions were, "Do what you have to do to keep anyone from getting into this place, because God help us if the fedayeen get their hands on this stuff." Every night for the rest of the time we were with that unit, at least one of Jackson's units would catch Iraqis or fedayeen trying to steal truckloads of ordnance.

The morning after one such "event" I filed this report:

When we arrive, the platoon commander who triggered the ambush is reviewing with his soldiers what happened. The bodies of fourteen men, nearly all dressed in black, are lying on or near a rutted dirt road that enters the ammo dump from the east. According to the battalion S-2, who has collected identity documents from the bodies, only two of the dead are Iraqi. Of the remaining twelve, four are Jordanian, three are Syrian, two are Egyptian, one is a Saudi, and the other two are Lebanese.

The foreigners and their two Iraqi guides, all armed with AK-47s, had disembarked from two pickup trucks about two hundred meters from the nearest ammunition bunkers and walked straight up the road into the killing zone of the night-vision-equipped platoon-sized ambush. The carnage was completely one-sided. There were no American casualties.

U.S. Army engineers and ordnance specialists inspected the depot over the course of several days, with us in tow. What they found were more than five hundred ordnance bunkers and revetments and ninety-five steel structures filled to the top with every conceivable type of ammunition and explosive from around the globe.

Much of the ordnance was in very good shape. Some of it—including Jordanian artillery rounds, Italian land mines, and Saudi small-arms ammunition—was nearly new. In one shed, several hundred green wooden boxes were labeled "Ministry of Procurement, Amman, Jordan," and had shipping tags with delivery dates in January 2003. Several steel buildings contained hundreds of cases of man-portable, shoulder-launched surface-to-air missiles: SA-7s, SA-14s, and SA-16s.

The unguarded anti-aircraft missiles and the tens of thousands of land mines and RPGs created the greatest anxiety among the specialists trying to inventory the site. These weapons can bring down a military helicopter or commercial jet. The mines and RPGs can take out a Bradley fighting vehicle and even an M-1 tank. Many of the surface-to-air missile and RPG cases had been broken open and emptied.

I asked one of the experts what they planned to do with all the ordnance. "I don't know," he responded. "We haven't got enough TNT, Det-Cord, and blasting caps to blow all this. Worse yet, there are probably seventy-five to one hundred sites just like this one elsewhere around the country."

★ ★ ★ ★ ★ ★ ★ ★ ★ ★ ★ ★

SATURDAY, 26 APRIL 2003

On the 25th, twenty-six-year-old Army 1LT Osbaldo Orozco became the first Fort Hood soldier to die in Iraq when his Humvee flipped over while on a combat patrol. That same day, Tarik Aziz—Saddam's former deputy prime minister and the only Christian in the Baath Party inner circle—was captured. As in so many other cases, he was found after a tip from an Iraqi civilian.

Early on the morning of 26 April, the FOX News foreign desk called on my satellite phone and told us that we could head home. Though it had only been two weeks since the fall of Baghdad,

When I left Iraq on the 26th of April, people were still cheering for American troops

it was already becoming clear that the nature of the campaign in Iraq was changing. Conducting "pacification" and civil affairs operations were becoming increasingly dangerous as foreign Jihadists continued to flood into the country.

Before heading to Kuwait for a flight home, we stopped in Tikrit to interview MG Ray Odierno, commander of the 4th ID. His parting words aptly summarized the situation for U.S. troops two weeks after the fall of Baghdad:

> "In many respects this is tougher than beating Saddam's army. We really don't know who the enemy is. He dresses like, looks like, and lives among the civilian population. We are going to need their help if we're going to defeat them—and that means we have to convince the Iraqi people that we're on their side as liberators, not as conquerors. That could prove to be a very tough task."
>
> **—MG Ray Odierno**

Events over the next several months would prove General Odierno to be right on the mark. About the only point he might have added was how hard it would become to keep America's people and political leaders behind the troops.

South of Baghdad, a soldier searches an Iraqi civilian at a security checkpoint

MISSTEPS AND THE RISE
OF THE INSURGENCY

★ ★ ★ ★ ★ ★ ★ ★ ★ ★ ★ ★

As Griff and I journeyed home, the USS *Abraham Lincoln* was headed there too. After ten months of combat operations, including Operation Enduring Freedom in Afghanistan and Operation Iraqi Freedom in Iraq, the aircraft carrier and its crew of 5,500 had traveled over 100,000 miles in support of the War on Terror.

Recognizing the skill and dedication required for such a commitment, President Bush decided to say "well done"—not only to the sailors on the *Lincoln* but to all of his troops. A former pilot, the President flew aboard in the cockpit of a Navy S-3B Viking, taking the controls for part of the trip. By landing on a moving carrier—an extraordinarily difficult feat—he paid the crew on board the *Lincoln* the ultimate compliment: he put his life in their hands.

President Bush with the flight deck crew on the USS *Abraham Lincoln*

Then, the commander-in-chief made a dramatic speech commending both the crew and all the troops who had helped end Saddam Hussein's rein of terror.

> "The transition from dictatorship to democracy will take time, but it is worth every effort. Our coalition will stay until our work is done and then we will leave and we will leave behind a free Iraq."
>
> **—President Bush**

Unfortunately, the media fixated not on the words of the president's speech but on a banner behind him that read "Mission Accomplished." It had been hung by the crew of "Honest Abe" who were glad to be coming home. The media seized on the image of the president in a flight suit standing before the banner and pilloried him. It was a major public relations gaffe that gave adversaries of the administration new ammunition, and it could have been prevented by the president's staff. But this misstep was followed by a far more grievous error.

Five days after what the potentates of the press derisively called his "Mission Accomplished Speech," President Bush appointed L. Paul "Jerry" Bremer as administrator for the Coalition Provisional Authority. The CPA had been created shortly after the capture of Baghdad to oversee the reconstruction of Iraq and provide leadership for reconstituting a new civil government.

Though accepting the assignment in Baghdad placed him at considerable risk, Bremer's appointment was controversial from the start. The person he replaced as CPA administrator, Jay Garner, a retired U.S. Army lieutenant general, had been criticized in the U.S. media for moving too slowly on reconstruction and "de-Baathification"— getting rid of former regime loyalists. But even before Jerry Bremer arrived, he was denounced by the press for being "too political" and "too close to the Bush administration."

L. Paul Bremer arrives in Iraq

In fact, Jerry Bremer came to the CPA with better credentials for combating terrorism than almost anyone President Bush could have chosen. In 1986, when I left my post on the National Security Council staff as the U.S. government's coordinator for counter-terrorism, Jerry Bremer was my replacement. He had a redefined mission and title: Ambassador-at-large for Counterterrorism. He had also served as chairman of the National Commission on Terrorism. After the 9-11 attack he cochaired a task force that drew up plans for creating the new Department of Homeland Security.

Bremer's instructions from the White House and the Pentagon included requirements for the CPA to "actively oppose Saddam Hussein's old enforcers . . . and eliminate the remnants of Saddam's regime." This guidance hobbled reconstruction by preventing the interim government from using talented administrators and technocrats who had joined the Baath Party simply to keep their civil service jobs under Saddam.

But the greatest damage to the prospect for peace in Iraq was the failure to immediately recall the remnants of the Iraqi military. Bremer's directive of 23 May 2003 effectively dissolved the entire Iraqi military system. The order told nearly 500,000 trained and armed young men that they were not part of the "New Iraq." Without options for legitimate employment, thousands of them became the "hired guns" for sectarian militias and Al Qaeda.

Bremer's rebuttal, in a FOX News interview, that "there was no Iraqi army to disband. The Iraqi army basically self-demobilized" was true, as far as it went. But it ignored what he might have done about it, as well as the lessons of history.

In May of 1945 when Germany surrendered, GEN Dwight Eisenhower issued orders to arrest all Nazi Party members. He instructed all German military personnel to return to their barracks with their weapons. In the zones occupied by U.S., British, and French forces, military police collected the Mausers and panzerfausts and issued shovels and wheelbarrows. The defeated army was put to work cleaning up the destruction. They were fed, clothed, and paid a modest sum by the U.S. Army, and they started rebuilding their

BAGHDAD, 18 April 2003 – Lt. Gen. William Wallace tells his soldiers to stay vigilant as Operation Iraqi Freedom transitions into a peacekeeping and humanitarian stage. "Don't let your guard down," Wallace said. "Show the people of this country the proper respect, but be careful. There's still a bunch of knuckleheads running around." He went on to praise the troops for giving "back to the Iraqi people the society and culture that is rightfully theirs."

country. George Patton, the military governor of Bavaria, went so far as to grant amnesty to low-level Nazi functionaries just to get public works—water, sewage, electricity, and the civil police—functioning again.

The same could have been tried in Iraq. In May of 2003, the Coalition effectively controlled all information being disseminated to the Iraqi people—print, broadcast, and many of the leading clerics. It would have been simple for the CPA to put out the word that every Iraqi soldier who returned to his barracks with his weapon would receive one hundred dollars at the end of thirty days.

It was never tried. Instead of becoming a work force rebuilding Iraq, many from the defeated Iraqi army became bomb builders, terrorists, and new recruits for Shiite and Sunni warlords. It was an unmitigated disaster.

By July of 2003, armed bands were operating throughout the countryside and in nearly all of Iraq's major cities. In Baghdad, Washington, and European capitals, critics of the Bush administration cited the "rise of an insurgency." The words "quagmire' and "Vietnam" appeared with increasing regularity in the press.

In reality, the parallels between Iraq and Vietnam are practically nonexistent—on the battlefield. But in the press and politics, it didn't matter that there were few similarities, except that ground combat remains a brutal, vicious experience for all who engage in it.

In Vietnam, U.S. troops faced nearly a quarter of a million conscripted but well-trained, disciplined, and equipped North Vietnamese Army (NVA) regulars and upwards of 100,000 highly organized Viet Cong (VC) insurgents on a constant basis from 1966 onward. Both the NVA and the VC "irregulars" were well indoctrinated in communist ideology; received direct aid from the Soviet Union, Communist China, and the Warsaw Pact; and benefited from logistics and politico-military support networks in neighboring countries. During major campaigns against U.S. and South Vietnamese forces—of which there were many each year—both the NVA and the VC responded to centralized command and control directed by authorities in Hanoi. None of that has been true in Iraq.

Since the summer of 2003 in the land between the Tigris and Euphrates rivers, enemy combatants have been a combination of disparate Sunni Jihadi-terrorists, disenfranchised Baathists, Shiite militias aligned with Iran, fanatical foreign Wahhabi-subsidized Mujahadeen linked to Al Qaeda, Muslim Brotherhood-supported radicals, and well-armed, hyper-violent criminal gangs, often with tribal connections that are stronger than any ideological, religious, or political affiliations. Though many Jihadists receive indoctrination, munitions, and refuge from a network of mosques and sectarian Islamic groups, centralized command, control, and logistics support is virtually nonexistent.

Operating in small independent "cells" instead of organized, disciplined military units, the enemy in Mesopotamia has no ability to mount any kind of protracted offensive against U.S. or even lightly armed Iraqi government forces. Increasingly dependent on improvised explosive devices (IEDs) and suicide-bomb attacks to inflict casualties, the opposition in Iraq is more "anarchy" than "insurgency."

The second great myth about the campaign in Iraq is the casualty rate. This is always the most difficult aspect of any war to address, because all comparisons seem cynical. For those of us who have held dying soldiers, sailors, airmen, Guardsmen, or Marines in our arms—and the families of those killed—this is particularly painful. Yet, the casualty rate is one of the oft-cited reasons for why we were "forced" to get out of Vietnam, and why we are once again being urged by the press and politicians to "end the bloodshed" in Iraq. While no one should ever claim "my war was tougher than your war," here's a reality check:

• Over the course of the entire Vietnam War, the "average" rate at which Americans died as a consequence of armed combat was about fifteen per day. In 1968–69, when my brother and I served as rifle platoon and infantry company commanders—he in the Army and I in the Marines—thirty-nine Americans died every day in the war zone. In Iraq, the mortality rate for U.S. troops due to enemy action is less than two per day.

- During the 1968 "Tet Offensive" in Vietnam, there were more than 2,100 U.S. casualties per week. In Iraq, the U.S. casualty rate from all causes has never exceeded 490 troops in a month.

- As of December 2007, after more than fifty-seven months of combat, fewer than 4,000 young Americans have been killed by enemy action in Iraq. That's roughly the same number killed at Iwo Jima during the first ten days of fighting against the Japanese.

Every life lost in war is precious, and every loss is grievous for their friends and families. Unfortunately, our media seems intent on using every one of those killed to make the point that they died for nothing. It's a technique that was perfected during Vietnam. Those who shape American public opinion apparently intend to make it true for Iraq.

On 27 February 1968, after a month of brutal fighting and daily images of U.S. casualties on American television, Walter Cronkite, then the host of the CBS Evening News, proclaimed that the Tet Offensive was proof that the Vietnam War was "no longer winnable." Four weeks later, Lyndon Johnson told the nation that "I shall not seek, and I will not accept the nomination of my party for another term as your President." It didn't matter that Tet had been a decisive victory for the U.S. and South Vietnamese.

The war in Vietnam wasn't lost during "Tet '68," no matter what Walter Cronkite said. Rather, it was lost in the pages of America's newspapers, on our televisions, our college campuses—and eventually in the corridors of power in Washington.

By mid-2003 we had reason to pray that the campaign in Iraq wouldn't be lost the same way.

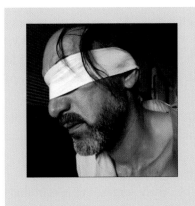

"The thugs we're fighting in Iraq aren't, for the most part, organized soldiers. They're mostly criminals and cowards. They talk real tough when they're strutting around on television with their guns and their buddies behind them. But kick in their door in the middle of the night and stick a gun in their face, and they cry like little girls and wet themselves."

— *An unnamed Special Operations soldier in Iraq, 2004*

Smoke billows from a building hit with a TOW missile launched by soldiers of the Army's 101st Airborne Division (Air Assault) on 22 July 2003 in Mosul, Iraq. Saddam Hussein's sons Qusay and Uday were killed in the battle as they resisted efforts by coalition forces to apprehend and detain them.

DYING TO KILL US

★ ★ ★ ★ ★ ★ ★ ★ ★ ★ ★ ★

Daytime summer temperatures in the "land between the rivers" average more than 105 degrees. By July 2003 the anti-war rhetoric in Washington and European capitals was just as hot. Coalition efforts to jump-start reconstruction were slowly getting underway but few of the "good news" stories made it to air or on the front pages. Even when Saddam Hussein's vicious sons, Uday and Qusay, were killed in a gunfight with U.S. troops in Mosul, the media found reason for criticism.

Uday, the elder sibling, had been responsible for recruiting foreigners to fight for his father's regime. Qusay had headed the Amn Al Khass, Iraq's internal intelligence and security force. Both brothers had a well-deserved reputation for extraordinary cruelty and had been accused of torture, numerous rapes, and scores of murders.

On 21 July, an Iraqi civilian tipped off a young U.S. Army sergeant in Mosul that the deposed dictator's sons were hiding at a particular address in the city's Al Falah district. In less than twenty-four hours soldiers from the 101st Airborne, commanded by MG David Petraeus, and Special Operators from Task Force 20 had confirmed the information and cordoned off the neighborhood.

To prevent civilian casualties the troops evacuated the surrounding homes and businesses and urged the fugitives to surrender. Instead of doing so, they opened fire on the U.S. troops surrounding the building. In the subsequent assault both brothers, their sole bodyguard, and Qusay's teenage son were killed. Five U.S. troops were wounded.

The success of this operation was quickly obscured by protests in the media that U.S. troops had used "excessive force" and complaints that Saddam's sons should have been "taken alive for their intelligence value" and then "tried for their crimes."

With the summer heat in Iraq came a wave of "suicide bombers"—individuals carrying explosives on their bodies—or driving vehicles laden with ordnance and intent on dying in the Jihad. On 19 August a terrorist driving a Russian-made flatbed truck pulled up next to the Canal Hotel, headquarters for the UN mission in downtown Baghdad. Beneath a tarpaulin on the truck were a five-hundred-pound bomb and dozens of mortar and artillery rounds, land mines, grenades, and plastic explosives—all readily available throughout Iraq. Unchallenged, the driver parked the lethal load beside a brick wall surrounding the hotel and detonated his cargo. The blast killed twenty-five people, including the UN special representative to Iraq, Sergio Vieira de Mello, and wounded more than one hundred others.

The remains of a suicide truck bomb in Baghdad

Scenes of the carnage, some of it videotaped as the bomb exploded, were broadcast around the world almost instantly.

Over the course of the next several months there were scores of such suicide attacks that killed hundreds and maimed thousands of noncombatants. On radical Islamic Web sites the perpetrators were called "martyrs." President Bush described them as "the enemies of civilization." By the time our FOX News *War Stories* team—cameraman Griff Jenkins, senior producer Pamela Browne, and I—returned to Bayji with Pepper Jackson's 3rd Bn, 66th Armor, in October 2003, suicide bombers and IEDs were the number-one killers of American troops and Iraqi civilians.

Jackson's troops and the rest of the 4th ID didn't let the increasing risk from suicide bombers and IEDs deter them from continuing their hunt for Saddam and his cronies. And on 13 December their patience and perseverance were rewarded.

American soldiers trapped him like a cornered rat hiding in a hole. And when he was caught, Saddam Hussein—the blustering, bloody tyrant who asked others to die for him—didn't even try to defend himself with the weapons at his disposal. Just days before the capture, I interviewed MG Ray Odierno, the 4th ID's commander. He assured me that his troops were going to find Saddam near Tikrit. They did.

Saddam was responsible for two horrific wars and the deaths of hundreds of thousands. His record was replete with the kind of atrocities that brought the United States into two world wars, a bloody campaign in Korea, and the war I fought in—Vietnam. He had raped, tortured, robbed, starved, and murdered his own people. He acquired and used weapons of mass destruction against his neighbors and countrymen. He had attempted to assassinate an American president and trained and supported Hamas, Islamic Jihad, Hezbollah, and Muslim Brotherhood terrorists who killed Americans.

The image of Saddam as a filthy, decrepit, coward captured—not killed—by an American soldier was a powerful message to repressed people all over the globe that this is the way brutal despots go. Placing him on trial before the people of Iraq, who subsequently sent him to the hangman's gallows, sent a clear signal to totalitarians—be they in Damascus, Tehran, Pyongyang, or Havana—that they are accountable to the people they have tortured.

Though tens of thousands of Iraqis celebrated Saddam's capture, the jubilation was less than universal. Critics in the European press decried the "humiliation" of videotaping "a former head of state" being examined by a U.S. military medical officer. The "mainstream media" in America speculated that the capture was "timed to improve Bush's poll numbers" and opined that Saddam would be tortured. Madeline Albright, who had been secretary of state in the Clinton administration, asked on FOX News: "Do you suppose that the Bush administration has Osama bin Laden hidden somewhere and will bring him out before the election?"

The surreal reaction to Saddam's capture was revealing. Media elites could have focused on the extraordinary courage, tenacity, and discipline of U.S. and coalition troops who had defeated Saddam's army and then captured the "Butcher of Baghdad." Instead, many of the most powerful shapers of public opinion persisted in denigrating the young Americans serving far from home in harm's way and insisting that they were engaged in a fight that couldn't be won. None of this was missed by those who were intent on spreading their Jihad and driving "the infidels" from what they called "the lands of the Prophet."

Despite pervasively negative press coverage, most of the U.S. troops I have covered simply refuse to be disheartened. But there is also no doubt in my mind that it has made their task much more difficult.

An Iraqi man takes his aggression out on one of the many large public murals of Saddam Hussein– he is hitting the mural with his shoe, which in Muslim culture is akin to spitting at someone

U.S. Army SSG Christopher Pearce sits next to a young boy during a visit to Shiek Burhan Al Asee's house during a patrol of the Riyahd village

★ ★ ★ ★ ★ ★ ★ ★ ★ ★ ★ ★ ★

10

BLOODY ANBAR

"THE MOST VIOLENT PLACE ON THE PLANET"

★ ★ ★ ★ ★ ★ ★ ★ ★ ★ ★ ★ ★

The 31 March 2004 press wire photos and videotapes from Fallujah were horrific. They showed children in Fallujah, Iraq, dancing gleefully while teenagers tore at the immolated bodies of four American security contractors who had been killed in an ambush. The perpetrators had set up cameras to document the atrocity and had provided tapes to radical Islamic Web sites. Numerous Arabic television networks immediately broadcast the horrific images. From his hideout on the Pakistan-Afghanistan border, Osama bin Laden claimed that "Al Qaeda in Iraq" had conducted the operation.

This Iraqi interim governing council approved the draft of a new constitution, a key step in returning full sovereignty to the Iraqi people

The murders at the end of March finished a month that had begun with considerable hope. Though a wave of suicide bombings had killed hundreds of Iraqi civilians during January and February, on 8 March the Interim Governing Council (IGC) approved a draft constitution and transitional administrative law. The IGC, comprised of Iraqis from across the political and sectarian spectrum, affirmed a bill of rights. This assured, among other things, freedom of religion, speech, education, and assembly, along with universal suffrage.

For Sunni radicals like Abu Musab al Zarqawi, the Jordanian who headed Al Qaeda in Iraq, or Moqtada al Sadr, the fanatical Shiite cleric commanding the Mahdi Army, the freedoms promised by the new constitution—and particularly women's equality—were abhorrent. They, along with disenfranchised Baathists and thousands of foreign Jihadists, set out to make sure that democracy in Iraq would fail. In Al Anbar province, the largest in Iraq, they almost succeeded.

Shortly after the murders in Fallujah, Christian Galdibini, my FOX News cameraman, and I arrived in Al Anbar. We were there to cover the Marines and soldiers who were engaged in the most intense fighting since the liberation of Baghdad a year earlier. The cities of Fallujah and Ramadi, the provincial capital, were the heart of the "Sunni Triangle," areas west and north of Baghdad in which most of Iraq's Sunni minority lived. After several days of covering gunfights in and around

Fallujah, we arrived in Ramadi and embedded with 2nd Bn, 4th Marines, out of Camp Pendleton, California, and the Army's 1st Brigade Combat Team from Fort Riley, Kansas.

In an earlier war, the command arrangement in Ramadi would have been considered unusual: a U.S. Marine Corps infantry battalion was assigned to a U.S. Army brigade, which in turn was part of the MEF. But in fact, as the Silver Star citation for the U.S. Army brigade commander sergeant major attests, it was a task organization that worked amazingly well, particularly given the shocking ferocity of the enemy.

The President of the United States takes pleasure in presenting the Silver Star medal to Ron Riling, Command Sergeant Major, U.S. Army, for conspicuous gallantry and intrepidity in action while serving as CSM for the 1st Brigade, 1st Infantry Division, in support of Operation IRAQI FREEDOM, near Ramadi, Iraq, on 6 April 2003. On that date CSM Riling and his brigade commander were notified that Marines attached to their brigade were pinned down by enemy fire. He quickly organized his forces and began moving to the embattled Marines. When his own elements entered the main town of Ramadi, they immediately came under direct fire coming from every direction. The Marine squad had been pinned down by snipers and was in desperate circumstances when CSM Riling's physical-security detachment arrived on the scene. The squad leader was dead, lying in the middle of the street, and three of the seven Marines were seriously wounded. The senior remaining Marine was a corporal. CSM Riling's force fought its way through withering enemy fire and linked up with the Marines where they were absorbed into the team and fought their way out together. After CSM Riling's team evacuated the injured Marines and recovered a Marine squad leader's body, another Marine platoon in the area came under attack by insurgents armed with RPGs. CSM Riling directed two Bradley fighting vehicles from the brigade's reserve into the fight to squelch the attacks.

In the midst of one hyper-violent engagement, Lt. Col. Paul Kennedy, the commanding officer of 2nd Bn, 4th Marines, described the province as "the most violent place on the planet Earth." Jim Booker, his sergeant major, nodded and said, "You're telling me." They were right.

Practically every day—and most nights—for month after month there were furious gunfights on the mean streets of Ramadi. The action was nearly

Lt. Col. Paul Kennedy

always a sudden, close-quarters, adrenalin-pumping experience for the U.S. troops engaged. Depending on the neighborhood, the enemy could be Baath Party loyalists, a criminal gang, or members of Al Qaeda in Iraq. The zealots in Zarqawi's Al Qaeda organization were a mixture of foreign fighters and young Iraqis. They were well armed and vicious, whether their target was an Iraqi police or military outpost, a U.S. convoy, or Iraqi civilians.

The Silver Star citation for SgtMaj Jim Booker aptly describes the courage required of those who struggled to bring law and order to the province.

The President of the United States takes pleasure in presenting the Silver Star medal to James E. Booker, Sergeant Major, U.S. Marine Corps, for conspicuous gallantry and intrepidity in action against the enemy while serving as SgtMaj, 2nd Bn, 4th Marine Regiment, 1st Marine Division, I MEF, U. S. Marine Corps Forces, Central Command, in support of Operation IRAQI FREEDOM from February to September 2004.

SgtMaj Booker courageously exposed himself to enemy fire while leading Marines and eliminating enemy forces in several battalion engagements. On 31 March 2004 the forward command element came under intense machine gun and RPG fire. With utter disregard for his own safety, SgtMaj Booker dismounted the vehicle, engaged the enemy, and forced their withdrawal. He pursued his attackers down several darkened city streets and mortally wounded a RPG gunner who was engaging the Command Group. SgtMaj Booker subsequently led a search that resulted in the arrest and capture of an eight-man cell and several weapons. On 10 April 2004, the forward command element came under fire from insurgents during cordon and search operations. He calmly led a team of Marines in a counter-attack, personally clearing several buildings, eliminating one insurgent fighter, and facilitating the evacuation of a severely wounded Marine. SgtMaj Booker's efforts enabled the forward command element to regain freedom of maneuver and inspired Marines to fearlessly engage the enemy. By his bold leadership, wise judgment, and loyal dedication to duty, SgtMaj Booker reflected great credit upon himself and upheld the highest traditions of the Marine Corps and the United States Naval Service.

Lt. Col. Paul Kennedy and SgtMaj James Booker during a gunfight in Ramadi

During these engagements it was evident that the enemy was incapable of taking on a Marine battalion or an Army brigade in a toe-to-toe fight. But the terrorists were convinced that if they could inflict enough casualties on U.S. troops, American resolve would weaken and the politicians in Washington would have to withdraw from the fight, leaving Iraq without any prospect for a democratic outcome.

Terror leaders like Zarqawi and al Sadr kept such hope for good reason. After several probes into Fallujah, U.S. troops were ordered by Baghdad to withdraw from the city on 30 April, leaving it in the control of the terrorists. In the aftermath, public opinion polls in the U.S. showed that approval for the campaign in Iraq had plummeted.

The drop in support for the American commitment in Iraq reflected the way the media covered the conflict. Photos and videotape of Humvees blowing up and burning on Iraqi roads—many shot by Arab cameramen traveling with the terrorists—were quickly printed and broadcast throughout the U.S. and Europe. The willingness of the mainstream media to use these images meant that for the first time in our nation's history, most of what Americans were seeing from the battlefield was coming from the enemy.

BATTLEFIELD INNOVATION

★ ★ ★ ★ ★ ★ ★ ★ ★ ★ ★

During a well-publicized exchange in December 2004, Defense Secretary Donald Rumsfeld said, "As you know, you go to war with the army you have, not the army you might want or wish to have at a later time." The comment created a firestorm of criticism in the press, but he was right.

In fact, well before he made the remark, combat-experienced soldiers, sailors, airmen, Guardsmen, and Marines fighting in Iraq and Afghanistan were adapting to every change in enemy tactics. By the time we returned to Iraq in April 2004, everyone we saw "in theater" was equipped with the newest body armor, complete with bullet-stopping ceramic armor plates.

As suicide bombers became the terrorists' primary offensive weapon and IEDs became their defensive weapon of choice, Marine and Army units improvised. Those units that didn't have "up armored" Humvees and trucks made their own. Motor transport mechanics were transformed into master welders who cut steel plates with torches and fit the "homemade" armor to the vehicles.

The troops called this improvised metal plate "farmer armor"

New unmanned aerial vehicles, small enough to be hand-launched by a rifle platoon on patrol, were being flown over the "battle space." Engineers and explosive ordnance disposal (EOD) experts had been provided with remote-controlled robots for disarming IEDs. And every soldier heading outside a forward operating base was equipped with the latest gunsights and the newest generation of night-vision equipment and communications gear. These were upgrades since the campaign began just a year earlier.

An EOD robot looking for explosives in Iraq

In addition to equipment and weapons innovations, combat-experienced small unit leaders and their troops developed what they called "street smarts." They learned the tricks of fighting a nameless, often faceless enemy most effectively at the lowest possible risk to U.S. and coalition personnel.

An incident I reported from Ramadi while I was embedded with 2nd Bn, 4th Marines, reflects the "combat savvy" of our troops.

A TOW missile streaks toward a VBIED . . .

Just after 9:00 p.m. the Iraqi police report discovering a 1975 Ford station wagon parked in the median of "Route Michigan"—the four-lane highway connecting Ramadi with Fallujah. The police suspect that the abandoned car is a Vehicle-Borne Improvised Explosive Device, or VBIED—in short, a car bomb. Minutes later, the QRF, comprised of an EOD team and a detachment from Weapons Company, is en route and armed for bear just in case it's all a set-up. Over us we can barely hear—but not see—an unmanned aerial vehicle scanning the route ahead, looking for any signs of an ambush.

... and safely obliterates it

We arrive at the site, and after placing security around the Marine vehicles, the EOD team unloads a small, tracked robot with a tiny TV camera on a telescoping arm. But before the robot can defuse the explosives, mortar rounds start impacting in the field off to our right. It won't take the terrorist gunners long to figure out that they missed us and adjust their fire. Staying here in the open isn't an option, but neither is leaving a VBIED behind.

I'm lying in the gravel on the left side of the road with my camera rolling as Sgt Jeremiah Randall from Weapons Company calls out, "Get the robot back and let's tow it." As the robot is being reeled in and I'm wondering who is going to be crazy enough to hook a chain up to a Ford station wagon full of Iraqi artillery rounds, another Humvee rolls up beside me. My tape is still rolling when the warning, "Firing TOW!" is shouted immediately above me.

My camera catches the "pop" of the wire-guided anti-tank missile being ejected from its tube, the ignition of its rocket motors, and its fiery trajectory toward the VBIED. The warhead performs as advertised, and there is a massive explosion as the artillery rounds hidden in the back of the car detonate. With my ears still ringing, I hear Sgt Randall's only comment over the radio: "Scratch one VBIED."

The Marines went back to base with no casualties.

"NO GREATER FRIEND, NO WORSE ENEMY"

★ ★ ★ ★ ★ ★ ★ ★ ★ ★ ★ ★ ★

Major General James Mattis had adopted the ancient Roman dictum, "No Greater Friend, No Worse Enemy," for the 1st Marine Division during the initial invasion of Iraq. By the summer of 2004, it was a maxim being practiced throughout Al Anbar. It didn't hurt that Lt. Gen. Jim Conway, the commander of I MEF, and Mattis were still "in country" and leading the same commands. The slogan—and all that it meant—was also well-known to the troops fighting in Al Anbar.

> Before a battalion-sized operation in Ramadi, Lt. Col. Kennedy told his company commanders to "hunt down" the terrorists and reminded them that the enemy "can't stand up to a Marine unit in a gunfight. They aren't as well trained, lack fire discipline, and aren't in shape. If you have to . . . send out invitations. Watch out for the IEDs and when they show themselves, shoot straight. Use only the force you need to eliminate the threat. Avoid civilian casualties and keep your communications up. And remember the division motto: 'No greater friend, no worse enemy.' Let them figure out which one they want you to be."

The "No Greater Friend" part was reserved for the Iraqi people who were in the crossfire between coalition forces and the terrorists. The units with which we were embedded conducted hundreds of civil affairs and information operations intended to build trust with the local civilians. There were frequent exchanges with the "locals" about water purification systems, electricity, job creation projects, schools—and always, the security of their homes and neighborhoods.

As a byproduct of these missions, U.S. commanders collected valuable intelligence about plans for disrupting reconstruction projects and upcoming elections, the location of IED "bomb factories," Al Qaeda "safe houses," and terrorist "propaganda mills" where they produced DVDs of their atrocities and made them available to radical Islamic Web sites—not to mention the rest of the media. One such site produced the grisly 11 May 2004 video of Nicholas Berg, a U.S. civilian hostage, being beheaded by his captors. As we discovered later, similar videos were being made in torture chambers inside Fallujah between April and November when the city was finally retaken by coalition forces.

"It's a gut-churning experience because you don't know if the guy on the other side of the door is going to meet you with an IED or an AK-47. These guys act all tough on the videos they make, as long as they have a mask on and all their buddies around. But you kick down their door in the middle of the night to arrest them, and they cry like little girls and beg for mercy. That's when you realize these men aren't soldiers, they're criminals and punks."

—U.S. Special Operations soldier

These "meet and greet" operations were much more than just handing out soccer balls and candy to children on the street. Human exploitation teams and intelligence specialists accompanying the civil affairs units also uncovered corruption that might otherwise have gone undetected. After hearing complaints in these sessions about Ramadi's police chief, Lt. Col. Paul Kennedy launched a quiet investigation into the chief's activities. The probe proved not only corruption but collaboration with criminal gangs who were preying on Iraqi civilians and shooting at U.S. troops. The chief went to jail.

Lieutenant Jeffrey Craig, a platoon commander, said the reason for these operations was "to speak with the people who don't normally want to be seen talking to us. We give them information about why we're here, what we're doing, and reasons to believe in the coalition and the future of Iraq. In return we gather intelligence about what's happening in their neighborhoods."

Armed with information collected during the day, the troops often returned by night to track down terrorists in their lairs. We accompanied U.S. Army and Marine units on dozens of these missions, some of which included U.S. Special Operations units. Though we weren't allowed to videotape their faces or reveal their names, our cameras were there to document the action.

Weapons cache found at the Coalition for Iraqi National Unity headquarters in Ramadi, Iraq

NO GOOD NEWS?

★ ★ ★ ★ ★ ★ ★ ★ ★ ★ ★ ★

Many of the so-called "insurgents" who fought the establishment of a stable government in Iraq weren't in it for political reasons; they were violent criminals preying on innocent Iraqi civilians. Throughout Al Anbar, violent, well-armed criminal gangs turned kidnapping for ransom, extortion, murder-for-hire, and armed robbery into a growing industry. The combination of criminal activity, sectarian death-squad murders, and increasingly lethal reprisals precipitated a cycle of violence that could be exploited by Sunni terrorists like Zarqawi and Shiite warlords like al Sadr. They told the Iraqi people that strict adherence to their tenets of radical Islam would protect them far better than the "U.S. occupiers" or the "puppet government in Baghdad."

The U.S. and international media, reporting from inside the capital's green zone, predicted that the country was on an irreversible descent into civil war and that the coalition could do nothing to stop it. That message was reinforced by the continued uproar over prisoner abuse at the Abu Ghraib detention facility, south of Baghdad. Outrageous photographs of Iraqi detainees being abused by American military guards had first circulated on 29 April. President Bush described the behavior at Abu Ghraib as "abhorrent," and the Pentagon announced that those responsible would be court-martialed. But that wasn't enough for the press and the president's opponents in an election year. By mid-May Abu Ghraib was a full-blown, nonstop scandal. Little other news from Iraq got any "ink" or air time.

Unfortunately, this meant that the American people were unlikely to hear or read about the courage and tenacity of the U.S. troops doing battle in Al Anbar—men like Sgt Kenneth Conde, a squad leader with the 2nd Bn, 4th Marines, in Ramadi. Conde was leading the point squad during a nighttime raid when his platoon was ambushed. In the opening minutes of the ensuing gunfight, he was hit in the shoulder. His Corpsman applied a battle dressing to the wound, and he stayed in the fray, leading from the front of his squad. By the time it was over they had killed six terrorists and captured a pile of enemy weapons and ordnance. Sgt Conde, because of his grievous wounds, could have had a ticket home, yet he decided to stay in the field. A few days after the action, he was awarded a Purple Heart. At the ceremony, I asked him why he decided to stay. "There was no other choice for a sergeant in the Marine Corps," Conde explained. "You have to lead your Marines."

HEARTS AND MINDS

★ ★ ★ ★ ★ ★ ★ ★ ★ ★ ★ ★

On 28 June 2004, two days ahead of schedule, Paul Bremer, head of the U.S.-led Coalition Provisional Authority, formally transferred sovereign power to an interim Iraqi government. This was an entity selected by Iraqis, not Americans or the U.N. The new prime minister, Iyad Allawi, promised to hold elections for a permanent government in January 2005, providing that the U.S.-led coalition remained in Iraq.

The change in Baghdad placated neither the enemy nor critics at home. If anything, radical Sunni and Shiite leaders were infuriated by the prospect of progress toward a representative government. On Islamist Web sites they promised to increase the violence. And they did.

Critics of keeping U.S. forces on the ground in Iraq stepped up their rhetorical attacks. They increased the volume on calls to "cut our losses" and "get out of Iraq" before U.S. elections in November. For the troops on the ground facing radical Shiites and Sunnis, it was just more of the same.

When our *War Stories* team—producer Greg Johnson, cameraman Mal James, and I— returned to Ramadi in July 2004, Paul Kennedy's 2nd Bn, 4th Marines, were still there, and so were the terrorists. Literally within minutes of arriving we were in a gunfight that went on for hours. It was 115 degrees in the shade—and there was no shade. During the long, hot summer of 2004, these kind of engagements occurred throughout Al Anbar province. The terrorists didn't make any distinction as to branch of service or rank.

On one torrid afternoon COL Buck Connor, the U.S. Army Brigade Combat Team commander, was nearly killed when his convoy was ambushed inside the city. The result was an extraordinary demonstration of Marine and Army teamwork and firepower, all documented by our cameras. Two heavily armed AH-1 Cobra attack helicopters and fixed-wing aircraft loaded with laser and GPS-guided bombs overhead provided air support. Backed up by armored Humvees and Bradley fighting vehicles, U.S. Marine and Army infantrymen slugged it out with the terrorists house to house and room to room.

Capt. Mark Carlton

By the time it was over, a dozen enemy combatants were dead, four were wounded and taken prisoner, and fifteen others were detained. Nearly one hundred enemy weapons and truckloads of ammunition and explosives were captured. During the fight, eleven Marines were wounded. These included Capt. Mark Carlton, the Fox Company commander, who suffered scores of shrapnel wounds from an enemy RPG. He was one of more than a dozen of the officers in 2nd Bn, 4th Marines, who were wounded—and decorated for their courage—while we were with them.

In the midst of one engagement, I ran to take cover behind a Humvee and literally ran into Maj. Dave Harrill, the battalion operations officer. Despite AK-47 rounds whizzing by and RPGs impacting in the street, he was standing beside Lt. Col. Kennedy as each of them talked over radio handsets. While changing the tape in my camera, I asked, "How's it going?"

Harrill shrugged and said, "Just trying to win some hearts and minds. Tough to do while they're trying to kill us."

His citation for the Silver Star sums up what it was like for thousands of soldiers and Marines serving in Al Anbar that summer.

The President of the United States takes pleasure in presenting the Silver Star medal to John D. Harrill III, Major, U.S. Marine Corps, for conspicuous gallantry and intrepidity in action against the enemy while serving as Operations Officer, 2nd Bn, 4th Marine Regiment, 1st Marine Division, I MEF, U.S. Marine Corps Forces, Central Command, in support of Operation IRAQI FREEDOM from February to September 2004. Maj. Harrill's leadership and heroism while under fire contributed materially to the battalion's success in preventing the fall of Ar Ramadi, Iraq. Throughout enemy attacks and offensive operations, he calmly led the battalion command element and coordinated maneuver of the battalion's combat units, while

personally neutralizing enemy automatic weapon and RPG fire, resulting in the enemy's defeat. During a major insurgent attack against coalition forces, Maj. Harrill led the forward command element into the aim point of the enemy attack. Despite constant enemy fire, he focused the combat power of six companies as they battled in eight separate locations over a seven-hour period. Maj. Harrill's superior tactical acumen enabled the complete destruction of assaulting enemy forces. By his bold leadership, courageous actions, and loyal devotion to duty, Maj. Harrill reflected great credit upon himself and upheld the highest traditions of the Marine Corps and the United States Naval Service.

THE FIGHT FOR FALLUJAH

★ ★ ★ ★ ★ ★ ★ ★ ★ ★ ★ ★

On 7 November 2004, five days after George W. Bush was reelected president of the United States and eighteen months after Saddam Hussein was toppled from power, interim Iraqi Prime Minister Ayad Allawi ordered the restoration of law and order in Fallujah. The following morning, a combined U.S. Marine, U.S. Army, and Iraqi military force launched "Operation Phantom Fury," a multibattalion attack to retake the city. The decision precipitated a firestorm of protest in the U.S. and the longest and bloodiest sustained battle in Iraq since the start of the campaign. For the U.S. units involved, it was the heaviest urban combat since the battle for Hue City in Vietnam during Tet, 1968.

By the time the operation began, Fallujah had become a stronghold for Abu Musab al Zarqawi and his Al Qaeda in Iraq. Hundreds—some estimated thousands—of foreign Jihadists had crept through the coalition cordon around the city to help reinforce Al Qaeda defenses. Though tens of thousands of civilians had fled Zarqawi's oppression, those who remained were forced to live under the strictest form of Islamic law.

The attack, spearheaded by two U.S. Marine regimental combat teams, RCT-1 and RCT-7, was supported by two U.S. Army mechanized battalions—2nd Bn, 7th Cavalry Regiment (1st Cavalry Division), and the 2nd Bn, 2nd Infantry Regiment (1st ID). The Army's M-1 Abrams tanks, Bradley fighting vehicles, and organic artillery added a heavy armor punch that proved to be crucial in the house-to-house, block-by-block fighting.

Lt. Gen. John Sattler, commanding the I MEF—and the overall commander for the operation—committed four new Iraqi infantry battalions to the attack. He integrated them within his RCTs. The Iraqi units were fresh from training and not as well equipped as their U.S. Marine and Army counterparts, but their bravery and tenacity impressed the Americans they fought alongside.

In urban combat, most of the action is at the small unit level. That's how it was inside Fallujah. Fire teams, squads, and platoons advanced on a narrow frontage down streets that required clearing every room in every building. Many of the structures had sophisticated barricades, firing ports, and even escape tunnels constructed by Zarqawi's zealots.

One Marine said: "We encountered two types of enemy combatants—those who wanted to live and those who stayed there to die. The first kind were mostly Iraqis. But it was the second kind—those who *wanted* to die—that made this fight so tough. They were the worst. If we didn't kill them, they would surely kill us."

As the attack progressed through the heart of the city, the soldiers and Marines uncovered entire buildings that had been used by Al Qaeda as slaughter houses—not for animals but for people. Zarqawi's thugs had used video cameras, DVDs, and computers to store the grisly images of torture, rapes, and beheadings. The atrocities were so graphic that one civil affairs NCO described them as "more sickening than anything I could imagine happening to another human being."

Dozens of soldiers, U.S. Navy medical corpsmen, and Marines were cited for courage during the bloody fight for Fallujah. Though most of the heavy fighting was over in ten days, Marines were still being engaged by cells of suicidal terrorists until just before Christmas. Perhaps the most telling example of how vicious the fighting was is the Navy Cross citation for 1stSgt Bradley Kasal.

Though we didn't know it at the time, the furious fight for Fallujah was the beginning of the end for Al Qaeda in Iraq. Abu Musab al Zarqawi had escaped—some said dressed as a woman—but his home base was gone. Hundreds of his foreign fighters were dead, and his computers, communications equipment, and reams of documents were being searched by U.S. intelligence experts. The battle had cost the lives of more than fifty Americans killed and three hundred wounded. But as 2004 ended, for the troops on the ground there was hope that the Iraqis might just pull off what most "experts" thought was impossible before Fallujah—free and fair elections.

The President of the United States takes pleasure in presenting the Navy Cross to Bradley A. Kasal, 1st Sergeant, U.S. Marine Corps, for extraordinary heroism while serving as 1stSgt, Weapons Company, 3rd Bn, 1st Marine Regiment, RCT-1, 1st Marine Division, I MEF, U.S. Marine Corps Forces, Central Command, in support of Operation IRAQI FREEDOM on 13 November 2004. 1stSgt Kasal was assisting 1st Section, Combined Anti-Armor Platoon as they provided a traveling overwatch for 3rd Platoon when he heard a large volume of fire erupt to his immediate front, shortly followed by Marines rapidly exiting a structure. When 1stSgt Kasal learned that Marines were pinned down inside the house by an unknown number of enemy personnel, he joined a squad making entry to clear the structure and rescue the Marines inside. He made entry into the first room, immediately encountering and eliminating an enemy insurgent, as he spotted a wounded Marine in the next room. While moving toward the wounded Marine, 1stSgt Kasal and another Marine came under heavy rifle fire from an elevated enemy firing position and were both severely wounded in the legs, immobilizing them. When insurgents threw grenades in an attempt to eliminate the wounded Marines, he rolled on top of his fellow Marine and absorbed the shrapnel with his own body. When 1stSgt Kasal was offered medical attention and extraction, he refused until the other Marines were given medical attention. Although severely wounded himself, he shouted encouragement to his fellow Marines as they continued to clear the structure. By his bold leadership, wise judgment, and complete dedication to duty, 1stSgt Kasal reflected great credit upon himself and upheld the highest traditions of the Marine Corps and the United States Naval Service.

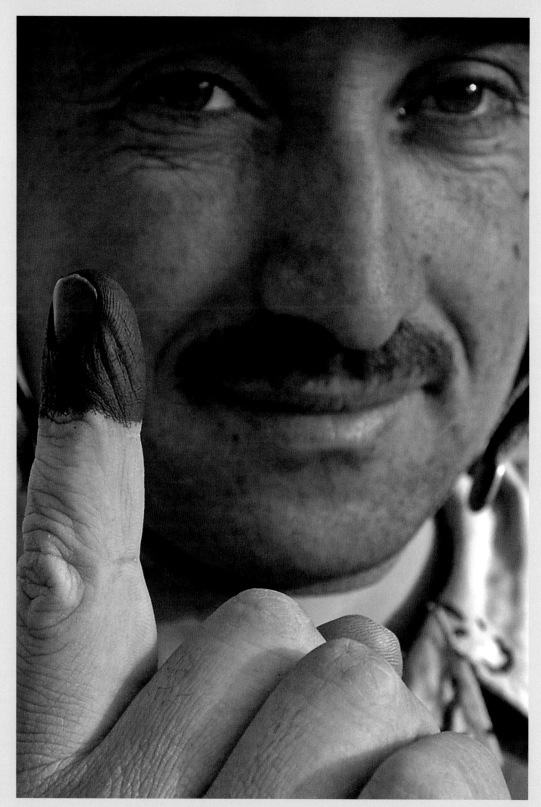

★ ★ ★ ★ ★ ★ ★ ★ ★ ★ ★ ★ ★

11

WILL DEMOCRACY WORK?

THE ELECTION IN AFGHANISTAN

★ ★ ★ ★ ★ ★ ★ ★ ★ ★ ★ ★ ★

9 OCTOBER 2004

In the last week of September 2004, *War Stories* producer Steve Tierney, cameraman Mal James, and I arrived at Bagram Air Base in Afghanistan. The 25th ID was in the midst of being augmented by a brigade of the 82nd Airborne Division and elements of the 10th Mountain Division in order to provide security for the first free and open elections in the country's history.

With producer Steve Tierney in Afghanistan

We all took up "residence" in what was once a Soviet troop billet. We were promptly assaulted by lice, fleas, centipedes, biting flies, and venomous scorpions. A battalion medical officer explained that we were the first Americans to occupy the building. Only half in jest, Mal suggested that the site had been used by the Russians for bizarre biological warfare experiments. Going on patrols with U.S. soldiers setting up security outposts for the upcoming elections was a respite from being eaten alive by the crawling critters.

As the day for the elections approached, correspondents from the U.S., European, and Arab media flooded into the country. Nearly all of them forecast that the elections would be a dismal failure. That was certainly what the remnants of the Taliban and Al Qaeda were preaching—and backing up their prediction with the threat of death for any woman caught going to the polls. The prognosticators of gloom and doom calculated that a "largely ignorant" society "with no tradition of democracy" would simply stay home on election day. Some said that the voters would be "confused" by so many candidates (there were sixteen) for president.

It turned out that they were all wrong. On 9 October 2004, more than eight million Afghanis—nearly 70 percent of the nation's registered voters—braved Taliban and Al Qaeda threats, mud, and minefields to cast a ballot at one of 4,800 polling sites.

In some places, there was over a foot of snow on the ground, but the voters came anyway, many wearing their best clothes to mark the dignity of the occasion. Well before the polls opened, entire families were waiting patiently in mile-long lines for the chance to cast a ballot and dip a finger into a container of indelible purple ink.

The election turnout was a stunning rejection of the radical Islamist agenda. Though the Taliban and Al Qaeda tried to intimidate voters—particularly women—from going to the polls, it didn't work. In Konduz, while a group of women were standing in a long line to vote, an IED detonated a few hundred yards away. The women defiantly stayed in line.

When all the ballots were counted, Hamid Karzai—with more than 50 percent of the votes—was named the first democratically elected president of Afghanistan. MAJ Scott Nelson, U.S. Army, a spokesman for the Multinational Force Headquarters in Kabul, put it this way: "Terrorists . . . suffered a resounding defeat at the hands of millions of Afghans voting for freedom."

MAJ Nelson was right on. And less than four months later, a nearly identical scenario was played out in Iraq.

IRAQI VOTE I: NATIONAL ASSEMBLY ELECTION

★ ★ ★ ★ ★ ★ ★ ★ ★ ★ ★ ★ ★

"By our efforts we have lit a fire as well—a fire in the minds of men. It warms those who feel its power, it burns those who fight its progress; and one day this untamed fire of freedom will reach the darkest corner of our world."
— PRESIDENT GEORGE W. BUSH, SECOND INAUGURAL ADDRESS, 20 JANUARY 2005

30 JANUARY 2005

The media "run up" to Iraq's first free and fair election on 30 January was almost identical to the coverage before the Afghan elections. For weeks before the ballot, the U.S. press and political opponents of the Bush administration in Congress predicted a "minimal" turnout and "invalid" results because the "Sunni population will boycott" the balloting.

An Iraqi woman prepares to vote by dipping her finger into ink

The vote to elect members of provincial legislatures and a 270-member National Assembly was specifically targeted by Abu Musab al Zarqawi and his Al Qaeda organization in Iraq. Al Qaeda propaganda organs made it known through radical Islamic Internet postings, videos rebroadcast on Arabic television, and in graffiti scrawled on walls that "we have declared a fierce war on this evil principle of democracy and those who follow this wrong ideology." Zarqawi went on to brand anyone who took part as an "infidel."

Iraqi men display their inked fingers after voting

U.S. intelligence officers noted that as the elections approached, radical Islamic Web sites operating in Pakistan, Syria, Saudi Arabia, Iran, Hamas-controlled territory in Palestine, and Hezbollah-controlled areas in Lebanon were all advocating the same thing: "stop the Iraqi elections." Quiet overtures to Arab governments nominally on "our side" in the War on Terror were less than effective in shutting down these sites. Though U.S. government officials won't say one way or the other, it's unlikely that the leaders in any of these countries looked forward to democratic elections anywhere in this part of the world.

To counter the blitz of anti-election propaganda, the government of interim Iraqi Prime Minister Iyad Allawi and the U.S. embassy in Baghdad launched a major "get out the vote" effort. Television, radio, and newspaper ads produced by pro-democracy organizations encouraged people to turn out on election day. In one TV commercial, an elderly Iraqi man was confronted on the street by a group of masked, armed thugs. The man was soon joined by a handful of his neighbors, then more, until the mass of ordinary citizens greatly outnumbered the terrorists who set off running from the crowd of unarmed but courageous Iraqis.

The voiceover said in Arabic, "On January 30th, we will meet our destiny and our duty. We are not alone and we are not afraid. Our strength is in our unity. Together we will work and together we will prevail." No ad like this could possibly have been broadcast under Saddam's rule—or under Al Qaeda.

A week before the election, a poll taken by the Arabic-language paper *Asharq Al-Aswat* indicated that more than 70 percent of the thirty-three thousand people queried intended to vote in the election. Nonetheless, the U.S. media persisted in predicting that the vote would fail. "Is a 50 percent turnout enough?" one reporter asked at a State Department briefing the day before the Iraqi ballot. Apparently the reporter was unaware that in U.S. congressional elections, fewer than 45 percent of those eligible to vote bother to cast a ballot.

Working with the Interim Governing Council in Baghdad, the U.S.-led Multinational Military Force designed rigorous security procedures for protecting polling places, voters, and international observers on election day. But because there were too few "vetted" and trained Iraqi police and military units to guard the six thousand polling places, coalition military personnel were called upon to shield numerous voting locations. In provinces like Al Anbar, heavily contested by Al Qaeda, most of the election sites were protected by American or other non-Iraqi coalition units.

The presence of Western troops guarding ballot boxes and the threat of violence—particularly in Anbar province—very likely did suppress turnout. But countrywide, 58 percent of those who were registered ignored the risk by placing an indelible ink-stained fingerprint next to the name of their chosen candidates.

Despite nine suicide bombers and more than a dozen mortar attacks on polling places around the country, more than eight million Iraqis cast ballots in the first multiparty election held in Iraq for more than half a century. The January 2005 election marked the first time in the entire five-thousand-year history of Mesopotamia that every man and woman, regardless of tribe, religion, or ethnic origin, was allowed to cast a ballot.

Even Arab television networks like Al Jazeera noted this "grand moment in Iraqi history" —as President Bush put it in a press conference the day after the election. The accomplishment was even more remarkable, considering that more than seventeen thousand provincial and national candidates had been willing to put their lives on the line in vying for office.

Three days after the Iraqi election, while ballots for local candidates were still being counted and validated, President Bush delivered his 2005 State of the Union Address. Seated next to Laura Bush in the balcony of the House chamber was Sofia Taleb al-Suhail, an Iraqi woman who had just voted in a free election for the first time in her life. Behind the First Lady were Janet and Bill Norwood, the parents of Marine Sgt Byron Norwood, who had been killed during the assault to liberate Fallujah. Mr. and Mrs. Norwood stood

to a sustained ovation when President Bush introduced them. But the applause became thunderous when Sofia reached out to hug the mother of the fallen Marine. It was a powerful and touching moment to remind all who watched about the sacrifice young Americans were making to help bring freedom to the people of Iraq.

IRAQ VOTE II: THE CONSTITUTIONAL REFERENDUM

★ ★ ★ ★ ★ ★ ★ ★ ★ ★ ★ ★

15 OCTOBER 2005

The responsibility of the 270-member Iraqi National Assembly elected on 30 January was very straightforward: to select a president, two deputy presidents, a prime minister, and a cabinet. And of equal importance, the assembly was charged with the Herculean task of drafting a new Iraqi constitution by 15 August and submitting it to a popular referendum by mid-October.

Having failed to stop the first election, Al Qaeda, Baath Party sympathizers, and radical sectarian militias redoubled their efforts to stop the process dead in its tracks. And they almost succeeded.

In the weeks after the January elections, violent attacks against the Iraqi police and coalition forces increased dramatically. Car bombs, truck bombs, IEDs, suicide attacks, and pitched battles against U.S. troops and Iraqi civilians increased in both frequency and lethality.

On 28 February a suicide car bomber in Hillah, sixty miles south of Baghdad, killed more than 120 civilians and wounded at least 150 more as they waited in line for government job interviews. It was the deadliest single attack on noncombatants since Saddam Hussein murdered thousands in his wave of repression after Operation Desert Shield in 1991. The message to the people was clear: the coalition cannot protect you.

In April, Prime Minister Iyad Allawi stepped down as prime minister and was replaced by a fellow Shiite, Ibrahim al-Jaafari. The new governing coalition immediately gridlocked over important constitutional issues, such as how much power minority Sunnis and Kurds would have in a democratic Iraq. Because most of the nation's known oil reserves are in Kurdish and Shiite controlled areas of the country, resolving those issues proved to be nearly impossible.

By May 2005, when our FOX News *War Stories* team—Mal James, Greg Johnson, and I—returned to Iraq, the remnants of Al Qaeda that had escaped Fallujah were reconstituting themselves in Al Anbar along the Euphrates River valley and north of Baghdad in Diyala province. To the south and east of the capital, Shiite militias were on a killing spree—"cleansing" entire districts and neighborhoods of any Sunni they could find. At the end of the month, Baghdad estimated that nearly seven hundred Iraqis had been killed by terror attacks.

On 28 August, the Sunni legislators in the National Assembly rejected a draft of the new Iraqi constitution and threatened to leave the government. Three days later nearly one thousand Shia pilgrims, marching to a religious shrine in Baghdad, died in a stampede created when rumors spread that Sunni suicide bombers had infiltrated the procession.

In Washington the press and the politicians blamed the increasing carnage on the stalled political process and the lack of progress on a new national charter. Apparently the critics had forgotten—or did not know—that it took four arduous years for Germany and seven for Japan to assemble sovereign governments after World War II. And in the United States, twelve years passed between Patrick Henry's cry of "give me liberty, or give me death" and the ratification of the United States constitution in 1787.

A car bomb is detonated in south Baghdad

In Iraq, there was no one in the country's first freely elected legislature who had any firsthand experience with democracy. As they struggled to create a constitution, they had to contend with gunfire, suicide bombings, assassinations, bitter sectarian rivalries that went back more than a millennium, and horrendous bloodshed. Yet, in eight and one-half months after Iraq's first election, the often fractious, frequently deadlocked Iraqi National Assembly managed to draft a charter for their country that could be put before the people.

As the date for the constitutional referendum approached, there were again dire predictions that Sunnis would boycott the vote, as they had in January; and that Al Qaeda and sectarian violence would limit turnout. Once again, the critics were wrong. More than 62 percent of all registered voters braved the threat of death from IEDs, mortar attacks, and suicide killers to go to the polls.

The masters of the media forecast a minimal turnout, again. But once again they were wrong. Nearly ten million people cast votes in the referendum, with nearly four out of five voting "yes" for their new constitution. Even the Sunnis came this time.

The constitution that the Iraqi people overwhelmingly affirmed provided for free, fair, and direct legislative elections every four years by secret ballot. It established a democratic system of government with an independent judiciary, checks and balances on power, and protection of women's and minority rights. It established a framework for determining how Iraq's vast oil wealth would be distributed to all the Iraqi people. It also meant that Iraqis would go to the polls yet again in December.

IRAQ VOTE III: THE NEW GOVERNMENT

★　★　★　★　★　★　★　★　★　★　★　★

Back in Iraq with Mal James, cameraman

15 DECEMBER 2005

When cameraman Mal James, producer Greg Johnson, and I returned to Iraq again in December 2005, we went straight back to Ramadi—capital of Al Anbar province—the country's largest and the heart of the so-called Sunni insurgency. There, we embedded with the 3rd Bn, 7th Marines, out of Marine Corps Base, Twentynine Palms, California. Well over half of these young Americans had previously seen action in Iraq or Afghanistan—and in some cases, both.

We chose to go to Ramadi again because Abu Musab al Zarqawi had pledged to turn election day in the provincial capital into a "bloodbath." Though he had made similar vows during the first two votes, this was also the city with the lowest turnout in the country.

Lt. Col. Roger Turner's 3rd Bn, 7th Marines, was assigned to the 2nd Brigade Combat Team of the 28th ID, from the Pennsylvania National Guard. The brigade commander, COL John Gronski, a Pittsburgh native, met us at the brigade LZ when we got off the helicopter in the middle of the night. My first question to him was about the upcoming elections.

"I think you will be surprised," he said. "In the first election last January, less than 5 percent of the people here voted. Last October it was about 25 percent. This time it's going to be a whole lot more."

I asked Lt. Col. Turner the same thing when I saw him the following morning: "Will they vote?"

"The people here now know that there is a lot at stake for them," he replied. "Boycotting this election won't help them, no matter what Zarqawi says. His tactics have backfired. Turnout is going to be a whole lot bigger than anyone expects."

The U.S. troops referred to 15 December as "E-Day." The "E" of course stood for "election." But it could easily have been "E" for the "elaborate" plans made to provide for safe elections while reducing visible American presence. By agreement with the provincial governor and officials in Baghdad, there would be no U.S. patrols or security units in the streets on election day.

To prevent car bombers, all motor vehicles except Iraqi security forces and election officials were banned from being driven from sunrise until sunset on the 15th. An Iraqi armored brigade, equipped with Soviet-era tanks, was dispatched from Baghdad. And hundreds of blue-clad Iraqi "provincial police" armed with AK-47s were "deputized" to provide security at polling places.

There were also quiet measures taken to "backstop" the Iraqi security. The night before E-Day, sniper teams and quick-reaction units surreptitiously moved out to preassigned positions where they could "overwatch" the polls and other key locations within the city. These small units—none was larger than a platoon—were ordered to stay out of sight but to be ready to respond instantly in case they were needed.

Mal James and I joined a Marine rifle platoon that was co-located with an Iraqi army company at a "strongpoint" in the heart of one of the most vicious neighborhoods in the violent city of Ramadi. A few yards up the heavily barricaded street was a polling place, due to open at 7:00 a.m.

A U.S. Marine sniper watches over a street in Fallujah, Iraq

Here's a portion of my report for FOX News the following day:

The polls opened here in Ramadi with a bang. Just down the street, at an intersection, an IED detonated beneath the treads of an Iraqi Army tank—thankfully without serious casualties. Afterwards, for a time, the streets were nearly empty. But then, using the loudspeakers on the minarets towering over the mosques, imams, sheiks, and tribal leaders urged people to get out and vote. One local imam told his followers, "God will bless you with a great life if you go out and vote." That and similar messages were broadcast from mosques all around town.

Terrorists like Zarqawi told the people to stay away from the polls or they would be killed. They came anyway—leaving the electoral sites with smiles and purple fingers. There were lines that wrapped around the block and extended for hundreds of people. Ten polling places ran out of ballots and had to send out for more.

At the end of this historic day, there was not a sound of gunfire, but instead, as the polls closed, there was a call to prayer. It was even an occasion for celebration as the neighborhood children were out in the streets, after dark, playing soccer with equipment given to them by Americans in uniform.

A soldier hands out soccer balls to local children

By the time the polls closed late on 15 December, more than twelve million Iraqis had voted—an astounding 70 percent of the electorate. Despite threats of terror and reprisals they trekked to nearly 6,500 polling stations and patiently waited in long lines to elect a 275-member National Assembly—the first freely elected, constitutionally determined legislature in the Arab world. For the very first time the Iraqi people—not the United Nations, not a foreign colonial power, not Americans—had drawn up their own national charter, nominated candidates, and elected their own government.

When election day was over, LCpl Jeffrey Heath stood in front of our FOX News camera while I asked him if the day had been a success. His reply: "Absolutely. This is why we're here—to help the Iraqi people gain the kind of freedoms that we take for granted back in the States." I couldn't have said it better myself.

Of course, holding an election isn't the last step in establishing a democracy; it's the first. An effective democracy requires rule of law, functioning courts, a balance of power, and civil institutions of government that are responsive to the needs of the people. Real democracies respect individual liberties and protect its citizens from violence—violence from criminals, hostile neighbors—and from their own government. All of that is a colossal challenge in a country besieged by sectarian strife, foreign terrorists flooding over its borders, and suicidal violence. Such an environment is not only deadly for people who are simply trying to provide for their families in Iraq; it is also lethal for the American troops helping to bring security and stability to the country.

As if to make that point, just three days after the election, LCpl Samuel Tapia, a mortar gunner in Weapons Company 3rd Bn, 7th Marines, was felled by enemy fire in Ramadi. He was on a patrol with Combined Anti-Armor Team Blue when a single shot from a sniper killed him, not three hundred yards from where people had lined up to vote on 15 December.

The balloting that LCpl Samuel Tapia helped protect had elected a government in Baghdad that was an imperfect democracy in its formative stages. It was susceptible to internal partisan political fratricide, homicidal suicide terrorists, IED makers, and Jihadists seeking to exploit Sunni-Shia-Kurdish rivalries. And it was very vulnerable to a failure of will in the United States.

The young warriors manning lonely outposts in Ramadi understood all of this. But they also knew that in helping to secure three elections in Iraq, they had been eyewitness participants in a dramatic moment in history. What they could not comprehend was the criticism to which they were subjected by much of the media and descriptions of the enemy as "opponents of the occupation,"

or "militants." The U.S. troops in Al Anbar know that the foes of freedom and democracy in Iraq are not "freedom fighters." They are terrorists, thugs, criminals, and cowards.

The troops were stunned to learn that politicians at home were less interested in the outcome of the Iraqi elections than they were in condemning their commander-in-chief for eavesdropping on terrorist phone calls. The soldiers and Marines we were with were equally disappointed that the elections had done nothing to squelch the clamor to "bring the troops home."

After my final report from Iraq before heading home for Christmas with my family, a young Marine approached me and asked, "What do you want for Christmas?"

It was the middle of the night, and we were standing atop a heavily sandbagged "strongpoint" known as "Outpost Horea" in downtown Ramadi, Iraq—long the bloodiest city in this very bloody country. In the dark, the Iraqi soldier standing watch beside the American looked toward us as a cold breeze rustled through the camouflage netting over our heads.

"What do I want for Christmas?" I repeated, somewhat surprised by the question. "I want you to get home safely."

The twenty-one-year-old Tennessean, girded in sixty-five pounds of armored flak jacket, night-vision-equipped helmet, grenades, and several hundred rounds of ammunition, reflected on that for a moment and replied, "So do I."

Then, quietly, from the young Iraqi soldier beside us, words in broken English that stunned me: "As do I—but not too soon."

That exchange, just days after a historic election, reflected the dramatic transition sweeping through Iraq at the end of 2005. While politicians and the mainstream media in the United States were focused on negative news, young Americans and their Iraqi counterparts were courageously going about the dangerous task of building a new nation from the ashes of Saddam's dictatorship and the ravages of Jihadist terror.

But as I left for home at the end of 2005, it was far from certain that politicians on Capitol Hill in Washington could muster the same tenacity as our troops. It was apparent that if Congress "pulled the plug" on Iraq, the elections they had helped secure would prove to be a brief flirtation with democracy and the country would descend into anarchy. And none of them wanted that as the legacy of their sacrifice.

★ ★ ★ ★ ★ ★ ★ ★ ★ ★ ★ ★ ★

12

TURNAROUND

CLOSING THE TERROR PIPELINE

★ ★ ★ ★ ★ ★ ★ ★ ★ ★ ★ ★ ★

By the time cameraman Mal James, senior producer Greg Johnson, and I returned to Iraq in May 2005, the terrorists who had been repudiated in the January elections were doing all they could to prevent the next Iraqi ballot. This was the constitutional referendum in October. Oil rich Wahhabi supporters of Sunni terror groups and Iranian-government backers for radical Islamists in the Middle East had good reason to be concerned.

On 14 March 2005, two months after the first Iraqi vote, over a million Lebanese—including Sunnis, Druze, and Christians—took to the streets of Beirut to demand that the Assad regime in Damascus quit interfering in Lebanon. The largely peaceful street demonstration in an Arab capital was a powerful sign of what "power to the people" could mean not only in Lebanon but in Syria, Iran, and Iraq.

A "house-borne IED" is detonated by U.S. Marines during Operation Matador

In the aftermath of the Beirut demonstrations, foreign money, specialized ordnance, and "volunteers" for anti-coalition forces began pouring into Iraq from Iran, Syria, and Saudi Arabia. Along the length of the Euphrates River valley, Abu Musab al Zarqawi resuscitated Al Qaeda in Iraq from the defeat it had suffered in the November 2004 liberation of Fallujah. To the east, Shiite militias and death squads, many with direct connections to Tehran, began running rampant through neighborhoods from Mosul in the north, south through east Baghdad, all the way to Basra.

As Iraqi civilian and coalition casualties increased, so did negative publicity and calls by Washington's political elite to "get out now." As usual, there was little "good news" from Iraq. And when there were insufficient "bad news" stories about U.S. troops, the media just made them up.

Shortly after we arrived in Iraq, *Newsweek* magazine published a fictional account about U.S. military interrogators desecrating the Koran at the military detention facility at Guantanamo Naval Base in Cuba. The most outrageous charge was that a guard had flushed a copy of the Koran, the holy book of Islam, down a toilet.

We first heard about the allegation over a loudspeaker on a nearby mosque while we were covering a U.S. Marine civil affairs team operating in a small village along the Euphrates River. After listening for a few minutes, the "terp" (interpreter) for the Marines gave us a rough translation along with the salient observation, "This isn't good."

He was right. Within twenty-four hours there were deadly riots and demonstrations throughout the Muslim world. In Pakistan, Afghanistan, and Iraq, imams, quoting the *Newsweek* article, incited violence by accusing "American infidels" of defiling Islam's holy book. Radical Islamic Web sites and propaganda organs sped the story globally—often embellished with other false charges—and issued calls for martyrs to join the Jihad.

Newsweek editor Mark Whitaker eventually recanted the phony report, saying, "We regret that we got any part of our story wrong and extend our sympathies to victims of the

With Producer Greg Johnson during Matador

violence and to the U.S. soldiers caught in its midst." But by then it was too late for the scores of Muslims who had been killed and wounded in the melees.

In the midst of this uproar, the Marines were doing their best to staunch the flood of foreign terrorists flooding down the Euphrates River from Syria into Iraq. On 7 May RCT-2 launched an offensive, code-named "Operation Matador," aimed at interdicting "known infiltration routes, and disrupting sanctuaries and staging areas" in the Euphrates River valley.

Our FOX News team headed for Al Qaim—the place the Marines called "the Wild West"—about a mile from the Syrian border. A young Marine combat cameraman, LCpl Aaron Mankin, jumped on a CH-53 helicopter with us. We flew from Fallujah to Al Qaim, the forward operating base of 3rd Bn, 2nd Marines, commanded by Lt. Col. Tim Mundy. Two years earlier we had been embedded with his older brother, Sam, in the advance on Baghdad and beyond.

Mundy's forward operating base was situated at a rail yard on the edge of Al Qaim at the far western edge of Anbar province, on the banks of the Euphrates River. From the roof of Mundy's battalion command post we could see into Syria. The nearby city, surrounded by the Western Desert and out of reach of any authority, had a long history of smuggling, gun-running, and cross-border banditry. One of the Marines described the sullen inhabitants of the riverside town of khaki-colored buildings as "much like the bar-room scene in the movie Star Wars."

On 07 April 2005, Al Qaeda terrorists had assaulted the main Al Qaim police station and then ambushed an Iraqi army unit en route to reinforce the beleaguered garrison. Three days later the Marine base was hit by a barrage of 122-mm rockets. Increasingly bold attacks on Mundy's resupply convoys and security patrols convinced Marine commanders that it was time to "shut the back door to Abu Musab al Zarqawi's terror recruiting pipeline."

Mundy's battalion was reinforced with additional M-1 tanks, armored assault vehicles, LAVs, engineers, a joint Army-Marine-Navy Seabee bridge detachment, Special Operations troops, and Company "L," 3rd Bn, 25th Marines—a Marine Reserve rifle company from Columbus, Ohio. On 7 May, Mundy's Marines swept out of their forward operating base in an armored column protected by Marine F/A-18s and AH-1 Cobras overhead.

To ensure that his armor could operate on both sides of the river, Mundy ordered his engineers and bridge detachment to place a floating span across the waterway. Then, to close an expected enemy escape route he seized the bridge at Karabilah. The fight to take and hold this key crossing became an epic battle, as the Silver Star citation for Lt. Brian Stann attests.

The President of the United States takes pleasure in presenting the Silver Star Medal to Brian M. Stann, 1st Lieutenant, U.S. Marine Corps, for conspicuous gallantry and intrepidity in action against the enemy as 2nd Mobile Assault Platoon Leader, Weapons Company, 3rd Bn, 2nd Marines, RCT-2, 2nd Marine Division, II MEF (Forward) in support of Operation IRAQI FREEDOM from 8 May to 14 May 2005. During Operation MATADOR, Lt. Stann led his reinforced platoon on an assault through a foreign fighter and Mujahadeen insurgent defense-in-depth to seize the Ramana Bridge north of Karabilah, Iraq. On three separate occasions, he traversed four kilometers of enemy-occupied urban terrain in order to maintain his battle position. With each deliberate attack he controlled close-air support and the direct fire systems of tanks and heavy machine guns, destroying enemy positions along the route. At one point, the enemy massed on his platoon and fired over thirty RPGs, machine guns, detonated two IEDs, and attacked the unit with three suicide VBIEDs. Lt. Stann personally directed two casualty evacuations, three vehicle recovery operations, and multiple close air support missions under enemy small arms, machine gun and mortar fire in his 360-degree fight. Inspired by his leadership and endurance, Lt. Stann's platoon held the battle position on the Euphrates River for six days, protecting the Task Force flank and isolating foreign fighters and insurgents north of the river. Lt. Stann's zealous initiative, courageous actions, and exceptional presence of mind reflected great credit upon himself and upheld the highest traditions of the Marine Corps and the United States Naval Service.

By dawn on 8 May, Mundy had effectively split his reinforced battalion into two armored task forces, one on each side of the river. As the two units began a parallel sweep through the sprawling settlements that lined the water's edge, the terrorists had nowhere to run.

The tactic took Zarqawi and his "mujahadeen" by surprise. In heavy contact on 8 and 9 May, seventy-five terrorists were killed and more than two dozen were captured in gunfights on both sides of the river. Intelligence officers subsequently showed us documents, travel credentials, and passports from Saudi Arabia, Syria, Lebanon, Algeria, Morocco, Yemen, Chechnya, and Jordan. There were also some identity papers from Iraq, but not many.

The terrain in which these battles were fought was surreal. Close to the river, the Marines encountered lush vegetation and numerous civilians in small agricultural communities. But as soon as we moved more than a kilometer from the water, the landscape looked like the moon. Not a blade of grass grew on the high bluffs overlooking the river. Movement through the desert churned up plumes of fine dust behind every column.

Before entering a village, a Psychological Operations detachment using loudspeakers announced to the occupants in Arabic that the settlement was surrounded and that civilians should assemble at a certain place. For the enemy, there was a different message: "If you are opponents of the democratic government, lay down your arms or come out and fight like men. If you want paradise, come out and fight. Don't be a coward and hide behind women."

Each time we stopped for more than a few hours, we went on the air to report for FOX News and for FOX News Radio via our satellite equipment powered from an armored vehicle or Humvee. On 10 May, Zarqawi's propaganda mill attempted to refute reports of his losses and the collapse of his sanctuary.

The inside of the armored assault vehicle turned orange and filled with thick, black smoke. The vehicle leapt into the air, violently throwing us about. Everyone was flung upward. I came down hard on my right side.

In the front of the troop compartment all I could see was a wall of fire and the silhouettes of still figures within the flames. The Marines in front most certainly were killed by the blast.

The rest of the troop compartment was immediately engulfed in flames. Smoke filled the cabin and billowed out, rolling into the afternoon air. As if we were in a foundry, the intense heat was immediately upon us.

I knew we had to get out.

— 1st Lt. Paul L. Croom II

In communiqués posted on radical Islamic Web sites, Al Qaeda asserted, "Do not believe the lies. We report to you, our brothers in the unification, that our mujahadeen in Al Qaim are well, enjoying victory or martyrdom for the way of Allah. The Americans are unable to count their losses due to the large number."

Apparently the accusation about "hiding behind women" hit home because the Al Qaeda organization also claimed that "the crusader's media lies when they accuse our mujahadeen of taking shelter behind other human beings." The posting concluded with a promise to deliver "hell with boiling volcanoes to the enemies of Allah." On 11 May, the "boiling volcanoes" part of this message seemed to come true for 3rd Bn, 2nd Marines.

We had halted outside a small hamlet, waiting for the villagers to assemble so the structures could be searched. As one of the armored assault vehicles, carrying almost half of 1st Platoon, "L" Company, 3rd Bn, 25th Marines, moved into position on the cordon, it rolled over a massive IED planted in the dirt road beside the village school.

There was a huge explosion beneath the twenty-three-ton vehicle, and it was instantly enveloped in flames from its ruptured fuel tanks. Six of the twenty men in the vehicle were killed by the blast. But for the fourteen wounded Marines inside, including Lt. Paul Croom and combat cameraman Aaron Mankin, survival meant escaping from the fiery cauldron.

Within seconds, ammunition inside the vehicle—small arms, 40-mm grenades, and anti-tank rockets—began "cooking off" in the intense heat, sending deadly projectiles ricocheting in all directions. As the Marines inside the vehicle struggled to escape the flames, their comrades raced to save them. One of them, Sgt Dennis Woullard, had been blown out a forward hatch by the

explosion. He and other Marines, disregarding the immense danger, raced to save their injured comrades. In a matter of minutes U.S. Army H-60 cas-evac helicopters were landing on the school soccer field to evacuate the wounded. Sgt Woullard's citation for the Silver Star describes the kind of courage that was commonplace that terrible day.

The President of the United States takes pleasure in presenting the Silver Star Medal to Dennis Woullard Jr., Sergeant, U.S. Marine Corps (Reserve), for conspicuous gallantry and intrepidity in action against the enemy while serving as Radio Chief, 1st Section, 3rd Platoon, Company A, 4th Assault Amphibian Bn, RCT-2, 2nd Marine Division, II MEF (Forward) from 8 to 11 May 2005. On 8 May 2005, in Al Ubaydi, Iraq, Sgt Woullard volunteered to assist an infantry squad conduct clearing operations during Operation MATADOR. After clearing several residences without incident, and during a breach of a front door, his team was immediately attacked with heavy machine gun and RPG fire from within. Every member of the team was wounded. Despite his wounds, Sgt Woullard evacuated two Marines from the residence, and then joined in an assault to recover the remaining trapped Marine. Sgt Woullard repeatedly exposed himself to heavy fire and assaulted into the house. He rescued the trapped Marine, shielding him with his body as he carried him to an Amphibious Assault Vehicle (AAV) where he administered first aid until en route to the battalion. On 11 May 2005, near the Syrian border, Sgt Woullard's AAV was attacked with an IED that killed or injured all the Marines on board. Although again wounded and disoriented from the explosion, Sgt Woullard struggled to the rear of the vehicle and opened the personnel hatch. With complete disregard for his own safety and exposed to the intense heat and exploding ammunition, he repeatedly returned to the burning vehicle to evacuate the severely wounded Marines. By his superior leadership, unrelenting determination, and total dedication to duty, Sgt Woullard reflected great credit upon himself and upheld the highest traditions of the Marine Corps and the United States Naval Service.

When Operation Matador ended on 14 May, more than 125 Al Qaeda terrorists were dead and 39 of Zarqawi's key lieutenants had been captured. Tons of enemy weapons, ordnance, and documents were retrieved along with six VBIEDs designed to be used in suicide attacks.

The operation had cost the lives of nine Marines. Another forty were wounded. Eight of those killed were from "Lima" Company 3rd Bn, 25th Marines. In 168 hours of day and night combat, the company's 1st platoon suffered 60 percent casualties.

In all the warfare I have experienced, the horrific explosion beneath the AAV on 11 May 05 is the most gruesome combat loss I have ever witnessed. The bravery of those who rescued their fellow Marines that terrible day is unforgettable.

Abu Musab al Zarqawi once again escaped the noose, probably by fleeing into Syria. But Operation Matador shut down the "main Al Qaeda invasion route into Al Anbar," as Lt. Col. Tim Mundy put it. The loss of long-established sanctuaries, bomb factories, and staging areas severely hurt Al Qaeda. The terror organization was rendered incapable of disrupting the constitutional referendum in October or the elections for a permanent government in December of 2005.

Unable to confront the "American infidels" head-on, Zarqawi reoriented his attacks to concentrate on "softer targets"—unarmed civilians. Though we didn't know it at the time, the turnaround in Al Anbar had begun.

RAMADI: IED CENTRAL

★ ★ ★ ★ ★ ★ ★ ★ ★ ★ ★

A gunfight after an IED attack in Ramadi

In October 2005, five months after Operation Matador, British Explosive Ordnance specialists, tipped off by a local citizen in Basra, set out to disarm what they expected to be a "run of the mill" IED. What they discovered confirmed what intelligence sources had been telling them for weeks—that Tehran was shipping technologically advanced detonators into Iraq and teaching Shiite terror groups how to make deadlier warheads.

Immediate action during an IED attack on
a Marine patrol in Ramadi

When the British Explosive Ordnance team disassembled the weapon, they found Iranian-built circuitry in the detonators. Of greater concern was the unique construction of the deadly device. Explosives, scraped out of an Iraqi artillery shell, had been packed into a common metal pipe less than four inches in diameter. A hole in the sealed end of the pipe allowed for the placement of an electric blasting cap, which in turn was connected to an electronic detonator controlled by an infrared sensor.

But this was no simple "pipe bomb." The "business end" of the device was a concave copper disc, designed to form a semi-molten slug that would hurtle out of the tube at supersonic speed. Properly constructed and placed, this "explosively formed projectile"— or EFP—could penetrate the armor on the flanks of a British Challenger or American Abrams tank. Nine months later, Iranian-supported Hezbollah fighters used these devices with deadly effect against Israeli armor in southern Lebanon.

By the time Mal James, Greg Johnson, and I joined Roger Turner's 3rd Bn, 7th Marines, in Ramadi to cover the December elections, the provincial capital was described in the U.S. media as an Al Qaeda stronghold. Though Al Qaeda wasn't yet using explosively formed projectiles, they had perfected the art of using IEDs as a defensive weapon and suicide bombs as an offensive measure against coalition troops. For the Iraqi civilians who didn't toe the Zarqawi line, they had an even simpler tactic: murder.

While Al Qaeda focused on deterring voter turnout through intimidation and horrific atrocities, the soldiers and Marines in Ramadi devoted themselves to making the city safe enough to even hold elections. Part of the effort involved keeping roads and streets open. This required constant patrols through IED-infested neighborhoods.

In the past, a U.S. military patrol or convoy through the heart of Ramadi would almost inevitably have resulted in several hours of "gunfight footage." But now the challenge was to negotiate IEDs placed by Al Qaeda bomb makers to inflict maximum casualties on the Americans.

When we went on operations, my cameraman, producer, and I tried to stay dispersed and ride in separate vehicles. On one occasion as Mal and I were accompanying a QRF responding to a unit in contact, an IED detonated beside the Humvee in which Mal James was riding. His reaction describes what happened:

In a split second, the Humvee filled with dust and smoke, and there was this incredible "thud," and I could feel the air compress inside the vehicle. As soon as you realize what's happened, you have this great fear . . . is there going to be a fireball come through the vehicle?

That was my great worry, of being engulfed by a fireball. And then we suddenly stopped, and everybody got out . . . . (It seems the most unnatural thing in the world to do—you've just been attacked—to actually get out; that's what the Marines do.) They got out, and they took those zealots on. In seconds, the scene was locked down, secured. Then, minutes later, we were back in the vehicle screaming down the road. We hadn't even gotten to the battle; we'd been attacked, survived, and moved on.

As fast as terrorists placed IEDs, the Marines of 3rd Bn, 7th Marines, and the soldiers of 2nd Brigade Combat Team, 28th ID, set out to disarm them. The danger the Marines and soldiers faced on these daily operations is reflected in the Silver Star citation awarded to Cpl Jeremy Stagner, who drove an ambulance for an EOD team.

The President of the United States takes pleasure in presenting the Silver Star Medal to Jeremy L. Stagner, Corporal, U.S. Marine Corps, for conspicuous gallantry and intrepidity in action against the enemy while serving as casualty evacuation driver, Company L, 3rd Bn, 7th Marines, 2nd Brigade Combat Team, 2nd Marine Division, II-MEF (Forward), in support of Operation IRAQI FREEDOM on 1 November 2005. While he was cordoning

an IED, Cpl Stagner witnessed an explosion caused by a second IED that destroyed an EOD vehicle. Almost immediately, he saw a Marine emerge from the vehicle covered in flames, and obviously in extreme pain. Completely disoriented, the Marine attempted to put the flames out by flailing his arms wildly. As his attempts progressively failed, he began to run in circles and cut sharply in different directions, trying to create enough wind force to extinguish the fire. Without hesitation, while he was under enemy small arms and RPG fire, Cpl Stagner grabbed a fire extinguisher, ran forty meters over open terrain to the burning Marine,

and extinguished the fire. Despite secondary explosions from hand grenades and C-4 in the vehicle, as well as continued exposure to enemy fire, he moved the Marine to the casualty-evacuation vehicle. Cpl Stagner then located a corpsman and, exposing himself to the enemy a third time, provided suppressive fire to cover the corpsman's sprint to the casualty. His heroic actions were instrumental in preventing the loss of additional lives. By his bold leadership, wise judgment, and complete dedication to duty, Cpl Stagner reflected great credit upon himself and upheld the highest traditions of the Marine Corps and the United States Naval Service.

Detecting and disarming IEDs, hunting down Al Qaeda terrorists, and securing elections weren't the only missions in Ramadi. COL John Gronski's 2nd Brigade Combat Team, 28th ID, also had the task of recruiting a new police force.

In the aftermath of the unexpectedly large election turnout on 15 December, the coalition launched a major effort to rebuild the Iraqi police force in Al Anbar province. Abu Musab al Zarqawi, having failed to keep people from going to the polls, pledged to stop the police recruiting drive. Mike McLaughlin, a U.S. Army lieutenant colonel on the 2nd Brigade Combat Team staff, was given the task of setting up the process for selecting the new applicants.

He established a screening center at a closed glass plant, immediately across the Euphrates Canal from the Marine base at "Hurricane Point" on the outskirts of Ramadi. After numerous meetings with the governor and local sheiks, the drive kicked off on 2 January. For three days all went well, with roughly 250 potential recruits screened and processed each day. But early on the morning of the 5th, one of the sheiks whom McLaughlin had befriended warned that Al Qaeda suicide bombers were planning to attack the recruiting center.

McLaughlin rushed to the glass factory and found a large crowd of several hundred young Iraqi males already jammed into the courtyard of the screening center. In order to warn his U.S. and Iraqi "screeners" of the danger without starting a panic among the recruits, he waded into the crowd. That's when a suicide bomber detonated an explosive device beneath his robe, killing and wounding more than thirty civilians and Iraqi and U.S. soldiers. A lethal piece of shrapnel from the bomb struck LTC McLaughlin in the head. This excerpt from the narrative accompanying his Silver Star citation describes what happened next:

One of his soldiers, SPC Gibson, himself wounded in the shoulder by shrapnel, immediately checked LTC McLaughlin for wounds, who in turn, in an act of extreme selflessness, stated that he was OK, but to concentrate on saving the lives of his men. LTC McLaughlin succumbed shortly thereafter to his wounds. Throughout the period, LTC McLaughlin displayed extraordinary personal courage, selfless service, and dedication to duty. He was a charismatic leader who always led from the front, and was the consummate professional, fully committed in word and deed to empowering the Iraqi people to pursue political and economic progress and to end the insurgency in Al Anbar province. His actions are in keeping with the finest traditions of military service and reflect great credit upon himself, the 2nd Brigade Combat Team of the 28th ID, and the United States Army.

Mike McLaughlin didn't die in vain. In the months ahead, the police force that he played a key role in recruiting would help drive Abu Musab al Zarqawi and his Al Qaeda organization out of Ramadi. But no one could see that in the days after his death.

THE AWAKENING

★　★　★　★　★　★　★　★　★　★　★　★　★

"The sons of Al Anbar from Fallujah to Al Qaim have risen up to fight the terrorists."
— Governor Maamoun Rashid, Ramadi, Iraq

"The brave Sons of Anbar have awakened to the need to defend our country. With the help of your country we will defeat the terrorists here."
— Sheikh Abdul Sattar Baziya, Ramadi, Iraq

When cameraman Mal James, Producer Andrew Stenner, and I joined Lt. Col. Bill Jurney's 1st Bn, 6th Marines, and COL Sean MacFarland's 1st Brigade Combat Team, 1st Armored Division, in Ramadi in December 2006, the press was describing the situation as hopeless. Though the Iraqi people had pulled off a successful election a year earlier, the country's first democratically elected government had failed to bring political reconciliation, stability, or economic recovery.

On 22 February, Sunni suicide bombers destroyed the golden-domed al Askari Mosque in Samarra, a revered Shia shrine. Within days, Moqtada al Sadr's Iranian-supported Mahdi Army and a dozen or more other Shiite militias were on a Sunni-killing spree.

Then, on 8 June, a unit of the U.S. Special Operations Command tracked down Abu Musab al Zarqawi in an isolated safe house five miles north of Baquba. A precision air strike killed the Jordanian as he tried to escape. But the death of the founder of Al Qaeda in Iraq didn't stop the sectarian slaughter.

By August, when thermometers along the Tigris and Euphrates rivers climbed to 130 degrees, the beheaded bodies of dozens of Iraqis were being found daily—amid growing carnage from suicide bombers. In the weeks leading up to the U.S. Congressional elections, there was a near total breakdown of law and order in the Iraqi capital and the words "civil war" were appearing regularly in the U.S. media.

On 5 November, two days before the U.S. election, Saddam Hussein was convicted of crimes against humanity and sentenced to hang. The verdict had no discernible impact at the ballot box. Opponents of the Bush administration's Iraq policy routed Republicans at the polls and promised to "end the war immediately" after being sworn in.

All of this was preamble to our late-night arrival at the Camp Ar Ramadi LZ after a much-delayed helicopter flight from Baghdad. We were met at the LZ by Marine Maj. Megan McClung, the 1st Brigade Combat Team's public affairs officer. She offered a cup of hot coffee and helped us load our backpacks, camera gear, and satellite broadcast equipment aboard a dust-encrusted Humvee and took us to meet COL Sean MacFarland, the brigade commander.

Just hours later, this widely respected and much admired Marine officer and two brave U.S. Army soldiers, CPT Travis Patriquin and SPC Vincent Pomante, were killed by an IED while escorting a *Newsweek* reporter to a security outpost in downtown Ramadi.

The tragic loss of these three Americans, like the four who were killed in a CH-46 crash near Taqaddum Air Base the day we arrived, were cited by critics as "proof" that the campaign was "unwinnable." Just days later a classified Pentagon intelligence report leaked to the media concluded that U.S. and Iraqi forces were "no longer capable of militarily defeating the insurgency in Al Anbar province." The assessment was wrong, and we showed why in our reports.

With Sheikh Sattar at an Iraqi Police Training Center

Since mid-summer the soldiers and Marines in Al Anbar had been working closely with a coalition of local sheiks led by Abdul Sattar Baziya, the most powerful tribal leader in Ramadi. His father and older brother had been murdered by Al Qaeda terrorists for cooperating with the coalition.

Sattar used his considerable influence to expand on what his father had started. By the time I met him for the first of several interviews, he was justifiably proud of what he called "The Awakening." He and a dozen other tribal leaders were recruiting local police officers and soldiers for the Iraqi Army and were working closely with the Americans to bring law and order in the province and rebuild essential infrastructure.

Civil Affairs teams, Military Transition teams, and Police Training teams had been formed from personnel in the 1st Brigade Combat Team and 1st Bn, 6th Marines. Their assignment was to work day-to-day with the Iraqis. New police security stations manned by Iraqi Army units—mostly Shia—and Iraqi police—mostly Sunni—and a single platoon of U.S. troops were being opened in neighborhoods long controlled by Al Qaeda.

Pushing into Al Qaeda safe-havens to establish new, permanent police security posts was dangerous for the Iraqis and Americans involved. The avenues of approach were inevitably lined with IEDs, and Al Qaeda was sure to attack the outposts.

Mal and I accompanied Bill Jurney's Marines as they set up a new police station in an abandoned four-story building in the heart of a neighborhood that had been under Al Qaeda control for more than two years. The operation, launched from Hurricane Point after dark, included Marines, U.S. Army tanks, EOD specialists, engineers, Navy Seabees, Iraqi police and army units, and truckloads of filled sandbags.

Within hours the building was secured and thousands of sandbags had been hauled inside to fill every window and build a barrier for security outposts on the flat-topped roof. Before dawn the escort force withdrew back to Hurricane Point, leaving a Marine Rifle platoon led by a lieutenant and nearly two hundred Iraqi police and soldiers behind to greet the new day.

Inside the building billeting arrangements were determined by security requirements, not creature comforts. A joint U.S.-Iraqi command post was set up in a room on the third floor, with wires running to antennas on the roof. Three-man security and sniper outposts were established on every corner of the roof. Every position had an American, a Sunni policeman, and a Shia soldier.

Mal and I took up residence in a windowless room on the ground floor, sharing space with the twelve-man U.S. Marine QRF. We unrolled foam mattresses from the bottom of our backpacks, set our cameras beside the bedrolls, and stretched out on top of our sweat-soaked flak jackets. Using our helmets for pillows, we went fast asleep with our boots on, waiting for the inevitable response.

It came after dark on our second night in the outpost. The local Al Qaeda cell, no doubt concerned that this new security station was interfering with their extortion, kidnapping, and burglary operations, decided to use the building for target practice. Apparently, every Jihadi who had ever wanted to fire a 60-mm mortar or a RPG was invited to the shoot-em-up.

I'm a very light sleeper, especially in the field. As the first mortar rounds hit the roof, I jumped up, threw on my flak jacket, fastened my helmet chin strap, grabbed my camera and a night lens, and headed for the stairs to get up to the roof. Half the QRF bounded for the roof while the other half headed out to preassigned positions in front of the building.

The attack was over in minutes. It had probably been staged to cover the withdrawal of the Al Qaeda cell from the neighborhood.

The effect of the new police station was dramatic and immediate. Iraqi police and soldiers accompanied by Marines began patrolling the neighborhood the morning after we moved in. Two days later a delegation of local parents, escorted by an Iraqi police lieutenant, came to the station and asked for help reopening a long-abandoned school.

Al Qaeda terrorists had told local authorities—on pain of death—not to allow this little female academic institution to unshutter its doors. Apparently, little girls learning math and science posed a significant threat to radical Islamic Jihadists.

In less than a week, Bill Jurney's Marines—aided by U.S. Navy Seabees, soldiers of the "Ready First" Brigade Combat Team, and Sheikh Sattar's local police—found desks, chalkboards, and school books and reopened the school. I went there with Maj. Scott Kish, the local Civil Affairs Group chief. It was an unusually cold day, and he noticed that the classrooms had no heat. That afternoon he delivered portable heaters, commenting that these actions "spawn success" because they "encourage Iraqis to take charge of their own destiny."

Opening police stations and girls' schools on the mean streets of Ramadi may not appear to be great victories to the critics of this war. However, they are precisely the kind of events that resulted from Sattar's "Awakening." They're also significant to the U.S. troops who help make them happen.

While we were visiting the school, I asked a young Marine corporal what he was doing in Iraq. "We're here to win," he responded, looking squarely into our TV camera—a more intimidating experience for him than the enemy fire he often faced on the streets of this beleaguered city.

By the end of 2006, Iraqi soldiers and police were regularly operating with U.S. Army and Marine units

When I pressed this twenty-year-old from the heartland of America to tell me what "winning" meant to him, he was straightforward: "That's when these people don't need me to guard this street so their kids can go to school—when they can do it themselves."

The belief that the Iraqi people would be able to "do it themselves" was evident in numerous other actions we documented—events that contradicted much of what the American people were being fed by the mainstream media and partisan political opponents at home. According to conventional wisdom, the Iraqis were unwilling to fight for themselves and were on the brink of a suicidal Sunni vs. Shia civil war. But that's not what we found on this trip to Al Anbar. A few examples from our reports:

While we were at the 17th Street Police Station with Bill Jurney, the Iraqi Police battalion commander, Lt. Col. Jabbar Inad al Namrawee, came to inspect his police officers. A week earlier, Al Qaeda terrorists had attacked another of his stations. Col. Jabbar led an all-Iraqi QRF into the battle. In the ensuing gunfight he was shot in the leg by an Al Qaeda attacker. By the time the battle was done, more than a dozen terrorists were dead and his "Sons of Al Anbar" had earned new respect from Ramadi's war-weary civilians.

When I asked Col. Jabbar how his wound was healing, he pulled up his pant leg and showed me the new "battle dressing" that a Navy Corpsman had applied over the entry and exit holes from the AK-47 round that had gone through his calf. They were Sponge Bob band-aids.

——— ———

We went with COL MacFarland and Sheikh Sattar to Camp Phoenix, where hundreds of young Sunni police recruits were being drilled in law enforcement tactics by Iraqi Army NCOs, most of them Shiites. The training was being supervised by U.S. Army soldiers and civilian police officers from Pittsburgh, New York City, Cincinnati, and Los Angeles.

While we watched, one of the Iraqi recruits failed to complete a task. The Iraqi NCO supervising the drill had the young man drop down and do twenty push-ups. Sattar smiled, turned to me, and asked, "Can you still do that?"

— — —

Ramadi is less volatile today, but it is still a dangerous place. We were on a joint Marine-Army-Iraqi "presence patrol" through a very rough part of town when the call came over the radio, "Rocket-propelled grenade! Eleven o'clock! Street level." Everyone in the vehicle looked to the left front. An instant later there was a flash as an RPG was launched, followed by the command, "Engage!" As the projectile detonated on a pile of sand in front of our Humvee, the U.S. Army M-1 tank beside us opened fire, not with the main gun which would have done enormous damage, but with the coaxial machine gun.

The result: a terrorist who will never again try to kill an American soldier, Marine, or an Iraqi policeman. When I asked the young tank commander about his decision to use the lighter weapon on the RPG shooter, the soldier replied, "Yeah, it was the right thing to do. It's only 'collateral damage' when it's someone else's house."

The Sunday before we departed Ramadi, our FOX News team attended services in the 1st Bn, 6th Marines, chapel at Hurricane Point. Christmas was just a few days away. The roomful of armed men sang "Silent Night," led by a machine gunner with an angelic voice. Chaplain Stall-Ryan spoke about the birth of the Prince of Peace.

Out on the streets of the city, the "Sons of Al Anbar," recruited by Sheikh Sattar and trained by Americans, were manning security stations and outposts that hadn't existed in my previous trips. Though there were still vicious bomb builders and suicidal fanatics, there were far fewer of them.

As we filed out of the chapel, I asked one of the Marines if he had a message for the folks back home. He reflected a moment and replied, "Tell 'em that things are better here than they know. We've turned things around."

HERO VALUES

★ ★ ★ ★ ★ ★ ★ ★ ★ ★ ★ ★ ★

It has been the great blessing of my life to grow up and spend most of my now-considerable years in the company of heroes. For me, heroes are people who put themselves at risk for the benefit of others.

Whether it was my parents' generation that persevered through the Great Depression and then fought and won World War II or those who serve in today's all-volunteer military, they all embody certain essential values that make them iconic in our culture. These values are courage, commitment, compassion, faith, and good humor. Anyone who spends time with these modern heroes has seen countless examples. Here are some of the best from my many months with those who have "been there, done that."

COURAGE

★ ★ ★ ★ ★ ★ ★ ★ ★ ★ ★ ★ ★

Courage is evident in more than the citations for bravery on the battlefield, many of which appear in this book. It isn't something you are born with . . . and it can't be given to you. Courage is a decision you make. It doesn't come from something you are; it's something you do.

Courage is a squad of young soldiers or Marines who hold their fire when a sniper shoots at them from a crowd of innocent civilians.

Courage is American troops having the integrity not to steal something from an Iraqi or Afghan house that they have entered in the middle of the night.

Courage is Iraqi Christians who attend worship despite threats and attacks on their churches.

Courage is Afghan women who refuse to leave a voting line even when a suicide car bomb explodes nearby. To do so, they say, would be to give the terrorists a victory.

Courage is Iraqi men who continue to volunteer for service as policemen and soldiers at great risk to themselves and their families. It's evident when Shiite and Sunni men put aside their differences to rid their country of terrorists.

Courage is visible in the eyes of Afghan parents who have been threatened for sending their daughters to a newly opened school, and they keep sending them anyway.

Courage is going back to a lonely outpost or on patrol or with a convoy after you have lost a buddy.

Courage is often the ultimate in self-sacrifice, as the Medal of Honor citation for Marine Cpl Jason Dunham attests:

For conspicuous gallantry and intrepidity at the risk of his life above and beyond the call of duty while serving as a Rifle Squad Leader, 4th Platoon, Company K, 3rd Bn, 7th Marines (Reinforced), RCT-7, 1st Marine Division (Reinforced), on 14 April 2004. Cpl Dunham's squad was conducting a reconnaissance mission in the town of Karabilah, Iraq, when they heard RPG and small arms fire erupt approximately two kilometers to the west. Cpl Dunham led his Combined Anti-Armor Team toward the engagement to provide fire support to their battalion commander's convoy, which had been ambushed as it was traveling to Camp Husaybah. As Cpl Dunham and his Marines advanced, they quickly began to receive enemy fire. Cpl Dunham ordered his squad to dismount their vehicles and led one of his fire teams on foot several blocks south of the ambushed convoy. Discovering seven Iraqi vehicles in a column attempting to depart, Cpl Dunham and his team stopped the vehicles to search them for weapons. As they approached the vehicles, an insurgent leaped out and attacked Cpl Dunham. Cpl Dunham wrestled the insurgent to the ground and in the ensuing struggle saw the insurgent release a grenade. Cpl Dunham immediately alerted his fellow Marines to the threat. Aware of the imminent danger and without hesitation, Cpl Dunham covered the grenade with his helmet and body, bearing the brunt of the explosion and shielding his Marines from the blast. In an ultimate and selfless act of bravery in which he was mortally wounded, he saved the lives of at least two fellow Marines. By his undaunted courage, intrepid fighting spirit, and unwavering devotion to duty, Cpl Dunham gallantly gave his life for his country, thereby reflecting great credit upon himself and upholding the highest traditions of the Marine Corps and the United States Naval Service.

HERO HUMOR
I'm Not a Mailman

For military men and women serving in harm's way during the holidays, there is nothing like getting mail from home to warm lonely hearts. Fortunately, families of these heroes never let them down when it comes to sending packages during the holidays.

On one trip, we were documenting the mountains of mail that had just arrived as troops loaded bags and boxes to be delivered to a rifle company. I shouted to one of the senior NCOs overseeing the detail and asked him, "do me a favor and walk toward the camera while we film all of you unloading the mail." Full of Christmas cheer, he glared into the camera and growled, "I'm not a ——— mailman!"

Never Fall Asleep First

"Sleep's a crutch"—or so declared the label on a bag of "Ranger Coffee" I was given recently. The caffeine it contained would have been welcome on any of my trips to the war zone, where I and my crew regularly pulled twenty-plus hour days. It's hard to complain, though, since the troops we cover seem to view sleep as a nasty habit that needs to be broken. They often get by on little more than chewing tobacco and Red Bull.

On our December 2006 trip to Iraq, we went through a grueling series of patrols, briefings, and night missions interspersed with live shots, stand-ups, and call-ins for FOX News. Andy Stenner, my producer, made the mistake of sacking out before the rest of us.

But with this group, you never want to fall asleep first.

We made sure Andy was comfortable and had some "friends" to snuggle with. The resulting photo was the source of laughs all over the newsroom. He paid me back by taking pictures of me every time I dozed off, no matter where it was.

HERO HUMOR
Shot at Without Result

Mal James and I were with a dozen heavily armed Marines and Iraqi policemen in Ramadi, Iraq, one afternoon when an enemy sniper "cranked off" a round in our direction. The videotape shows me walking toward the camera and my reaction as the shot passed wide of its mark. By the time the sniper fired a second time, I was out of the frame—and on the ground. Old men can move surprisingly fast when properly motivated.

The moment recalled Winston Churchill's line, "Nothing in life is so exhilarating as to be shot at without result." But the most impressive response was that of the Marines and Iraqi police accompanying the unarmed contractors. There was no burst of return fire from the Marines, no aimless barrage from the Iraqi policemen. Instead, as the camera continued to roll, they hustled everyone to cover. The Marines could be seen on the videotape scanning distant windows and rooftops through their rifle sights. Later, Marine gunner Bob Tagliabue summed it up best: "We go to the practice range. The terrorists don't."

COMMITMENT

★ ★ ★ ★ ★ ★ ★ ★ ★ ★ ★ ★

Every one of our soldiers, sailors, airmen, Guardsmen, and Marines currently serving has volunteered to do so in time of war against an implacable enemy. Without being conscripted, they left the comfort of home, the warmth of friends, and the affection of their families to serve in harm's way.

Despite the relentless criticism of a generally hostile media, the overwhelming apathy of their fellow citizens, and the on-again-off-again support of politicians, they have reenlisted and returned to combat at higher rates than any military force in our nation's history.

Some people here at home claim, "I support the troops; I just don't support what they are doing in Iraq or Afghanistan." Those who believe that statement need to try this experiment. When you get home after work, walk in the front door and tell your spouse: "I love you . . . but I really don't like the way you drive, cook, look after the house, or care for the kids—and that needs to change right now." Then see where you sleep that night.

Most of the young Americans in our military are in their early twenties. They are accountable for hundreds of millions of dollars worth of equipment and the lives and safety of innumerable others. In a combat zone they go to work every day carrying lethal weapons and the means to summon

massive destruction from afar on a moment's notice. By the time they have received an honorable discharge, they will have been entrusted with more responsibility than their civilian peers will ever be given.

Though they rarely see "gratitude" mentioned in print or on the air, the men and women in our armed forces earnestly believe that they are protecting us from a ruthless foe who would repeat the horror of 9/11 against us if given the chance. And those who serve in our military today know that their pitiless adversary has been taught to hate and is dying to kill any American.

If that weren't enough, those on the front lines in the war against radical Islam also carry on their shoulders the hopes and dreams of Muslims who yearn for freedom and safety after years of brutality and oppression. And back home, the biggest decision many of their peers have to make is what movie to see on a Friday night.

During the opening stages of Operation Iraqi Freedom, I asked Col. Joe Dunford to describe the seven thousand Marines, soldiers, and sailors he was leading in RCT-5 in the attack north to Baghdad. "They're just incredible," he replied. "They look out for each other, they trust each other, and they're ready to do whatever they're called upon to do."

I have met many of those troops in trips to Iraq, Afghanistan, and the Philippines. They are still serving. Now that's commitment.

HERO HUMOR
Will Work for Food

Each time the Marines established a new U.S.-Iraqi security station in terrorist-controlled neighborhoods, they had to fortify the building they were going to occupy with sandbags. But tens of thousands of sandbags don't fill themselves. The Marines solved the problem in Marine Corps fashion.

Immediately outside the mess hall at Hurricane Point the engineers dumped a mountain of sand. Next to it they placed pallets of green sandbags and a half-dozen shovels. Every person on the base—officers, troops, and FOX News personnel—had to fill two sandbags in order to get a meal. There were no complaints—at least that we heard. One wag put it this way: "We're Marines. We work for food."

Freedom Comes in Forty-Pound Bags

Mal James, my superb combat cameraman, and I accompanied the Marines as they opened a new police station in the heart of an Al Qaeda-controlled neighborhood in Ramadi. We moved out after dark—a Marine rifle platoon, a company of Iraqi Shiite soldiers, and a detachment of Iraqi Sunni policemen.

Within a few hours this combined unit of fewer than one hundred men occupied a four-story concrete building in the middle of an Al Qaeda-controlled neighborhood. Well before dawn they had packed every window full of sandbags and built sandbag barriers around the edge of the roof. Each of those forty-pound sandbags—thousands of them—had been filled by the Marines, loaded on flatbed trucks, brought to the site, and then carried up the stairs. Almost half of them were taken all the way to the roof. It was back-breaking, dirty work—carried out in the100-degree heat through a stifling, dust-filled haze lit only by the eerie dim glow of blue chem-lights. Mal and I did our share, joining the human chain that passed the sandbags from the ground floor and up the stairs. In the midst of it all, one of the Marines observed, "The recruiter never told me that freedom comes in forty-pound bags!"

COMPASSION

★ ★ ★ ★ ★ ★ ★ ★ ★ ★ ★ ★

Since 2001 I have spent more than a year covering U.S. military personnel fighting radical Islamists around the world. Whoever coined the phrase "nice guys finish last" didn't spend enough time with the men and women of our armed forces. On the battlefield, compassion and courage aren't mutually exclusive.

The care with which U.S. forces are carrying out this war stands in stark contrast to the ruthless tactics of our adversaries. Americans publicly debate the morality of certain forms of interrogation. Our enemies release to the public videos of hostages being tortured and beheaded.

I've also looked into Saddam's mass graves and seen the captured films and videotapes of innocent Iraqis having their tongues cut out and others being blindfolded, bound, and marched off the top of a three-story building. I have seen the Taliban's torture chambers in Afghanistan and have interviewed survivors of Abu Sayef atrocities in the Philippines.

I have seen and documented Iraqi schools turned into ammunition depots and mosques used as bunkers. In the village of al Hamira near Baquba in mid-2007, Al Qaeda operatives massacred every inhabitant and their livestock and beheaded more than a dozen children. The same mainstream media that gave front-page, lead-story status to Abu Ghraib and Haditha barely mentioned al Hamira.

Terrible things happen in all wars, and this one is no exception. War is the cruelest of human endeavors. Yet, when American military personnel are accused of being involved in wrongful behavior, they are investigated, and where appropriate, subject to trial and, if convicted, punishment. Restitution is paid to innocent victims of American destruction. But our radical Islamic enemies use innocent civilians as human shields, laud those who commit atrocities—and promise more of the same.

Wounded enemy combatants are routinely sent to the same hospitals where they receive the same outstanding medical care as wounded American troops. Sick or injured enemy combatants often enjoy more comfortable living quarters than the doctors and nurses who treat them.

In battle, I have seen Marines and soldiers risk their lives to rescue Iraqi civilians and care for injured or wounded noncombatants. Troops in the units with which I have been embedded put themselves at great risk to avoid civilian casualties or collateral damage. U.S. military personnel play soccer with kids, befriend the people, and build schools. I've seen soldiers and Marines give their last MREs to hungry children and take up collections among their peers to pay for sending

U.S. Air Force SrA Andrzej Wojcicki talks to an Afghan child at an internal displaced persons camp outside of Kabul, Afghanistan

disabled children to the U.S. for advanced surgery and rehabilitation. American military medical personnel routinely petition to adopt orphaned children who come through their field hospitals.

For the members of the U.S. military, compassion is not only a virtue—it's policy. For radical Islamists, compassion is a weakness. For the mainstream media, American compassion is generally ignored.

Yet, compassion—as much as the force of arms—is a key to winning not just the campaigns in Iraq and Afghanistan but the long, deadly struggle against merciless Jihadists. A U.S. Army chaplain in Mosul put it best: "That's the difference between the terrorists and us. Don't you understand? *That's* the difference!"

HERO HUMOR
Soccer Bombing

One of the best ways our troops are drying up the source of new terrorists is by befriending the Iraqi children. As the troops travel on patrols, the children come running and form a dancing, waving mob behind the Humvees, shouting "Mista! Mista!" (Mister! Mister!) as they distribute toys and soccer balls. These kids know that good things get delivered when the Americans show up.

But not all delivery methods are equally effective. On a helicopter flight between Baquba and Baghdad, an enterprising door gunner began tossing soccer balls out as the chopper flew over remote villages and farms. Popping an Iraqi farmer in the head with a soccer ball from a helicopter going 150 knots probably isn't going to win his heart and mind. Nor is a "smart ball bomb" bouncing through the front door of a little mud hut and ricocheting around inside going to make a family on the ground an ally.

Most of these desert people live without what we consider the essentials of daily life. It has to be unsettling to them when a screaming black monster the size of a house goes thundering overhead at nearly 200 miles per hour. Having a brand new soccer ball crash into their chicken coop from out of the sky doesn't exactly set their minds at ease.

In the aftermath, somebody rethought the soccer-bombing campaign. Sure, it's better to give than to receive, especially when you are talking about high-velocity projectiles. But when it comes to delivering soccer balls, it's best to do it from the ground.

HERO HUMOR
You Told Me It Would Be Hot

If asked to describe the weather in Iraq, the average American would probably respond "hot." And this is correct—most of the time. But you might be surprised to discover that the winter season in northern Iraq gets surprisingly cold. Just ask my combat cameraman, Mal James. He and I had been to Iraq during the summer of 2004, and the heat was so intense he ended up with an IV drip in his arm.

On a subsequent trip to Iraq to cover the troops as they prepared for another Christmas away from home, Mal was surprised to find that the weather wasn't just cold; it was frigid.

Mal James

One day at Hurricane Point in Ramadi a firefight broke out in the city. We decided to climb up on the roof of the building we were staying in to get some footage. The wind chill on that rooftop was approaching zero, and the gusts felt like they would tear the frozen flesh off your face. Mal piled on every stitch of clothing he'd brought with him. But even with sixty pounds of body armor, it still wasn't enough.

This photo I took of Mal captures the misery of that day quite perfectly. With teeth chattering, he declared, "You told me it would be HOT!"

I laughed and told him he looked like the poor kid on the school playground whom no one wants to play with.

Such is the glamour of a job in broadcasting.

The Press Corps

When members of the media are "embedded" with U.S. military units in a combat zone, they wear body armor and Kevlar helmets just like the troops. Chuck Holton's vest had the word "PRESS" stamped prominently across the back. This prompted a soldier to walk up behind him and press the word on his vest. Getting no reaction, he pressed "PRESS" again, then shrugged and said, "Hmm . . . nothing happened."

FAITH

★ ★ ★ ★ ★ ★ ★ ★ ★ ★ ★ ★

*"May the LORD my rock be praised,
who trains my hands for battle
and my fingers for warfare."*
—Psalm 144:1

*"The safest place for me to be is in
the center of God's will, and if that is
in the line of fire, that is where I will
be."*

—Father Tim Vakoc,
U.S. Army chaplain

War can bring out the worst in man. The crucible of combat tests a person's faith in himself, his fellow man—even faith in God. It is particularly so in this war on terror. At any moment a brutal, suicidal, and fanatical enemy can blow himself to pieces just to kill an American. Yet on Sundays in Iraq and Afghanistan, where our troops brave these dangers daily, tens of thousands of young Americans attend services where they pray for their enemies. Those who lead those prayers are garbed in the same sun-bleached camouflage as the troops kneeling before them. We call them chaplains. They are part of what makes us "different" from our enemy, and they are a remarkable lot.

My wife and I were married before a Navy chaplain assigned to the Marine base at Quantico. When I was wounded in Vietnam, it was Cmdr. Jake Laboon, our regimental chaplain, who called out "take this one next," as the triage corpsmen ran in to get another litter patient for emergency surgery. Chaplains Bob Beddingfield and Don Dulligan spent months in the field with my Marines, braving enemy fire to minister to them. As our children were born, other chaplains baptized them in chapels around the country. To say that these "men of the cloth" were an important part of my life in the service would be an understatement. And so it is today for the young Americans I see on my trips to Southwest Asia.

Chaplains hold services wherever and whenever they can

Chaplain John Barkemeyer celebrates mass for soldiers at their combat base in Ramadi, Iraq

The chaplains in Afghanistan and Iraq—and offshore in the Persian Gulf—are cut from the same bolt of cloth as those I recall from my days in uniform. They minister to a "flock" of Americans only a few months out of high school—all of whom know fear, whether they show it or not. By the time these worshippers return to the United States they will have confronted more hardship and danger than their civilian contemporaries will experience the rest of their lives.

Yet, despite all they have endured, the vast majority of these young Americans will complete full and productive lives. Thanks for that should go, in part, to chaplains like Navy LT Jamie Stall-Ryan. He's the type of chaplain who greets you warmly. When he asks how you are doing, you can see that he really wants to know. He's a "man's man," yet talks of Bible study classes and invites those in his "parish" to consider meaning and purpose in a place filled with chaos. He acquired a large-screen TV and a satellite dish for his chapel so the troops have a place to watch NFL football games. They know he will be there for them if things fall apart.

These spiritual leaders counsel young men and women who are confronting their own mortality. But there aren't enough chaplains to go around. As many as a third of all chaplain slots in the military are vacant. Units frequently deploy without a dedicated chaplain. For many troops, the only chaplain they will see are "circuit riders" who—like "saddlebag preachers" of old—brave ambushes to deliver comfort and spiritual reinforcement in dangerous places.

Father Tim Vakoc, an Army chaplain, was making the rounds ministering to soldiers deployed around Mosul in May of 2004 when his Humvee was hit by an IED. He became the first chaplain wounded in Iraq. He suffered terrible head wounds from the explosion and shrapnel. When I visited him in the VA hospital in Minneapolis, he was barely able to move. He has since been transferred to a nursing facility where he continues to make what can only be described as miraculous progress.

Chaplains like Father Vakoc have served as merciful messengers in America's military since the American Revolution. In the midst of the arduous campaigns in Iraq and Afghanistan, I have seen them tending the wounded, comforting friends of the fallen, and encouraging the weary. On numerous occasions I've heard chaplains like Carey Cash, Father Bill Devine, Frank Holley, and Brian Weigelt remind young warriors that despite the horror of combat, the incredible fatigue and the terrifying sights, sounds and smells of war, the God who made them did not intend that they descend into savagery.

After the brutal battle to liberate Fallujah, Chaplain Bill Devine told the troops at a memorial service for their fallen brethren in RCT-7, "There is nothing more Christian than what we are doing here." Father Devine wasn't making a political statement, nor were his words intended to inflame the passions of Islamic radicals who hate Christians and Jews. His words referred to the sacrifice of those who had fought against great odds so the Iraqi people could enjoy their God-given freedom.

In all my years in and around the military, I have never seen so many men flock to chapel services, Bible study groups, and prayer sessions. I have seen them put pocket Bibles into their flak jackets and gather in a prayer circle before and after dangerous missions. In the midst of terrible gunfights, I've heard these men take vulgar language to the level of a new art form. But when the shooting stops, I've seen them reading the Bible in a quiet moment.

The behavior of these young men thrust into the most dangerous circumstances reflects a faith forged in a culture that does not seem to comprehend who they are—or their spiritual underpinnings. But these troops don't seem to care what others think. They know who they are, where they are going, and why they are going there.

After a vicious engagement on the streets of Ramadi one hot afternoon, we returned to the company outpost. After making sure that all his Marines had replenished their ammunition and prepared their gear for the next mission, the company gunnery sergeant announced, "Bible study on the third floor at 17 hundred," or 5:00 p.m. The place was packed. The study leader was the great gruff bear of a sergeant whose squad I had been with during the patrol. Three weeks later he was dead.

By then I was back in the States, and I attended his funeral in Fredericksburg, Virginia, to tell his family what a fine man their son and brother was. But they already knew. And I know that I'm going to see Sgt Joshua Frazier, USMC, again.

With Marine Sgt Joshua Frazier shortly before he was killed in action

HERO HUMOR
Doesn't FOX Know How to Set Up a Camera?

In the Philippines, U.S. Special Operations troops have been quietly helping the government wage a successful campaign against the Abu Sayyaf and Jemaah Islamiyah Muslim terrorist organizations for years. I got a chance to see this progress for myself during a month-long trip to the region in mid-2007.

One day we did a live interview with a U.S. Navy SEAL. Because of the classified nature of his business, we weren't allowed to show his face on camera, so we positioned it to show only the back of his head.

A U.S. Navy SEAL in the Philippines

Before we went live on FOX, I handed the Special Operator my satellite phone so he could call home and tell his wife to turn on the tube. She was excited to be able to see her husband, safe and sound half a world away.

After the interview, he called her back to see what she thought of the interview, only to find her livid. "What's wrong with those stupid FOX people?" she asked. "Don't they know how to set up a camera? All we could see was the back of your head!"

Fan Mail Advice

When we're doing live broadcasts over our satellite uplink, we can also get instant feedback via e-mail. During a live "hit" on the *Hannity & Colmes* show one night, Alan Colmes, my favorite liberal, made a comment about an attack that had allegedly killed Iraqi civilians. In reply I made the observation that "those who haven't experienced ground combat have no idea how terrible it is. Combat is the most horrific experience a human can endure." Within minutes we received this e-mail from a concerned viewer: "Subject: Correction, please: 'Colonel North, on tonight's *Hannity & Colmes* you said, "Ground combat is the worst experience any human can have." This is not true. The worst experience any human can have is spending time with my mother-in-law. My best friend has served in Afghanistan and Iraq. He lost his right hand in Fallujah and has met my mother-in-law. I just called him. He agrees with me and says it is not even a close call. — Jim, San Diego"

HERO HUMOR
Won't Be Home for Christmas

It was the 22nd of December, and I was just finishing up another embed in Iraq. We were on a rooftop doing a live interview with a Marine. At the end of it I said to him, "You're not going to be home for Christmas. Is there anyone you'd like to say hello to?" The Marine grinned as he sent well wishes to his family, asking them to keep him in their prayers.

Fifteen seconds after the live shot ended, my satellite phone rang. It was my wife, Betsy. Apparently she'd turned on the television right at the end of the interview. "Did I just hear you say you won't be home for Christmas?"

I've missed more than my share of Christmases and other holidays, and I'd promised her that I would be there this time, no matter what.

"Of course not, honey," I replied, getting that sinking feeling that a man gets when his husband points are disappearing down a black hole. "I said I'd be there and I will," I assured her.

"You'd better be," she growled. "If you leave me here alone with eight grandchildren, you might as well stay in Iraq. You'll be safer there than in this kitchen."

I made it home for Christmas.

If I don't get home by Christmas, these will be my only friends

Soldiers carry a casualty to a U.S. Army H-60 medical evacuation helicopter in Tarmiyah, Iraq. Treatment for shock and blood loss on the battlefield and rapid air evacuation have saved the lives of countless wounded warriors.

★ ★ ★ ★ ★ ★ ★ ★ ★ ★ ★ ★

14

WOUNDED WARRIORS

Military medicine routinely gets a bad rap. In February 2007, the *Washington Post* published an article headlined "Soldiers Face Neglect, Frustration at Army's Top Medical Facility." The piece prompted a media circus, Congressional hearings, the sacking of two generals and the Secretary of the Army, firings at Walter Reed Army Medical Center, and wholesale accusations that the care our wounded warriors receive just isn't up to par. But as usual, there's another side to the story.

For the record, I admit to being biased. I probably wouldn't be alive today but for military medical care. A U.S. Navy medical corpsman saved my life when I was wounded in Vietnam. Navy surgeons have operated on me at aid stations, in field hospitals, and on hospital ships. I've been a patient at Walter Reed and the U.S. National Naval Medical Center at Bethesda, Maryland. And all that was before I started work at

FOX News, documenting American heroes fighting radical Islamic terrorism.

Since the War on Terror began in October 2001, nearly thirty thousand young Americans have been wounded in action. Thanks to improvements in armored vehicles, body armor, rapid casualty-evacuation, and advanced medical treatment, better than half of them have been able to return to duty within three days of being hurt.

Put differently, if a wounded soldier, sailor, airman, Guardsman, or Marine makes it to a casualty-evacuation helicopter alive, there is a better than 96 percent chance that he or she is alive today. That's better odds than surviving a serious car crash on a U.S. highway.

In countless engagements I have heard the call "Corpsman up!" or the shout, "Medic!" Almost invariably, no matter how dangerous the situation, a bright, brave, highly trained U.S. Navy medical corpsman or Army medic, skilled in treating shock and equipped to treat blood loss, is "on" the casualty in seconds. Within minutes, most casualties are on a casualty-evacuation helicopter headed for a field hospital equipped and staffed for advanced life support. If the wounds are severe enough, within hours the patient is en route to the Landstuhl Regional Medical Center in Germany aboard a USAF C-17 Nightingale.

U.S. military personnel requiring multiple surgeries, continued treatment, or protracted recovery are transported back to the United States for further care. Each time I return from being "embedded" in Iraq or Afghanistan, I try to visit the "wounded warriors" from that unit. Their stories provide a somewhat different perspective than that offered by the mainstream media.

A C-17 Nightingale transporting wounded from Iraq to Landstuhl Regional Medical Center in Germany

SGT LUKE CASSIDY

★ ★ ★ ★ ★ ★ ★ ★ ★ ★ ★ ★

"I was right outside a school that we'd just restored, telling our commander of the progress we'd made. We had driven about three hundred yards from the school when the IED exploded and shot through my engine block. I tried to keep the vehicle under control the best I could, because we were so close to a ravine. Everybody was able to jump out of the vehicle, so nobody was seriously injured."

Nobody, that is, except Luke.

Marine Sgt Luke Cassidy was seated on the edge of an examining table at Walter Reed Army Medical Center as he recalled the day terrorists tried to kill him. I had been with his Civil Affairs team in Ramadi. Not long before he was wounded, I had ridden with him in that same Humvee to the school. Years before, Luke's dad was a colonel at the Pentagon when I was on the National Security Council staff at the White House. Luke grew up in Virginia. After graduating from George Mason University, he became a Fairfax County police officer. He also enlisted in the Marine Reserves.

When Luke's Civil Affairs unit was activated in 2004, he volunteered for service in Iraq. Six months later, after fifteen surgeries, he was being fitted for a prosthetic limb to replace his left leg that had been traumatically amputated below the knee by a roadside bomb. "I also lost a toe, fractured my heel, had several shrapnel wounds in my right leg, shrapnel wounds in my hand and lost most of my hearing in my right ear," he added with a shrug.

As our FOX News cameras rolled, a prosthetic limb specialist adjusted the length of the new metal limb and fine-tuned the tension on the "foot." Then, with two Army medics and a nurse standing by just in case, he said to the wounded Marine, "Let's try it."

Luke pulled himself up between the parallel bars—identical to those used in gymnastics—and took his first tentative steps since the explosion five months earlier. As he walked, a great smile appeared on his face and tears flowed down his cheeks. "I promised my kids that we'd be able to play again," he explained. "You know, that's the most important part, being able to be there for my children."

It was a powerful moment, and Luke wasn't the only one in the room with tears in his eyes. The prosthetics specialist smiled and said, "That's why I come to work every day."

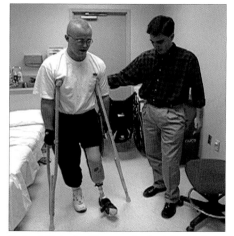

Marine Sgt Luke Cassidy, moments after taking his first steps on his new prosthetic leg

SGT GREGORY EDWARDS

★ ★ ★ ★ ★ ★ ★ ★ ★ ★ ★ ★

"Stay strong. Stay with me, Sgt Ed!" the Navy corpsman shouted. Then, as though giving an order, the "Doc" yelled at the shattered Marine on the litter, "You're not going to die on me."

The jarring of the Humvee ambulance sent stabs of white-hot pain through what was left of Sgt Gregory Edwards's broken body as the vehicle sped through Ramadi on the cratered highway that the Marines called "Route Michigan." Moments earlier Sgt Edwards had been leading his rifle squad from "A" Company, 1st Bn, 6th Marines, on a house-to-house search for an Al Qaeda bomb factory. They had done this countless times. They were good at it. But on 21 October 2006, they found what they were looking for—the hard way.

The explosion of a carefully planted IED mangled Sgt Edwards below his body armor. The first person to him was U.S. Navy Medical Corpsman Christopher Anderson. The man they called "Doc" Anderson immediately applied tourniquets to Edwards's shattered limbs and started an IV to ward off shock.

As they raced for the LZ to meet an inbound casualty-evacuation helicopter, Edwards looked up at the man who was checking his pulse and said, "Take care of my babies, Doc."

Anderson shouted back, "You're going to take care of your babies. You're going to be OK!"

Edwards lapsed into unconsciousness before the helicopter landed. His next recollection is awakening in a hospital bed in Washington, D.C. It was strangely familiar. When he realized that it was Walter Reed Army Medical Center, it was because he had been there before.

Sgt Edwards was on his third deployment to Iraq when new wounds sent him back to Walter Reed. In 2003 he had been part of the initial assault on Baghdad and saw the statue of Saddam Hussein toppled. He'd been wounded on his second deployment and spent time recovering at Bethesda and Walter Reed. When 1st Bn, 6th Marines, was slated for a third deployment, he insisted on going along.

This time, however, Gregory Edwards's road to recovery would never end. Though the doctors operated on him more than thirty times, they couldn't save his shattered legs. When all the surgery was done, he had one stump above the knee, a stump below the other knee, and only one functioning hand.

When I came home from my "embed" with 1st Bn, 6th Marines, in late December 2006, I went to see Sgt Edwards at Walter Reed. His only complaint about the medical care he was receiving was about the length of the prosthetic limbs for which he was being fitted. "Tell the sergeant major," he said, "when I put these things on I want to be two inches taller than I used to be."

As he recovered, Walter Reed arranged for his wife, Christina, and his daughters— five-year-old Caitlin and three-year-old Paige—to move into temporary housing near the hospital. Freedom Alliance, the Disabled American Veterans, and other charities provided financial support for the family.

Despite his horrendous injuries, multiple operations, and painful therapy, Sgt Edwards put himself on a punishing physical regimen, intent on learning to walk with prosthetic limbs by the time 1st Bn, 6th Marines, returned to Camp Lejeune, North Carolina, in April of 2007. He wanted to be there to greet them all, and "Doc" Anderson in particular. "If it wasn't for Doc, I wouldn't be here," he said. "I wouldn't be able to hold my daughters on my lap."

But Doc Anderson didn't make it home alive. On 4 December 2006 he was killed during a mortar attack in bloody Ramadi. When Hospital Corpsman Christopher "Doc" Anderson, fourth-generation sailor and son of a former Navy SEAL, was buried at Arlington National Cemetery, Sgt Edwards was there—though he described it as one of the most painful experiences of his life.

As his body continues to mend, Greg Edwards is putting the pieces of his life back together as well. He's learned to scuba dive through a program at Walter Reed. A nonprofit organization called "Homes for Our Troops" built a specially adapted home for his family in his home state of Alabama. When people thank him for sacrificing for his country, he says it makes him uncomfortable. He sent his Purple Heart medal to the family of the man who saved his life—his friend, Doc Anderson.

In the foyer of the National Naval Medical Center at Bethesda, Maryland, there is a life-sized statue of a U.S. Navy medical corpsman holding a wounded Marine. The plaque at its base reads: "The Unspoken Bond." For Greg Edwards, those three words say it all.

"I lost my legs for the people of Iraq, so their children will be able to run around, just like mine. If time was turned back, I'd do it all over again."

— Marine Sgt Gregory Edwards, father of two

2ND LT. ANDREW KINARD

★ ★ ★ ★ ★ ★ ★ ★ ★ ★ ★ ★

The highway bridge over the Euphrates River at Rawah, Iraq, makes the place strategically important. Perched on the banks of the river in western Al Anbar province, the town had been a safe haven for Al Qaeda terrorists coming down the waterway from Syria. Al Qaeda of Iraq used the bridge and highway to move car bombs north to Mosul and east to Tikrit—a route that allowed them to bypass Ramadi and Fallujah. Second Lt. Andrew Kinard's 1st platoon of Company "A," 2nd LAR Bn, was in Rawah to make sure they couldn't do that anymore. That's why, on 29 October 2006, the terrorists tried to kill him.

Six weeks into a seven-month long deployment, 2nd Lt. Kinard was leading seven of his Marines on a morning foot patrol searching for a terrorist bomb factory when an IED exploded directly next to his left leg. The blast blew him into the air—and he landed almost twenty feet from the crater. Three other Marines were wounded.

According to those who were there, before the grievously injured officer passed out from loss of blood, he ordered them to set up security, get a head count, and start treating the other injured Marines. The platoon corpsman rushed to stop the flow of blood but couldn't find enough undamaged tissue to apply the tourniquets. It didn't look good. The lieutenant was losing blood from almost every part of his body.

A cas-evac helicopter airlifted him to the Marine Air Base at Al Asad, then to the Army trauma hospital at Balad, north of Baghdad. Sixty-seven pints of whole blood—more than five times the amount in a healthy adult—were pumped into the failing officer's veins in a twenty-four-hour period.

By the time he could be flown to Landstuhl, Germany, he had gone into cardiac arrest—and been resuscitated—twice. Emergency surgeries went on nearly nonstop to plug the seemingly innumerable holes punched in his body by shrapnel from the bomb. The family was alerted, and a prayer vigil was held. Hundreds of people half a world away went to their knees and begged God for a miracle.

Some miracles happen immediately. This one took a while.

Four days after being blasted to pieces, Andrew Kinard was in the intensive care unit at the National Naval Medical Center, Bethesda, Maryland, with his family around his bedside, still praying. By the time I got back from Iraq, just before Christmas 2006, "Drew" as his Marine friends call him, had already endured more than two dozen surgeries.

He was also the talk of the hospital. Every nurse in the place knew his name and had been by to see him many times.

His doctor told me that the twenty-four-year-old lieutenant was "getting better" even though he had pneumonia, a blood infection, and perforations of his intestines from innumerable pieces of shrapnel. They had just done one of the many skin grafts necessary to prepare his stumps for prosthetic limbs.

When I walked into his room, his mother and his sister Katherine were with him. His dad—a doctor in Spartanburg, South Carolina—and two younger siblings, Courtney and Will, were all en route to spend Christmas with their badly battered Marine.

Without all the cards, posters, banners, Christmas stockings, lights, photos, and flags spread around the room, the space would have looked like a scene from a Hollywood science fiction movie. Monitors, electronic devices, compressors, pumps and assorted tubes, wires, and bags of various colored fluids surrounded the bed—all connected to Andrew Kinard. Tiny flecks of shrapnel were still visible in the left side of his face. He had no legs. His abdomen was an open hole. And he was smiling. "God is good," he said in greeting.

CNO Adm. Mike Mullen speaks with Marine Corps 2nd Lt. Andrew Kinard, United States Naval Academy (USNA), Class of '05 Adm. Mullen was present for the commencement and commissioning ceremony for the Class of 2007 at Navy/Marine Corps Memorial Stadium in Annapolis, Maryland.

Over the next eleven months of hospitalization, Andrew Kinard was living proof of that statement. When I asked him or his family "How can I help you?" the inevitable response was, "Just pray for recovery." And so he also became evidence of the power of prayer.

In April 2007 he flew to Marine Corps Base Camp Lejeune, North Carolina, for the 2nd LAR Battalion's return from Iraq. Wearing his Marine utility field uniform for the first time since he was wounded, he arrived to greet his comrades in a special "all-terrain" wheelchair.

Kinard was asked by a reporter on the scene to describe his recollections of the day he was wounded. He acknowledged that his memory of the moments after his injury had been dulled by shock and pain, then said, "A man asks himself, if something happens to me when I go into the face of battle, how will I react? Will I be brave?"

As they arrived home, the members of "Alpha" Company made it clear: Lt. Andrew Kinard was, without a doubt, their hero.

Then, one year to the day since he was wounded, the young officer came home. On 29 October 2007, dignitaries and thousands of well-wishers were on hand to welcome Andrew at First Baptist Church, Spartanburg. The following Sunday he spoke at all three services—thanking all for their unfailing prayers.

His recovery will continue for months or years to come. But on one of my visits to him in the hospital the man who had once played rugby at the Naval Academy said, "I don't need legs. I have my arms. I learned discipline at the Naval Academy. I have my faith—and a desire to serve. Maybe I'll go to law school."

Andrew has all of that—and more. He also has a great sense of humor. He has a T-shirt with the words "Marine for Sale" printed on the front. On the back it reads: "40% Off—Some Assembly Required."

"I am continuing to get stronger every day through therapy, and I have especially been encouraged by my improvements in learning to walk again. I have worked harder here than I ever did during my academy days or infantry training, yet I can credit these improvements only to the grace that God provides me each day. God is so good!

"I would like to thank all of the individuals, families, and churches that have prayed specifically for me throughout this entire ordeal. I truly believe in the power of prayer, and I am so grateful for the prayers lifted up for my sake. I ask that when you pray for me, please also pray for those wounded veterans that do not know Christ. I don't know where I'd be without my faith."

— Lt. Andrew Kinard, 25 June 2007

LCPL AARON MANKIN

★ ★ ★ ★ ★ ★ ★ ★ ★ ★ ★ ★

It was 11 May 2005, Al Qaim, Iraq, day five of Operation Matador. When the massive IED planted in the dirt roadway detonated, the explosion ripped into the assault amphibious vehicle like a bullet through warm butter. Fuel from the twenty-three-ton vehicle's ruptured fuel tanks ignited immediately, searing the men and weapons inside. Six of them were already dead—killed by the blast. For the rest, it was a matter of getting out of the inferno or die by flames and smoke—or by the ammunition being "cooked off" in the intense heat.

One of those trapped inside was a young Marine who didn't even have to be there. LCpl Aaron Mankin, a combat correspondent assigned to II MEF headquarters in Fallujah, had volunteered to accompany our FOX News team as we headed to western Al Anbar province to cover the operation along the Syrian border. His job was to write stories and shoot still photographs and video. As we headed out on the operation, I had told him to "be careful."

Mankin cracked back, "No, you be careful. I may have a camera in one hand, but I have a rifle in the other."

He was standing up in the back of the armored vehicle, his camera rolling on the Marines moving to cordon a suspected Al Qaeda terrorist haven, when the bomb went off. The force of the explosion knocked Mankin to the floor of the vehicle and slammed shut and warped the overhead hatch that he had been standing in. Those who survived the initial blast struggled out of the inferno through a narrow emergency access at the rear of the vehicle. By the time he dove out onto the ground, his clothing and exposed flesh were on fire and his lungs were seared.

As he rolled in the dirt to put out the flames, a Navy hospital corpsman, disregarding exploding projectiles just a few feet away, raced to extinguish the burning Marine. Aaron was quickly placed aboard a litter and loaded aboard a U.S. Army H-60 casualty-evacuation helicopter with three other wounded Marines.

One of the Army pilots who braved exploding ordnance to land near the flaming assault amphibious vehicle told me that he remembered Aaron because "I could smell his burned flesh in the cockpit" and his medic kept yelling at the grievously burned Marine, "Hey! Hey! Don't go to sleep! Stay with me!"

Concerned that Mankin would not make it, they took him straight to the Army Trauma Hospital at Balad. There, doctors cut away his burned clothing, applied antibacterial dressings to cover his burns, and put him on a ventilator to help him breathe. Then they shipped him on a USAF C-17 Nightingale to Landstuhl, Germany. Two days later he was in Burn Unit 1 at Brooke Army Medical Center in San Antonio, Texas.

Brooke—known as "BAM-C" in the military—is probably the finest burn center in the world. When Aaron arrived, the doctors determined that he had suffered second- and third-degree burns over 25 percent of his body. His nose, ears, and cheeks were literally charred—and the flames and debris that he had inhaled inside the burning vehicle had seriously damaged his airway from his mouth to his lungs. His lungs were already filling with fluid. The doctors kept him heavily sedated for days as they fought to keep the Marine from succumbing to the two great killers of burn victims: pneumonia and infection.

With the help of specifically tailored antibiotics and round-the-clock attention, Aaron beat the odds. When I saw him again, it was November of 2005—eight months since he was wounded. By then he had already endured nearly two dozen surgeries, the amputation of half his right thumb and index finger, and operations to extend motion in his wrists, arms, and mouth. Skin grafts had been performed to restore tissue on his hands, arms, and face. His father, Steve, describes his son's survival as an answer to prayer.

When I talked to Aaron, he was seated next to his mother. He told me, "My initial goal was survival. I wanted to see Diana, my girlfriend, again. I wanted to see my family again. Now I want to have a future—and a family of my own."

He also acknowledged that he was worried about what Diana would think of him. He had no nose, ears, or lips from the flames that had engulfed him. His face, hands, and arms were scarred. Would she, he wondered, still care about a man so disfigured?

Aaron need not have worried. He and LCpl Diana Kavanek had met when they were in training, before he shipped off for Iraq and she to Afghanistan. When she arrived back in the U.S. in December 2005, she flew immediately to San Antonio to see Aaron. They were married in February 2006, and their daughter, Madeline Paige Mankin, was born in January 2007.

Little Madeline's dad isn't done recovering yet. On 4 October 2007, Brooke Army Medical Center and the UCLA Medical Center teamed up to create "Operation Mend"—a collaboration of burn specialists and plastic surgeons. Aaron Mankin was chosen as their first patient. He has since had surgery to start the process of reconstructing his nose, ears, and mouth—and there's more to come.

In between operations Aaron works at Brooke Army Medical Center in the public affairs office as a patient-media liaison and counsels other wounded soldiers and Marines. As I was writing this book, his dad sent me a DVD of his son speaking at a church in Rogers, Arkansas, his hometown. In it, Aaron says, "From the start, I knew I'd get better. I always knew that it was a part of God's plan. God's been very faithful to me even though I don't deserve it. God gave me the chance to be part of something that will be remembered in the chronicles of history."

Aaron Mankin is a hero worth hearing.

"It makes you wonder why [military medics] that are smart enough to do something like that stay in the Army. I mean, they could've just as easily been making a lot more money in a safe and comfy hospital. I'm just glad that they do it. I'm sure that their reasons are similar to mine. They are patriotic; they enjoy the camaraderie in the Army and the sheer adventure of it. They believe in this country and are willing to stand up for it and do whatever it takes to make sure it stays safe. They are the kind of people who are willing to fight to make sure we feel safe when we go to sleep at night. They fight so we can feel comfortable when we go to the grocery store or to the shopping mall, without the fear of a terrorist attack. They are the people who hate violence more than any liberal protester but are prepared to use it to give that protester the right to speak his or her mind even if it may be directly against them. They get their reward in personal satisfaction instead of money, and they know they are doing an important job for our country, and doing it well."

— SSG Robbie Doughty, a Special Forces soldier who lost both legs in an IED attack in Iraq

Marine Capt. Brad Adams was riding in a Humvee near Fallujah in October of 2004 when a young boy riding a bicycle approached his vehicle. Hidden in the bike's basket was a command-detonated bomb—placed there by a terrorist who used the child as an unwitting delivery service. As the vehicle pulled alongside Capt. Adams's door, the terrorist triggered the bomb with a cell phone, killing the boy and blasting Adams's body with shrapnel. He underwent nine surgeries and recuperated for more than a month at the National Naval Medical Center in Bethesda. "The level of treatment we're getting here is outstanding," he said.

That sentiment is echoed by Cpl Nicolas Roberts, who was badly injured from a gunshot wound in Ramadi. When I met him, he'd undergone seven surgeries. Of his stay at Bethesda, he said, "I'm getting great care here—this is the best hospital in the world."

THE BOTTOM LINE

★ ★ ★ ★ ★ ★ ★ ★ ★ ★ ★ ★

At the beginning of this chapter, I admitted to bias because I have been a patient of military medicine and I have seen how well "the system" treats our wounded warriors today. Do some casualties "slip through the cracks"? Yes. Could things still be done better? Sure. But "better" is the norm, not the exception. The individual cases cited here are all known to me personally, and they are only a handful of the nearly thirty thousand soldiers, sailors, airmen, Guardsmen, and Marines who have become casualties during the War on Terror. But they really are typical.

The Wounded Warrior Regiment—which Marine commandant James Conway instituted in 2007—offers considerable promise in helping wounded Marines recuperate and then transition back to active duty or civilian life. Our FOX News team visited the Wounded Warriors at Camp Lejeune and didn't find anyone "slipping through the cracks."

Roughly 10 percent of the casualties in the War on Terror have been traumatic brain injuries. These kinds of injuries have occurred at about three times the rate as amputations. But both are usually caused by the same thing: IEDs and suicide bombs. Severe head trauma, in which the brain is injured because of blast, concussion, and/or penetration of the skull by shrapnel or a projectile, often results in terrible, life-long damage. Nobody writes or talks much about the wounded warriors with traumatic brain injuries because so many of them appear to be so hopeless. The next time you have a chance, go to a VA hospital and meet those who struggle to recover from such injuries, as well as those who minister to them.

Finally, a word about post-traumatic stress disorder (PTSD). For years I was convinced that PTSD was a "shrink's" lifetime self-employment program. Tell a soldier who has been in battle that "you have a problem" enough times, and soon he will have a problem. My solution for PTSD was a size 10 boot in the backside. Maybe this is not as dramatic as George Patton slapping a sobbing soldier in Sicily, but it had about the same effect. Then I saw PTSD up close and personal.

In the aftermath of the terrible carnage on 11 May 2005, on Operation Matador, where six Marines were killed by an IED and fourteen more were nearly incinerated, I saw grown men break down and cry. This happened not just at the memorial service but days later in the barracks, in the armory, and at the mess hall.

Speaking with doctors, nurses, and corpsmen at TQ Field hospital

After observing several of these incidents, I asked a Navy Reserve medical officer what was happening. In his civilian life he works in an emergency room. He offered this explanation that works for me. "Anyone," he said, "who has been in a serious automobile accident—let alone combat—has post-traumatic stress disorder. Everyone of us manifests that PTSD in different ways." He went on, "Some people get back in gear right away and push the memories of a terrible event out of the way, but they still have PTSD. Others need help dealing with it. And some never recover—just like any other trauma."

"Is there one kind of person who deals with PTSD better than another?" I asked.

The doc considered the question a moment, then replied, "I don't know the statistics, but from my experience, those who have strong families and a strong faith seem to handle trauma of all kinds better than those who don't."

Sounds like a pretty good prescription to me.

SrA Ashley-Louise Jacobsen hugs a young Iraqi girl

★ ★ ★ ★ ★ ★ ★ ★ ★ ★ ★ ★

15

THE "OTHER" HEROES

During the Global War on Terror, more than one million Americans have been deployed overseas. While women have always deployed in support of the men on the battlefield, this war moved women from the background to the forefront.

Behind the old Cadet's Chapel at the United States Military Academy at West Point, there stands a collection of stone monuments, memorials to the old soldiers who rest there. Among them is the grave of a woman named Margaret Corbin.

Margaret was given a soldier's pension after her heroic actions at the battle of Fort Washington, New York, in 1776. When her husband was killed while manning a cannon, "Molly" took his place next to the gun and continued loading and firing it herself until she was also wounded. Women weren't supposed to fight, but Molly did anyway. She became "the first American woman to take a soldier's part in the War for Liberty."

It's still official U.S. military doctrine: Women are barred from serving in "combat arms" military occupational specialties. But this technicality is overshadowed by the fact that in the War on Terror, the "front line" is everywhere. Just ask PFC Jennifer Eischens, a food service specialist who served in Baqouba, Iraq, with the 4th Infantry Division's 1-68 Combined Arms Battalion. Her missions often took place outside the chow hall.

In a Muslim society, it's culturally unacceptable for male soldiers to speak to Iraqi women. So Jennifer often accompanies infantry squads on their patrols around Baqouba to allow them to do their job without offending Iraqi cultural sensitivities. "It is a change of pace," Eischens says. "I like to go out on patrol—it makes the days go by faster."

PFC Jennifer Eischens

SSG Layla Elbel

If it were not for the uniform and helmet, blonde-haired, blue-eyed SSG Layla Elbel would have no trouble passing as the quintessential American girl. That is, until she opens her mouth and starts speaking fluent Arabic.

Elbel has a skill that makes her very valuable to the United States, and it is something she learned in grade school.

"Well, I grew up in Jerusalem, Israel," Elbel explains. "My parents sent me to Arabic school from kindergarten until eighth grade." Her parents are American missionaries.

So what was it like growing up a blond-haired American girl in an Arabic culture? Elbel says, "It was a lot of harassment, from the point that I was a woman in a male-dominated society. And I represented an American Western culture that they did not respect."

Elbel joined the military after high school. It did not take the Army long to discover that she was a gold mine—and not just linguistically.

"I have a cultural awareness that most soldiers who have learned Arabic through the military do not have," she says.

Not surprisingly, it wasn't long before she found herself in Iraq, with a challenging job as the base commander's personal translator.

"I went everywhere with him," she grins. "I listened to other interpreters and . . . [went] on all of his military operations. I was chosen for that position mainly because of my background."

Most U.S. soldiers rarely interact one-on-one with the Iraqi people. But Elbel's job gave her the rare opportunity to talk with them on a daily basis. This gives her a good sense of how the Iraqis feel about their situation.

"Many of the people that the colonel talked to daily cannot thank us enough for what the American soldiers have done in removing Saddam Hussein," she says. "They have a hope and a mission to accomplish now. They have very high expectations, and when they see American forces roll into their area, they automatically feel safe."

Elbel also offers some insight into why many Arabs dislike America. "I think many of the things that they hate about our culture are the same things that we Americans hate about our culture—the constant immorality, the deterioration of our TV shows. . . ."

Her job is both challenging and exciting. And she's done it so well that Special Operations recruiters came calling. Various government agencies wanted her, too. But there was just one problem.

"I've chosen against pursuing them, mainly because my faith in Christ has given me a passion for something different," Elbel says. "I've met some Iraqi women, and to the Western world, they have no hope. And the fact that I could not freely express to them the hope and the freedom that Jesus Christ has given me has been very painful."

So, a few months after her return from Iraq, Elbel chose to leave the Army to pursue another mission—working to bring freedom of a different kind to Arabic-speaking people.

Throughout the U.S. military, women are finding themselves in situations that—as far as their job descriptions are concerned—shouldn't happen.

Sgt. Leigh Ann Hester

Leigh Ann Hester was one of those. A sergeant with the 617th Military Police Company, a National Guard unit out of Richmond, Kentucky, she spent over a year in Iraq. On Palm Sunday, 2005, her squad was following a supply convoy near the Iraqi village of Salman Pak when the convoy was ambushed by as many as fifty heavily armed terrorists. Hester's squad responded by plowing into the kill zone with their Humvees, deliberately drawing the heavy enemy fire away from the civilian convoy drivers. When an RPG hit one of the Humvees, wounding those inside, Hester went into action. One of her squad mates, 5'2" specialist Ashley Pullen, laid down suppressing fire while Hester and another soldier entered a trench line full of enemy soldiers and began killing them with grenades and precision rifle fire.

When the smoke cleared, twenty-seven insurgents lay dead, another seven wounded. Hester's squad suffered only three casualties, none of them fatal.

For their heroic actions, three members of the squad were awarded the Silver Star. SSG Hester became the first woman in history to earn the award in close quarters battle.

"It really doesn't have anything to do with being a female," Hester said. "It's about the duties I performed that day as a soldier."

Sgt. Leigh Ann Hester reads the information panels of the Global War on Terrorism (GWOT) exhibit at the Army Women's Museum at Fort Lee, Virginia. The exhibit showcases the contributions women have made in the GWOT and features a life-size diorama of the actions of Hester and her squad-mates during an ambush by insurgents near Baghdad.

Maj. Megan McClung

And that's what is happening across all of the armed services. Maj. Megan McClung is another example. When I first met Megan, she was a thirty-four-year-old Marine serving as a Public Affairs officer in Ramadi. She was cheerful and efficient as she helped us get the footage we needed for our broadcast, and I could tell that she was tough as nails. She'd graduated from the Naval Academy in 1995 and was slated to spend a year in Iraq overseeing public affairs for the 1st Brigade of the Army's 1st Armored Division.

Soon after she left us that day, the awful news came that Megan had been killed by an IED in Ramadi. The date was December 6, 2004. Megan became the highest-ranking female to be killed in the global War on Terror.

Like other women who have died in this war, Megan didn't go looking for combat, but it found her anyway. For better or for worse, women are finding themselves on the front lines. And like Molly Corbin, they are proving themselves capable and confident warriors.

Above, U.S. Army MAJ Jennifer Bailey reads a book to Iraqi girls during a humanitarian mission

At left, SSG Gina Gray holds newly born Zuher, whom she helped deliver during Operation Ivy Cyclone when paratroopers of 2nd Bn, 503d Infantry (Airborne) were searching the house and discovered the mother needed help

These women are American heroes. There is another group who deserve the title as well—the families of our service members who wait and pray at home.

WHEN DAD IS AT WAR

★ ★ ★ ★ ★ ★ ★ ★ ★ ★ ★ ★

U.S. Army SPC Adam Darrah holds his daughter for the first time after returning from a yearlong deployment in Iraq

Maybe it's appropriate that Father's Day—a secular holiday supported by Calvin Coolidge in 1924 and officially designated as the third Sunday in June by Lyndon Johnson—is so close to Memorial Day. Both occasions have been observed with tens of thousands of dads absent from their children, serving in our armed forces far from home and often in harm's way. Some of those children and dads have never met face-to-face.

Today, Marine Corps recruiting ads would have the uninitiated believe that the only thing that matters is being a "warrior." And while that is certainly a crucial ingredient in being a Marine, there is another aspect that pervades all of the military services today—concern for the families of those who are serving.

While I was covering the 5th Marines in Iraq for Fox News, a sergeant major approached me after a live broadcast and asked if one of his young corporals could use my satellite phone to call home. "His wife gave birth last night," the grizzled veteran of two wars and many gunfights explained. "He wants to call so she and his new son can hear his voice." I handed him the phone.

The young corporal's new son won't remember that phone call. But hopefully, in the midst of one of life's inevitable challenges, the Marine corporal and his wife will recall that all-too-brief conversation as evidence of a father's love for the son he wouldn't be able to hold for a while.

That's always a challenge for those in our armed forces—reconciling the willingness to serve our country with the need to be a dad. Today, tens of thousands of soldiers, sailors, airmen, Guardsmen, and Marines who are fathers are serving overseas without their families. They serve in Iraq, Afghanistan, Korea, Japan, the Balkans, and at sea around the world, defending this country from the threat of terrorism and offering others the hope of freedom. Many, like that young corporal, will be working twenty-hour days and avoiding sniper fire when their child is born instead of handing out cigars and buying every stuffed animal in the hospital gift shop. For those fathers, the chance to hold their newborn will have to wait.

When he visited the sailors on board the USS *Abraham Lincoln* (CVN 72) on May 1, 2003, President George W. Bush pointed out that while these sailors were at sea, back home their wives had given birth to 150 babies. Similar stories abounded at every port hosting a welcome-home ceremony. When the USS *Reuben James* (FFG 57) and the USS *Paul Hamilton* (DDG 60) returned to Pearl Harbor, eleven fathers had the opportunity to see their newborn children for the first time. At Naval Air Station North Island in Coronado, more than one hundred sailors disembarked the USS *Constellation* (CV-64) and met the new additions to their families.

Understanding the importance of a father in a child's life, the military is trying to relieve some of the stress that families experience during long deployments. Programs like United Through Reading help fathers to serve both their country and their family. It may not replace the warm feeling of sitting on daddy's lap while he reads a bedtime story. But while on board ship, sailors can videotape themselves reading books to their children and ship the tapes home.

For the U.S. troops in Iraq keeping the peace and restoring order for the Iraqi people,

the hope is that their absence from home will only be temporary. For most of them it will be, but Iraq is still a dangerous place. Many young children—some of them not yet born—have lost their fathers during this war.

As President Bush once said in a Memorial Day address at Arlington National Cemetery, "Americans like these did not fight for glory, but to fulfill a duty. They did not yearn to be heroes, they yearned to see mom and dad again and to hold their sweethearts and to watch their sons and daughters grow." These men are called heroes and rightfully so.

But largely forgotten still are the many others who continue to sacrifice—the children left behind. Birthdays, ballet recitals, their first at-bat in a Little League game—these are just a few of the important events in a child's life that are performed or celebrated without the love and guidance from dad. Their sacrifice is the lonely home whose quiet night is pierced by the sound down the hall of Mom crying herself to sleep. In their teenage years, they go to the movies with their friends, only to see their dead father's courage mocked on the big screen by leftist producers and liberal actors. They struggle to save for college, trying to accomplish a goal they know would have made their father proud.

Nothing replaces a daddy. But for those children whose fathers have given the ultimate sacrifice in service to this country, say a prayer that they will find peace in the knowledge that their hero dad pledged his life for a cause he believed in. And for the rest of us, in addition to honoring our heroes in uniform, may we always be thankful for the ones who waited—and wept—for daddy.

Above, a soldier embraces his children after returning from a fifteen-month deployment

Below, a crowd of family and friends give a boisterous welcome home to soldiers with an Army Reserve unit from Las Alamedos, California, as they arrive at Fort Carson, Colorado, after a year-long deployment to Iraq

KEEPING IT TOGETHER AT HOME AND AT WAR

★ ★ ★ ★ ★ ★ ★ ★ ★ ★ ★

"It's the simple things. Seeing your kids asleep when they don't know you are there. Coming home and playing in the front yard with all the neighborhood kids. Those are the things I miss the most."

— LT. COL. BILL JURNEY, 2005, RAMADI, IRAQ

Lt. Col. Bill Jurney keeps tabs on the home front from Ramadi, Iraq

Behind every military member, there's a loving family waiting, hoping, and praying for their return. Though often overlooked, these "heroes on the home front" are essential for the strength of our military as a whole and for the defense of this nation.

For most American troops deployed in the fight against the terrorists, a day at war begins before dawn. After a quick clean-up and a bite to eat, these soldiers, sailors, airmen, Guardsmen, and Marines head out on patrols, humanitarian missions, or guard duty. Danger is a constant companion, but the source of their motivation is no secret—they hunt down the savages overseas in order to safeguard their loved ones at home.

The routine for anxious military families back in the States might not require body armor and Kevlar helmets, but theirs is often a day that is nearly as challenging.

Camp Lejeune, North Carolina, is home for Marine Lt. Col. Bill Jurney. When I met him, he was commanding the 1st Bn, 6th Marines, in Ramadi, Iraq. At the time Bill was well into his eighth long-term deployment as a Marine officer. He understands all too well the challenges that come with leaving a family behind. And while multiple deployments might help the Marines and their families get better at managing the time apart, it never gets easier.

"I will say—without question—our families have the tougher mission," Bill declared.

"By design, our team is put together, trained and equipped to accomplish the mission that's in front of us—as a team—and everybody has a role to play in supporting that mission. Our team at home was designed to have two individuals. And now that team only has one. We are not asking anybody to feel sorry for us for that. Most spouses of the United States Marines are pretty doggone strong-willed and independent. They have learned to adapt and live their lives and raise our families in our absence."

Lt. Col. Bill Jurney's wife Sue and their children Madison and Troy, on the front steps of their home near Camp Lejeune, N.C.

Back at home at Camp Lejeune, Bill's wife Sue agrees. "It's not just a job, it's a lifestyle. And it affects everybody in your family."

After eighteen years of being married to a Marine, Sue is no stranger to the hardships that come with the territory. That experience is vital as she volunteers her time supporting the other Marine families in the battalion. It's her way of assisting the war effort.

"Military spouses are sacrificing every day," she says. "The way they handle things at home is very important to the mission. Because if the guys over there are concerned and worried about how things are going at home, then they can't stay focused on their mission in Iraq."

Another of those wives is Jen White. She met her husband, Jody, when he was sacking quarterbacks as a linebacker for the University of Cincinnati. When I met them, he was a captain, leading the two hundred men of Charlie Company, 1st Bn, 6th Marines. During Jody's six deployments, Jen has paid the bills, kept the vehicles running, and kept their five children busy with school, sports, and other activities. And her husband is the first to admit she has the more challenging job: "If I had all five of my kids, she'd probably come home and the house would be leveled."

Sometimes the hardest part isn't the deployment itself, but the questions that come from the kids as Daddy is preparing to leave—again. Jennifer says, "Our oldest son had some really hard questions. He wanted to know about Daddy dying and what will happen, what will happen to us. That was a shocker for me."

Unfortunately, the media isn't making that job any easier. Lt. Col. Jurney brought it up in our interview in Ramadi: "You have embedded reporters who come with us. When they see something that is moving forward or progress, that'll be the last thing you'll ever see them print or talk about. Often times, I think [the families back home] typically only hear those negative aspects of what's moving forward, of some reporter who is embellishing and playing up to improve his ratings. And unfortunately, there are families who suffer the consequences of those actions. I don't think they get a balanced view."

For this reason, most of the families I spoke with say they do their best not to listen to the mainstream media. One young mother told me, "You try to avoid the news . . . I wait to hear from Mike because I know he's the one who will tell me what's going on."

Capt. White says that after six deployments, he's come to realize that his wife's ability to carry on in his absence makes his job easier. "She's been able to handle everything the Marine Corps has thrown at her."

Sue Jurney agrees. "When you think of a Marine, you think of tough and strong and courageous, the best of the best; and all those words could describe the corps of Marine wives."

"The advent of instant communications has made the deployment process much different . . . but—in many ways—it is harder. Megan and I 'chatted' almost nightly as she started her day and I finished mine. My last communications with her was just . . . after she had met you. That night . . . I went back to the computer to see if she would be ready to 'chat,' but I knew it wouldn't happen."

— Michael McClung, father of Maj. Megan McClung, writing to the author about the sadness that instant communication brought when his daughter was killed in Iraq

E-MAIL CUTS THE TIME BUT CAN'T CLOSE THE DISTANCE

★ ★ ★ ★ ★ ★ ★ ★ ★ ★ ★ ★

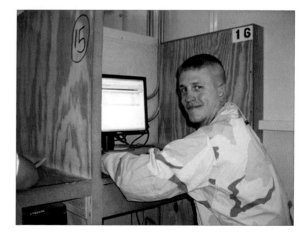

Loneliness is one of those unseen enemies that assault every military man or woman deployed far from home. And as long as there have been armies, there have been loved ones left behind who worried and waited for the troops to return.

In World War II, American soldiers left their home country and their loved ones often for years. Communications being what they were, phone calls home were almost unheard of. Many a fighting man went months without receiving any word from home, and a letter back to the States often arrived with portions marked out by military censors. In 1943, the military instituted V-mail, an innovative form of communication designed to make the mail service more efficient. Letters were scanned to microfiche after censoring, then shipped to the States by air and reprinted before delivery. This was instituted to save space on military shipping, but also to cut the delivery time from months to weeks.

Then, as now, the military understood the impact that communications with the home front have on unit and individual morale. This is what the generals at the Pentagon like to call a "force multiplier," which means that one warrior whose spirits are high is more effective than two who are lonely and depressed.

With this in mind, e-mail and call centers are high on the priority list, once a forward operating base is created. These days, it's not just that e-mail is faster than a postcard sent by boat or air mail; the quality of communications has increased exponentially. Most bases have Internet call centers where deployed personnel can chat via webcam with loved ones back home. Personal satellite phones, while still relatively expensive, allow many of our fighting men and women to participate in important moments that they would otherwise miss.

Internet terminals on most bases in Iraq and Afghanistan allow soldiers to stay connected with home

These advances are some of the most appreciated aspects of life in today's military. E-mail and other technologies offer big advantages over the communication channels used by their fathers and grandfathers. But today's troops know that though technology may cut the time, it will never quite close the gap. There hasn't been a program yet written that will allow a soldier to hug his wife or hold his baby girl over the Internet. Until it does, loneliness will continue to be an unwelcome companion to our men and women in uniform.

★ ★ ★ ★ ★ ★ ★ ★ ★ ★ ★ ★

16

GETTING IT DONE!

"A lot of us didn't believe at first that [the enemy] meant what they said when they vowed out loud that they would rule the world—including us. But little by little, and then a lot faster, they started showing us that unless we fought back, they would be in our own back yard. These enemies did their worst to [other countries, then] . . . they started on us. Suddenly, Americans in Omaha and Dallas and Chicago, deep inside our borders, realized that no place on earth is more than 60 hours flying time from any other. America's freedom was attacked.

That's why we're in this war. That's why you're in this army.

There will be no security, no safety, no freedom for any of us until we have won this war. Every one of us wants to get home, but we won't stop fighting until, this time, the victory has been completely won. When that glad day comes, you'll know you did your share.

Go on now, soldier; put up a good fight. It will be worth it all when it's all been done."

— EXCERPTED FROM WAR DEPARTMENT PAMPHLET 21-13, 10 AUGUST 1944.
Given to soldiers headed overseas in World War II

In August 1944, two months after the landings at Normandy, Allied troops were "bogged down" in the hedge rows of western France. In the Pacific, the Japanese were inflicting a terrible toll on U.S. soldiers, sailors, and Marines as they "island hopped" toward Tokyo.

To counter the war weariness of the American people—and the uncertainty of U.S. troops headed overseas—the War Department published "Army Life." This was a pamphlet containing the exhortation quoted on the previous page. The words are remarkably applicable to the situation today.

We Americans are an impatient lot. We require movies on demand, fast food from drive-through windows, express oil changes, rapid air travel, and high-speed Internet service. "Just-in-time" deliveries have become the norm in manufacturing. When we want it, we want it now.

Our eagerness for instant results has served as a stimulus to the U.S. economy, inspired scientific progress, and promoted extraordinary advances in technology. We now build homes and commercial structures in days and weeks that used to take months or years.

But when it comes to defeating a suicidal adversary on the battlefield and constructing institutions of democracy in a once-brutalized country—as we had to do in Europe and Japan, and are now doing in Iraq and Afghanistan—the desire for immediate outcomes is a vice rather than a virtue. That was the case with our own radical experiment in representative government. More than eleven years passed between the Declaration of Independence and the ratification of the U.S. Constitution. Japan didn't get back on its feet for seven years after surrendering in World War II. It's good to remember such things when thinking about the situation in Iraq and Afghanistan.

In December 2007 our FOX News *War Stories* team—cameraman Mal James, producer Andy Stenner, and I—accompanied by Chuck Holton, the editor of this book, went back to Iraq to evaluate for ourselves the progress being made "on the ground." What we found was stunning. Here's the short form:

• The "Awakening" that began in Al Anbar province and that we saw and reported on so vividly in December 2006 is spreading throughout Iraq. The tactic of establishing permanent joint Iraqi-U.S.-manned police and security stations in areas previously controlled by Sunni or Shiite terror groups and militias is succeeding everywhere it is being tried.

• Al Qaeda's response—increasing brutality against the Iraqi people—has failed miserably. It has thoroughly alienated much of the Sunni population against the Al Qaeda organization in Iraq, prompting Osama bin Laden to issue an unprecedented statement in October 2007, acknowledging "mistakes" that have been made and urging his followers, "I advise you myself, Muslims in general and brothers in Al Qaeda everywhere, to avoid extremism among men and groups."

• The Iraqi police and security forces continue to improve in both numbers and capability and are increasingly able to undertake unilateral operations. In response to the successes they have enjoyed, recruiting has increased better than 100 percent over 2006.

• The rate of all attacks against Iraqi civilians and coalition forces dropped by nearly 70 percent in the last four months of 2007.

• In December 2007, for the first time since 2004, the number of Iraqi civilians returning to their homes was higher than the number of people seeking refugee status internally or in neighboring countries. In short, the Iraqi people who fled the violence are coming home.

> "The enemies of Iraq will shrink at no act, however barbaric. They will do all that they can to shake the confidence of the people and to convince the world that this effort is doomed.
>
> "Together with our Iraqi partners, we must defeat those who oppose the new Iraq. We cannot allow mass murderers to hold the initiative. We must strike them relentlessly. We . . . must set the terms of the struggle, not our enemies. And together we must prevail."
>
> **— LTG David Petraeus, U.S. Army, in a letter to his troops on 11 February 2007, the day he assumed command in Iraq**

HOW IRAQ HAS CHANGED

★ ★ ★ ★ ★ ★ ★ ★ ★ ★ ★ ★

December 2007 – In Iraq for a ninth time with editor Chuck Holton

When, in December of 2007, our FOX News *War Stories* team returned to Iraq on our ninth trip, none of us were prepared for the dramatic changes taking place in the country. Thanks to the U.S. Army 3rd ID and U.S. Special Operations Command, we were able to assess what was happening in Baghdad, then east along the Iranian frontier, south to Hillah, in Babil province, west to Al Anbar, and north to Diyala province.

Without exception, everywhere we went there was ample evidence of Iraqis taking charge of their own destiny. Though no U.S. or Iraqi commander was willing to claim victory, one senior U.S. commander said to me, after being assured of nonattribution, "There is more fighting and dying to be done, but this battle is won."

What follows are a few excerpts from the reports we filed.

7 DECEMBER 2007 — ISKANDARIYAH, IRAQ

Many of the 3rd ID troops here are on their third year-long tour of duty in Iraq. These soldiers were part of the initial attack north from Kuwait in March 2003; they were here when Al Qaeda tried to stop the elections in 2005; and they have been here again since May 2007. What they have experienced along the way gives them a perspective that is much at odds from what we most often see expressed in our mainstream media and by America's most prominent politicians.

"If I thought we were losing, I wouldn't be here," said SSG Nicholas Ingleston of Williamstown, N.Y. He's an M1 tank gunner on his third tour of duty in Iraq. When I asked him why he had decided to re-enlist in the U.S. Army knowing that would mean coming back to Iraq a third time, this father of three replied, "I'm part of a team, and we came here to do a job and we're doing it."

Professional political pessimists and their apprentices in the press long ago declared this fight "lost" and U.S. efforts here a "failure." But if they cared to look, they would find, as Mark Twain once said of Wagner's music: "It's not as bad as it sounds."

When COL Terry Ferrell, the commanding officer of the 2nd Brigade Combat Team, 3rd ID, arrived here in June, this area was an Al Qaeda stronghold. Today, all that has changed.

We confirmed that "the awakening" in the Sunni population and the "concerned local citizens" program in Babil province have indeed, as Ferrell puts it, "lifted the blanket of fear on these communities." He told us, "We have crippled the Al Qaeda in this area and contributed to a dramatic turnaround in security for Baghdad." From all we see, he's spot on.

Interestingly, these kinds of stories are commonplace in most of Iraq. Unfortunately, these aren't the kinds of facts that make good copy for America's media elites. Reductions in enemy attacks; fewer U.S., coalition, and civilian casualties; and improvements in Iraqi military and security forces have driven news from Iraq out of the front pages of our papers and off broadcast news.

Publicly, U.S. commanders describe the situation as "cautiously optimistic" and say "the momentum is in the right direction." Privately, they say, "We are putting them [Al Qaeda and the Shiite militias] on the ropes."

Though disappointed by the lack of "good news" being reported in the U.S. media, the troops' sense of humor is undiminished. When Secretary Gates was in Baghdad in December, he announced that lack of congressional funding could result in "pink slips for up to 200,000 Defense Department employees." Hearing the story, one young soldier heading out on patrol commented, "Somebody call me if I get laid off."

CPT Nazzir said he waited to join the Iraqi Army until it was clear "who was going to win" the war against radical Islamic terror

10 December 2007 — Maderiya, Iraq, We walked through this agricultural community east of Bagdad, not far from the Iranian border, with COL Terry Ferrell, commanding officer of the 2nd Brigade, 3rd ID. He introduced me to CPT Fawaz Nazzir, of the Iraqi Army. I asked why he joined the new Iraqi Army eleven months ago. His reply was a testament to American resolve in prosecuting this campaign: "I waited," replied CPT Nazzir, "to see which side was going to win."

To some Americans that may sound like a cynical response but not to those who have spent years campaigning in Mesopotamia. "What would you expect given how uncertain our commitment was at home?" commented one U.S. officer on his third tour of duty here. He continued: "Until 'the surge,' nobody in Iraq knew whether we were going to finish this fight. AQI [Al Qaeda in Iraq] and the Shiite militias were all telling their followers that we were going to cut and run. 'The surge' proved that we weren't going to abandon them."

Not only did we not abandon them; we upped the ante, increasing the number of U.S. combat units in the country and significantly expanding training and support for Iraq's fledgling security forces. Much of the enhanced instruction, arming, and "know how" has come via U.S. Special Operations Command—soldiers, sailors, airmen, and Marines uniquely prepared and equipped to carry out unconventional operations. The result has been a dramatic reduction in terror attacks against Iraqi civilians and Coalition personnel. While the mainstream media and U.S. politicians were harping about the "lack of political progress in Baghdad," the Iraqi Army, police, and Special Operations Forces were being rebuilt from the ground up.

That's not to say that Iraq is no longer dangerous. It can still be lethal, particularly for Iraqis.

14 DECEMBER 2007 — HILLAH, IRAQ, BABIL PROVINCE
Just hours before we arrived here, an IED killed Lt. Gen. Qais Hamza al-Mamouri, the Babil province Chief of Police and the architect of the Reconciliation Movement in southeastern Iraq.

With Brig. Gen. Abbas, commander of the Police SWAT Force, and an officer of the U.S. Special Operations Command in Hillah, Iraq

For more than two hours, Gen. Abbas and I walked through the crowded streets of Hillah where Iranian-supported Shiite militia gangs once held sway over 500,000 Iraqis. Wading through throngs of citizens, Gen. Abbas promised them that, "We will continue to give every Iraqi equal protection from all criminals."

A vigorous opponent of Iranian influence in Iraq, Qais was also the author of an agreement among tribal and community leaders pledging to "provide security for all citizens without regard to sect, ethnicity, or political party affiliation." Though Babil province is predominantly Shiite, Qais had insisted that his police enforce the law impartially "for all Sunnis, Shiites, Kurds, and Christians."

Less than twenty-four hours after Gen. Qais was killed, a U.S. Special Operations officer took our FOX News team to the headquarters of the Hillah SWAT Police to meet with their commander, Brig. Gen. Mohammad Abbas al-Jubori, a Qais protégé.

According to our escort, "General Abbas has built Hillah SWAT into one of the finest police departments in the country. He's committed to a free and independent Iraq—where every man and woman is treated equally—despite Iraq's neighbors being less than enthusiastic about a democracy next door."

17 DECEMBER 2007 — RAMADI, IRAQ

Yesterday we were in Fallujah, the former Al Qaeda stronghold where Iraqi police in blue uniforms watched as we stood on a residential street, rebuilt from the rubble of vicious urban combat in 2004. Today we're in Ramadi.

When our FOX News team was here exactly a year ago, Sheikh Sattar—the chief instigator of the Sunni "Awakening"—was still alive, and the citizens of Al Anbar province were just beginning to cooperate with coalition forces. Last December, the city of Ramadi had a well-deserved reputation as the most violent place on the planet. The streets were full of IEDs, and there were daily attacks against U.S. soldiers and Marines by snipers, mortars, rockets, and roadside bombs. At home, the "experts" had decided that Iraq was descending into an abyss of sectarian conflict.

This year, U.S. Navy SEALs took us to dine with Sheikh Mohammad al Heiss, the new leader of the Sunni reconciliation movement. On a street where terrorists tried to kill us last year, we walked without flak jackets or helmets—something that would have been unthinkable only a few months ago.

Accompanied by the SEALs, we strolled down "Route Michigan," past the mosque where we had documented bloody battles and into the souk (an Iraqi version of a mall), so that I could buy Christmas presents for my wife and grandchildren. The only bad part of the trip this year was our interpreter telling me afterward that I got "robbed" on the scarves and hats for my grandchildren. But I know I got a good deal on the bracelet for Betsy.

One of many gunfights along "Route Michigan" in Ramadi, Iraq
The convoy we rode in had just been ambushed by Al Qaeda Mujahadeen, across the road from the Blue Mosque; the smoke is from a burning Humvee

20 DECEMBER, 2007 — BAQOUBA, IRAQ

It is nearly Christmas, and most of the young Americans we are with are going to miss the holiday with their families. For many, it is their third Nativity season away from home since Operation Iraqi Freedom began in 2003.

A year ago, the masters of the mainstream media were contending that the campaign in Iraq was "lost." The Associated Press, in a piece headlined "Many U.S. Troops in Iraq Oppose Escalation," baldly stated we were "embroiled in civil warfare between majority Shiite Muslims and Sunni Arabs that no number of American troops can stop." America's newspapers and television screens were full of stories about U.S. and Iraqi casualties, and liberal partisans were demanding that President Bush "bring the troops home—now!"

Then in February, the first U.S. "surge" troops arrived in Iraq. Within weeks, U.S. casualties spiked, and the potentates of the press proclaimed that the additional troops were "too little, too late." Radical Islamic Web sites agreed and predicted the toll of dead and wounded would force the Americans to abandon Iraq just as they quit Vietnam, Beirut, and Somalia. Osama bin Laden declared that the "American infidels" were being "driven from Mesopotamia."

They were all wrong. So was I. In January 2006, after nearly a month embedded with U.S. troops in Anbar province, I had written—and said on FOX News—that "dispatching more combat troops to Iraq isn't the answer. Adding more trainers and helping the Iraqis to help themselves, is." GEN Petraeus did both, and it was exactly the right move. The "surge" in combat power and trainers changed everything.

Since the beginning of December 2007, we have traversed the length and breadth of Iraq, interviewing hundreds of Americans and Iraqis, both civilian and military. In our travels, we have documented stunning progress in bringing security and civil law and order to this country. This week, Basra province reverted to full Iraqi control as British troops completed their withdrawal from Iraq's southernmost prefecture. Last night we accompanied a U.S.-trained-and-supported Iraqi special operations unit on a nighttime raid to apprehend a terror suspect, a feat that would have been impossible last year.

"The momentum is in the right direction," MG Rick Lynch, commanding general of Task Force Marne, told me—and his troops know it. As one young officer put it, "There is still fighting to be done, but the troops are volunteering to come back. They don't 're-up' for a losing battle."

From the ground up, this country is being transformed more rapidly than anyone believed possible, and America is gaining a new ally in the struggle against radical Islamic terror.

"Look, Mom, no Flak jacket"- preparing to do a "stand-up" at the Ramadi souk in December of 2007
In nine trips to Iraq, this was the first time I have been in the city without getting shot at

WHY DON'T WE HEAR MORE OF THIS KIND OF NEWS?

★　★　★　★　★　★　★　★　★　★　★　★

When it comes to Iraq, good news is no news. By autumn of 2007, the trends and indicators from Iraq were so positive that the mainstream media took Iraq stories off the front pages and the evening news and went searching for other negative stories about the U.S. armed forces to feed the American people. In October and November there were stories about high numbers of suicides, desertions, and divorces among members of our military and how difficult it had become to attract new recruits. A 17 November 2007 Associated Press headline blared: "Soldiers strained by six years at war are deserting their posts at the highest rate since 1980."

These young Americans believe in this struggle enough to reenlist

In fact, the suicide rate for U.S. military personnel is lower than that of the same age group in the U.S. population. The divorce rate in the military is slightly lower than the overall population. The desertion rate for the Marines has actually declined since 9/11. And as for new recruits, every branch of the U.S. armed forces exceeded their recruiting goals in 2007. Marine combat units in Iraq and Afghanistan had more requests for reenlistment than they were authorized to accept.

The recruiting and retention story is particularly heartening because many young people are discouraged from serving in uniform by family members, friends, and high-school guidance counselors. This is something that would have been considered shameful at one time in our country.

SGT Steven C. Ganczewski, a Ranger in editor Chuck Holton's unit, had been asked by a high-school guidance counselor why a young man with his "potential" would join the Army.

"Someone with his potential"—as if selfless service, even to the point of giving one's life for a cause greater than any one of us—is somehow beneath one's "potential." Thankfully, Patrick Henry and George Washington didn't feel that way in 1775.

The story made me wonder if those who discourage others from serving because it's beneath their "potential" would say the same thing to the man who said, "Greater love hath no man than this, that a man lay down his life for his friends" (John 14:13 KJV). That man, Jesus Christ, went on to do just that.

But SGT Steven C. Ganczewski understood that there are more important things in life than safety and a scholarship, despite what the guidance counselor had to say.

The media also made a great deal over the unwillingness of members of the State Department to accept assignments in Iraq. This confirms what I have been saying for years—that only those who wear our nation's military uniforms have the courage to really fight Islamic terror. In fact, in the battle for the people of Iraq, our men and women in uniform are America's best ambassadors. They work tirelessly to build a better future for the people of Iraq and Afghanistan. Marine SSgt Darin Patterson of the Fifth Civil Affairs Group put it this way: "It's always a step forward, whether it's just one inch or two inches; it has to start somewhere." This approach is being taken all over Iraq, and it is changing everything.

Just before Americans celebrated Thanksgiving in 2007, Muslim sheiks, imams, and civilians went to St John's Catholic Church in Baghdad to encourage their Christian neighbors to return home. In 2004, Al Qaeda of Iraq bombed the church, a prominent landmark in the capital's southern neighborhood. Their goal was to eliminate all of Iraq's Christian communities. Nearly all the Christians from the neighborhood around St. John's fled, becoming refugees. Many left the country.

As southern Baghdad was secured in the summer of 2007, the church was rehabilitated by U.S. Army engineers. More than a dozen Muslim dignitaries attended the first mass in the restored church as a way to encourage their Christian neighbors to come home.

Is Iraq still a dangerous place? No doubt. Though there are fewer of them, IEDs and suicide bombers—most of them from Saudi Arabia, Syria, Iran, Yemen, Chechnya, and Lebanon—still kill and maim. One suicide bomber on a bicycle attacked a police recruit formation. A few days earlier, eight Shia and Sunni sheiks were kidnapped after a reconciliation meeting in Baghdad. But the Iraqis didn't call for U.S. help in either incident. They could have done so, but they didn't have to.

Iraqi fire, police, and medical personnel were the "first responders" in the suicide bombing. Two days after the kidnappings, an Iraqi Special Operations Force [ISOF]—trained by U.S. Special Operations personnel like those with whom we were embedded—launched a hostage recovery unit to rescue seven of the eight kidnap victims alive. No U.S. military personnel were involved.

The "surge" has been about much more than thirty thousand additional U.S. troops in Iraq. The real "surge" is in the transformation of the Iraqi military and security forces. As they get bigger and better, more Iraqi civilians move away from supporting Al Qaeda and other criminal and extremist elements. In short, there is a momentum to success, and success breeds more success.

★ ★ ★ ★ ★ ★ ★ ★ ★ ★ ★ ★

The Troops

First and most important, the young Americans dispatched to fight the war against radical Islamic terror have never wavered in their courage and commitment. Their bravery and tenacity have been tested by brutal adversaries in some of the most difficult and dangerous conditions U.S.

troops have ever faced. Despite media and political opposition to Operation Iraqi Freedom, even before it started, and partisan opposition that worsened over the next five years, the young soldiers, sailors, airmen, Guardsmen, and Marines fighting the battles never quit. Persistence pays. Tenacity makes a difference.

Without the valor and self-sacrifice of the brightest, best-educated, best-trained, best-equipped, and best-led military in the world, and the sacrifices their families have made at home, victories in the war against radical Islam would be impossible. When the media and political opponents of the war were insisting on a pullout from Iraq, tens of thousands of those who had already "been there, done that" volunteered to go back again. Those who served in this crucible really are American heroes.

A Marine in front of a mine clearing vehicle with his military working dog, "Dollar"

Leadership

President Bush has never wavered in his support for the troops that he sent off to fight this war. Though he was admonished to "cut our losses" and "get out now," though his party lost control of the Congress in 2006, he was steadfast in his resolve not to have this war end like Vietnam. And his field commanders were cut from the same tempered steel.

Men like GEN David Petraeus, generals James Mattis, James Conway, and Ray Odierno were pilloried in the press, but they prevailed anyway. They motivated young soldiers and Marines to weather the IEDs, suicide bombers, and mind-numbing fatigue to press on despite criticism on the home front. These leaders ignored the bashing they got for being too aggressive and kept the pressure on the enemy. Leaders do make a difference.

Adaptability

The American military proved to be much more flexible than our adversaries on the battlefield or critics at home believed possible. Neither Al Qaeda of Iraq nor the Shiite militias nor their foreign supporters were able to change their weapons or tactics as fast as U.S. troops could adapt to new situations and developments on the ground. The campaigns in Iraq and Afghanistan have proven that the ability of young Americans to bring new ideas to the battlefield—not just in weapons and equipment, but in new "thinking"—is unrivaled.

The military's new line of mine resistant ambush protected (MRAP) vehicles has dramatically reduced the number of casualties from roadside bombs in Iraq

Tens of thousands of changes have been made in U.S. military weapons, equipment, organization, and tactics since the unprovoked attack on 9/11. The adaptability of commanders and units on the ground permitted us to capitalize on the brutal fanaticism of Al Qaeda and seize the opportunity presented by the "Awakening" in Al Anbar, and then spread the concept throughout the country.

As we saw firsthand in December 2007, the integration of Special Operations capabilities with those of conventional military units created a synergy that was devastating to the terrorists who were trying to maintain their hold on the Iraqi population. That same model is now being taught to the Iraqis.

The resilience of the Iraqi people also deserves recognition in accounting for a successful outcome in Mesopotamia. In three elections during 2005, the Iraqi people braved horrific threats of violence in order to cast ballots in overwhelming numbers. Those votes really have made a difference. Though political change in Baghdad has been slower than anyone wanted, the fact that women were empowered to run for office and vote has changed the entire dynamic in Iraq.

Ridding neighborhoods of thugs and murderers so children can go to school; reconnecting homes and businesses to electricity, water, and sewage; and providing jobs for millions of unemployed men—all these things are now feasible. Though it may take longer than anyone prefers, the country now has a future.

GEN Petraeus is fond of telling visiting reporters that we're "not yet successful, but we're succeeding" and that "the momentum is going the right way." U.S. troop reductions are already occurring, and more are to come. By July of

General David Petraeus greeting an Iraqi street vendor

2008, all thirty thousand U.S. personnel sent to Iraq during "the surge" are slated to be home. But what U.S. media elites have failed to note is that the real surge—Iraqis serving their country—will continue to change their country for the better.

Over the course of 2007, the Iraqi army grew nearly 110 percent to twelve divisions, forty-one brigades, 123 battalions, and four ISOF battalions. Nearly all of them have gained invaluable combat proficiency from their U.S. advisors and in engagements with the enemy. By the summer of 2008 the Iraqis will have trained and fielded another eight brigades for a total of 154 battalions, including six ISOF battalions. And an additional thirty thousand Iraqi police officers will be on the streets.

It's easy to get lost in the numbers. Here's the bottom line: By the time U.S. troops sent to Iraq for the "surge" come home, the Iraqis will have fielded a near 100 percent increase in police and security forces since January of 2007. The improvements are both quantitative

and qualitative. By the time the five U.S. "surge brigades" return home, the Iraqi Army will have fielded ten new brigades of their own, and the Iraqis aren't going to rotate home— they are there to stay.

CAN IT ALL STILL GO WRONG?

★ ★ ★ ★ ★ ★ ★ ★ ★ ★ ★ ★

There is no doubt that the momentum is, as GEN Petraeus puts it, "in the right direction." But things could still go wrong.

The first and most likely place for all the progress to come off track isn't in Baghdad; it's in Washington. Congressional demands for a "pull out now" in the heat of an election year, backed up by a cut-off in funding, could precipitate a disaster.

Iraq's neighbors are less than enthusiastic about a democracy next door. We have seen the sophisticated IEDs and rockets that Iran builds and sends into Iraq to kill and maim. Though Iraqi oil production now exceeds pre-2003 levels, the democratically elected government in Baghdad isn't doing enough to rebuild the country's crumbling infrastructure. A collapse of American resolve would likely encourage Iran, Saudi Wahhabis, and Syria to increase support for a resurgence in Al Qaeda and the Shiite militias. It is, in the words of one U.S. officer in Iraq, his idea for a "worst-case scenario."

The theocracy in Tehran could acquire nuclear weapons and give the U.S. an ultimatum, or worse yet, actually use one against U.S. forces in Iraq or in the Persian Gulf. That would of course be a prelude for a devastating U.S. military strike against the Iranian leadership and weapons-of-mass-destruction facilities. But it would change all of the hoped-for outcomes in the war against radical Islam.

Finally, all of the U.S. military officers I spoke with on my ninth trip to Iraq expressed concern that the government in Baghdad might not be up to the task of bringing about a functioning democratic government. While pointing to successes at the local level and in the provinces, they expressed frustration with the pace of sectarian reconciliation in dialog in the capital. Though few thought it likely, some said that they were concerned that "if the politicians don't get their act together, the army could take over." One general officer told me, "I don't even want to think about that happening," though clearly he had.

WHERE WE COULD DO BETTER

★ ★ ★ ★ ★ ★ ★ ★ ★ ★ ★ ★

We Need to Tell the Truth about Who "They" Are

There are two great inconsistencies about the radical Islamists who purport to lead the Jihad against us that need to be constantly emphasized for those we are attempting to help.

First, the Jihadist masterminds like bin Laden, Zarqawi, and

Musab al-Zarqawi

al Sadr aren't eager to find martyrdom. To the extent they can, they remain on the run and in hiding, relegating the glory of exploding bodies to their followers and their followers' children. We should constantly remind their followers that their leaders are cowards.

Second, the terrorists we face in Iraq, Afghanistan, and the Philippines are able to construct car bombs and use cell phones as detonators. They know how to use AK-47s and RPGs, and they know how to use video cameras to record their atrocities. But none of them are capable of building a car, a cell phone, or even a relatively simple automatic rifle. They can blow up a generating station, but they can't make a light bulb. We should regularly remind those who can read or listen that "Jihadists" seeking to "drive out the infidels" are destroyers, not builders.

We Need to Tell the Truth about What We Stand For

Islamic radicals like bin Laden, theo-fascists like those in Tehran, and dictatorial regimes like the one that previously occupied Baghdad count on an illiterate and impoverished citizenry. They know people with this mind-set can be incited to frenzy or suicidal terror by defaming Jews or Americans. The only cure for this misery-driven fury is education. Too many children in Muslim countries are indoctrinated on how to hate and kill and how to kill themselves. Teaching reading, math, science, and life skills commensurate with God-given abilities is a far less costly way of fighting the Jihad than the blood of American troops. Giving young Muslim children something to live for instead of reasons to die by killing an "infidel" may be the best long-term investment we can make in our own future.

We Need to Tell the Truth about the Best Antidote for Radical Islamic Terror

The number-one target of radical Islam is Muslim women. In Taliban-controlled Afghanistan, Al Qaeda strongholds in Iraq, and other countries and regions ruled by radical Islamists, boys

become men at age fifteen. But girls are considered women at age nine. They can be tried as adults in a criminal court, are liable for the death penalty, and can be stoned to death for adultery. Though the legal age of marriage for a girl is thirteen, a father can make a daughter marry earlier and order her to endure female genital mutilation.

Radical Islamic courts consider a woman's testimony to be worth half that of a man. Mothers may not act as financial guardians or make decisions about their children's residence, foreign travel, or medical care. Women must have permission from a father, husband, or male relative to travel.

Men have uncontested rights to divorce their wives, and they may practice polygamy. Women are not allowed to vote or participate in political debate. They receive half the inheritance of men. If a man dies childless, his entire estate goes to his parents or siblings, not his wife.

Specific evidence of radical Islamic violence perpetrated against tens of thousands of Muslim girls and women in the name of "Islamic purity" has been catalogued by the United Nations, the European Union, and numerous human rights organizations. In Iraq and Afghanistan, U.S. military commanders have filed innumerable reports of atrocities perpetrated against women and girls by organizations like Al Qaeda in Iraq and the Mahdi Army.

Nearly all of these events have been ignored by the mainstream media. Little has been said about the innumerable ways that U.S. soldiers, sailors, airmen, Guardsmen, and Marines have become the principal protectors of Muslim women.

Thanks to young Americans wearing flak jackets and helmets, hundreds of schools have been built for Muslim girls, scores of female health care clinics have been opened, and hundreds of thousands of women now work, have their own bank accounts, and use cell-phones. Millions of women have the right to vote and serve in elected office.

Just before the December 2005 election in Iraq, Mamoun Rashid, governor of Al Anbar province, told me, "Women don't vote to have their sons become suicide bombers." He's right. That's why the best antidote for radical Islamic terror is a woman's purple finger, signifying her right to vote.

We Need to Tell the Truth about Who We Are

Americans ought not be ashamed of who we are. We have brought freedom and opportunity to hundreds of millions around the globe. We send young countrymen around the world not for gold or oil or colonial conquest but to offer others the hope of the same freedoms we enjoy. Neither individual liberty nor Christianity are threats to Islam. These are threats only to the power of the radical Islamists. Informing people in predominantly Muslim countries about concepts like private property, personal choice, respect for the sanctity of life, and the freedom to make decisions in a system governed by rule of law isn't extreme pride; it's essential to their understanding of who we are.

As we prepared to head back to Iraq for our ninth trip in four years, President Bush awarded the Medal of Honor to Michael Murphy for "conspicuous gallantry and intrepidity, at the risk of his life, above and beyond the call of duty." But because

Murphy had been killed in action, his parents had to receive the medal awarded to their son.

LT Michael Murphy, a U.S. Navy SEAL, didn't die in Konar province, Afghanistan, fighting to expand American influence over others. He was fighting to give others the hope of freedom because he believed this would help give his countrymen a safer future. He was right. We ought to remind enemies and allies alike that we have a whole nation full of people such as Mike Murphy—men and women who will gladly volunteer to put themselves at risk for the love of liberty.

These are American Heroes.

The President of the United States in the name of the Congress, takes pride in presenting the Medal of Honor to Lieutenant Michael Murphy for conspicuous gallantry and intrepidity at the risk of his life above and beyond the call of duty as the leader of a special reconnaissance element with Naval Special Warfare Task Unit Afghanistan on 27 and 28 June 2005. While leading a mission to locate a high-level, anticoalition militia leader, LT Murphy demonstrated extraordinary heroism in the face of grave danger in the vicinity of Asadabad, Konar Province, Afghanistan. On 28 June 2005, operating in an extremely rugged enemy-controlled area, LT Murphy's team was discovered by anticoalition militia sympathizers, who revealed their position to Taliban fighters. As a result, between thirty and forty enemy fighters besieged his four-member team. Demonstrating exceptional resolve, LT Murphy valiantly led his men in engaging the large enemy force. The ensuing fierce firefight resulted in numerous enemy casualties, as well as the wounding of all four members of the team. Ignoring his own wounds and demonstrating exceptional composure, LT Murphy continued to lead and encourage his men. When the primary communicator fell mortally wounded, LT Murphy repeatedly attempted to call for assistance for his beleaguered teammates. Realizing the impossibility of communicating in the extreme terrain, and in the face of almost certain death, he fought his way into open terrain to gain a better position to transmit a call. This deliberate, heroic act deprived him of cover, exposing him to direct enemy fire. Finally achieving contact with his headquarters, LT Murphy maintained his exposed position while he provided his location and requested immediate support for his team. In his final act of bravery, he continued to engage the enemy until he was mortally wounded, gallantly giving his life for his country and for the cause of freedom. By his selfless leadership, courageous actions, and extraordinary devotion to duty, LT Murphy reflected great credit upon himself and upheld the highest traditions of the United States Naval Service.

★ ★ ★ ★ ★ ★ ★ ★ ★ ★ ★ ★

17

DISPATCHES FROM A FORGOTTEN WAR

To Americans of my generation and older, the Korean War is the "Forgotten War." For this generation, it's Afghanistan—or to be precise, Operation Enduring Freedom.

This long campaign against al-Qaeda and the Taliban in the shadow of the Hindu Kush didn't start as a "forgotten war." On Oct. 7, 2001, less than a month after the 9/11 attacks, Operation Enduring Freedom began with a salvo of Tomahawk cruise missiles and raids by B-1s, B-2s, B-52s, and waves of carrier-based aircraft. For the next month, the entire world was riveted as Afghan Northern Alliance troops—bolstered by U.S. special operations forces and CIA teams—swept south toward Kabul.

The liberation of the capital in November 2001 was an international press event. When the 15th Marine Expeditionary Unit landed at Forward Operating Base Rhino on Nov. 25 to cut Taliban/al-Qaeda escape routes into Pakistan, reporters clamored to cover the operation. For the next sixteen months, most of the so-called mainstream media provided at least some regular coverage of the hunt for Osama bin Laden.

Then came Iraq. The start of Operation Iraqi Freedom, in March 2003, created a virtual news vacuum in Afghanistan, and it has been pretty much like that ever since. Though there have been brief moments of media interest—such as the Oct. 9, 2004, election that brought President Hamid Karzai to power—the potentates of the press largely ignored developments in Afghanistan and focused instead on predictions of disaster in Mesopotamia.

By the spring of 2008, success in Iraq was an undeniable reality. But in Afghanistan, Taliban insurgents and foreign fighters, flowing across the porous border with Pakistan, commenced a vigorous offensive against the elected Karzai government. U.S. Army General David D. McKiernan, the new NATO commander in Afghanistan, asked for reinforcements. When our European "allies" balked, President Bush ordered 3,500 more American troops to the theater—most of them, Marines. Enemy contact and American casualties increased almost immediately, but the mainstream media, preoccupied with a hotly contested U.S. presidential race hardly noted what was happening in Operation Enduring Freedom.

A Taliban resurgence began in early 2008

In July, Senator Barak Obama paid a brief visit to Bagram Airbase north of Kabul. Though he was accompanied by scores of journalists, reports on the trip devoted considerably more broadcast time and column inches to the presidential candidate's basketball prowess than they did to the U.S. troops serving there. When the senator departed, the media left with him.

Just days after this "high-viz" political event, producers Greg Johnson and Andy Stenner and I departed for Afghanistan. In Dubai we linked up with cameraman Chris Jackson and after a seven-hour layover—during which we negotiated the transfer of our body armor and helmets through Dubai customs—we flew to Kabul. There we were met by Chuck Holton, who took so many of the magnificent photographs in this book and an officer from the Combined Joint Special Operations Task Force, who arranged for us to catch a U.S. military resupply flight south to Kandahar.

More than forty hours after leaving the U.S., we arrived at the austere headquarters of Marine Expeditionary Unit 24—a Marine Air-Ground Task Force or MAGTF—deployed from Camp Lejeune and New River Marine Corps Air Station in North Carolina. There Col. Pete Petronzio, the commander of 24 MEU briefed us on the mission of his 2,300 Marines and the heavy contact they had already encountered with the Taliban in southern Helmand Province.

That night we took a two-hour helicopter flight and then a bone-jarring, "dust-sucking," sixteen-hour cross-desert land convoy to "embed" with Battalion Landing Team (BLT) 1/6. On the way, a sudden sandstorm blew in and we had to "lay over" until dawn. Built around the 1st Battalion, 6th Marines, BLT 1/6 is the Ground Combat Element of 24 MEU—and they have seen plenty of ground combat.

Official information about the 33,000 U.S. soldiers, sailors, airmen, Guardsmen, and Marines here in Afghanistan are preceded by the "slug line"—"Operation Enduring Freedom." Our FOX News team dubbed our reports—"Dispatches from a forgotten war."

GARMSIR, HELMAND PROVINCE AFGHANISTAN
AUGUST 2, 2008

It is more than 115 degrees Fahrenheit. We're soaked with sweat. The Marines fighting here since April say it is cooler now than a month ago, when temperatures were above 125 degrees—as high as the thermometer will go. The bright sunlight is oppressive and fine dust, the consistency of talcum powder, permeates everything. Terrain more than a few hundred meters from the Helmand River looks like desolate lunar

Talking with 1/6 CO LtCol Anthony Henderson, USMC

landscape. In this climate, drinking at least ten liters of water a day is essential for survival. We all drank that much and more on the convoy from Forward Operating Base (FOB) Dwyer.

According to Lt. Col. Anthony Henderson, the commanding officer of BLT 1/6, nearly half the Marines in this unit were with us in Iraq. Some have made as many as five combat deployments. All of them are volunteers. Though U.S. forces don't keep score with "body counts," the Helmand Provincial Government credits the Marines with killing more than four hundred enemy combatants in this Taliban stronghold. No one here disputes the number.

Since arriving in Afghanistan in April, the Marines of 1/6 have had numerous gunfights with the Taliban. They don't swagger, but they know that they are making a difference even though this is the most difficult country to get around in I have experienced since Vietnam. As we arrived at "Strongpoint Bravo," we had no idea how much more challenging things were about to become.

STRONGPOINT "BRAVO," AUGUST 3, 2008

On the modern battlefield the U.S. military employs a wide array of sophisticated technology: satellites, manned and unmanned aerial vehicles, thermal imaging devices, electronic intelligence equipment, laser targeting equipment, radio jammers—and that's just the unclassified stuff. Yet, even with all this gear, the best way to keep an adversary off balance is to conduct patrols.

Patrolling, especially in a counterinsurgency environment, is essential for collecting intelligence, denying the enemy safe-havens and hunting down insurgents. Foot and vehicle-mounted patrols are a key component in "winning hearts and minds," and in Afghanistan patrols go on around the clock, "twenty-four seven." They are all inherently dangerous.

As we arrived at Strongpoint Bravo—a fortress constructed of dirt-filled Hesco barriers and bunkers—a squad-sized foot patrol was just returning from a reconnaissance mission. They were searching for improvised explosive devices and the Taliban terrorists who build them. They found neither.

Getting ready to go out on patrol

A few hours later Maj. Michael Little, the 1/6 Weapons Company Commander, asked if two of our FOX team wanted to "ride along" with a platoon-sized, five-Humvee "presence" patrol to a small agricultural community a few kilometers north of the strongpoint. Cameraman Chris Jackson and I donned our flak jackets and helmets, grabbed our camera gear, and reported to the dust-covered vehicle staging area.

Lieutenant John Branson issued a detailed patrol order describing the enemy and friendly situation, the mission of his patrol, and the tactics, techniques, and procedures to be used during the operation and we mounted up. I piled in behind Lt. Branson. Cameraman Chris Jackson took a seat in the right rear of the vehicle commanded by Sgt. Courtney Rauch and introduced himself to the driver, Cpl. Arnaldo Figueroa, Cpl. Donald, manning a .50 cal machine gun in the turret, and Cpl. Wright on left rear security.

Sergeant Rauch was a reassuring factor. I saw him in action in Ramadi in 2006. Big, tough, and smart, the amiable Pennsylvanian and his wife Vanessa were part of our FOX News documentary, "From the Frontlines to the Home Front." He exuded competence and the Weapons Section he now led reflected his experience, skill, and steady leadership. After checking all his men, they "locked and loaded," and we rolled out into the desert toward a scattered collection of mud-walled orchards, houses, and opium poppy fields.

We stopped three times within the first two hours, asking questions of the "locals" we encountered, checking documents, patiently probing about Taliban sightings through the interpreter, an Afghan-born American citizen known to the troops as "Frank the Terp." The patrol was about 500 meters from a walled compound when Sgt. Rauch saw something suspicious in front of us and signaled an immediate halt. It was too late.

The massive IED detonated directly beneath Sgt. Rauch's lead vehicle of our five-Humvee patrol. The blast blew Cpl. Donald out of the turret and Cpl. Wright and cameraman Chris Jackson out the left and right rear doors. Though heavily armored, the Humvee was immediately engulfed in flames.

Trapped in the front of the burning vehicle were Cpl. Figueroa and Sgt. Rauch. Despite his own wounds from shrapnel and the blast, Jackson immediately jumped up and scrambled back to the burning vehicle. With ammunition "cooking off" inside the Humvee, he somehow jerked the buckled armored door open and dragged Sgt. Rauch to safety. On the left side of the vehicle, Cpls. Wright and Donald did the same for Cpl. Figueroa.

Both badly wounded Marines were dragged to safety behind the next vehicle in the column. While two U.S. Navy medical corpsmen, Jose Pena and Gregory Cox, administered first aid, Lt. Branson deployed his Marines to secure a helicopter landing zone.

Within minutes of the explosion, a Humvee-mounted Quick Reaction Force (QRF) from the Marine strongpoint, an armed UH-1N "Huey" and an AH-1J "Cobra" gunship were headed our way. They arrived—accompanied by Chuck Holton—just as a CH-46 Sea Knight helicopter swooped in to evacuate the casualties while small-arms, rockets, and machinegun ammunition exploded in the diesel-fueled flames of the lead Humvee. Fewer than twenty minutes after the blast that almost killed them, the two wounded Marines were in the air, headed for the big British hospital at Camp Bastion.

Weapons company Marines carrying Sgt. Rauch to a CH-46 Cas-evac helicopter

The wrecked Humvee burned until well after dark. When the fire finally died out, a Vehicle Recovery Team removed the wreckage to deny the Taliban a chance to exploit the incident in their prolific propaganda. The only indication left behind was a fire-blackened hole in the dirt track.

It was well after midnight when we made it back to the strongpoint. Once inside the little base, the Weapons Company Corpsman examined the shrapnel wound in Chris Jackson's leg, cleaned it thoroughly and bandaged him up. After checking for signs of traumatic brain injury, the "Doc" offered to have him evacuated after first light. His response was classic "hero humor."

Cameraman Chris Jackson after surviving the IED

HERO HUMOR

Jackson's cameras and equipment in the Humvee were blasted to pieces and burned beyond recognition. He had a shrapnel wound in his right leg and undoubtedly a concussion from the explosion. Yet, he refused to be evacuated, claiming he had to stay in the field because "In every hour of videotape that Oliver North shoots there are five or six really good seconds. I know I can do better." That might have been true before the IED went off, but for a while, I had the only camera.

STRONGPOINT "BRAVO," AUGUST 4–7, 2008

Shortly before dawn, Lt. Branson awakened me and said, "We're going back out to where we got blown up yesterday, want to go along?" We went.

With a UAV overhead and fixed-wing close air support aircraft standing by if needed, eight Humvees converged on the mud-walled compound nearest to where the IED detonated. Using a bullhorn, Frank the Terp summoned the village elder to a shura—a meeting—in the open next to Branson's Humvee. Just to make sure everyone watching got the message, the Lieutenant secured the Stars and Stripes to the whip antenna of his Humvee.

To reach us, the local headman had to walk across a field of opium poppies. When he arrived, the Marine Lieutenant told him through the interpreter, "Yesterday some bad men planted an explosive device that damaged one of our vehicles and hurt two of my friends. We must find out who did this. If we do not, we will have to stop helping you with new wells, irrigation, and medical supplies. The school you asked for will never get built because the Taliban will come back in force."

Speaking with a villager to get information

The old man said nothing. He glanced around at the Marines dismounted from their vehicles, looked at the large American flag waving from the rear of Branson's Humvee, nodded his head and walked back to his family compound. The Marines loaded up and headed across the desert to their strongpoint.

The next day, with information provided by the locals corroborating other intelligence, the Marines apprehended six military-age males with explosive residue on their hands and clothing. Sometimes just showing the flag helps win "hearts and minds."

CAMP BASTION, HELMAND PROVINCE AFGHANISTAN, AUGUST 8, 2008

Camp Bastion is no five-star resort, but to us it felt like one

It took us nearly twelve hours of cross-desert movement in trucks and Humvees and a two-hour, middle of the night flight in a CH-46 helicopter to make our way from Strongpoint Bravo to Camp Bastion. This British-built fortress, perched on a plateau in southwestern Afghanistan, is well-named.

Surrounded by miles of open desert, the citadel has its own concrete runway, water supply, sewage, electricity, Level 3 trauma hospital, even fire mains—all constructed in the past thirty-six months. The heavily armed camp quarters British, Danish, Estonian, and Czech troops of the International Security Assistance Force. It's also home to Task Force 2/7—built around the legendary 2nd Battalion, 7th Marine Regiment. Based at Marine Corps Base Twentynine Palms, California, these troops came from the best possible place to prepare for this austere terrain and oppressive heat. Camp Bastion is also an outpost of sanity in an otherwise insane part of the world.

Life in Helmand Province has changed little in five hundred years

Helmand Province is the heartland of the Taliban, the Islamic radicals who won a bloody civil war to rule Afghanistan in 1996. Once in power, the Taliban imposed strict Sharia (system of law) and brutalized the largely impoverished Afghan population. Taliban leaders also provided a haven for Osama bin Laden's al-Qaeda to launch the 9/11 attacks. In November 2001, when they were deposed by the U.S.-backed Northern Alliance, many of the Taliban fled south to Pakistan and east to Iran. In the spring of 2008, they came back intent on overthrowing the democratically elected government of President Hamid Karzai. That's when the Marines of TF 2/7 arrived "in country"—ostensibly to train and mentor Afghan army and police forces.

It's been a challenging assignment for the 1,300 Marines, sailors, soldiers, airmen, and civilians of TF 2/7. The unit's area of operations is more than 28,000 square kilometers—roughly the size of Vermont. There is only one paved highway. Overland transport to some of the fifteen forward bases and combat outposts where TF 2/7 operates often takes more than twenty-four hours of continuous day and night movement through the desert. Until mid August, when four CH-53 transport helicopters and four Cobra gunships arrived, the task force had to rely on NATO aircraft for close air support, aerial resupply, and casualty evacuation. Parachute drops of food, water, and ammunition are often necessary.

Before they could train their first Afghan soldier or national policeman, the Marines had to fight their way into the districts where they were to do the mentoring. Since then, they have had to battle the Taliban to keep their overland supply lines open and their outposts secure.

Lt. Col. Richard Hall, the TF 2/7 commander and I once served together in 3rd Battalion, 8th Marines. He's a smart, no-nonsense, level-headed professional, not given to hyperbole. He describes the nearly nonstop gunfights, indirect fire, and improvised explosive device attacks as "a very dynamic, complex, and often hostile environment." That's putting it mildly.

Because there were no police stations or Afghan army units in most of the remote locations where TF 2/7 is operating, the Marines had to construct their own security outposts—a Herculean effort, given the lack of paved roads and primitive infrastructure. As Lt. Col. Hall put it: "We have simultaneously fought the Taliban, built more than a dozen defensive strong points, trained new Afghan National Police, and conducted civic-action programs to win over the local population. And we're getting it done. Our motto, 'Ready for all, yielding to none,' says it all."

By the time we linked up with them in early August 2008, the Marines and Navy medical corpsmen of TF 2/7 had suffered more than one hundred casualties from enemy action. Since they arrived, they have confronted the Taliban, unrelenting heat, innumerable exhausting patrols wearing 40 pounds of armor, and persevered in the roughest living conditions I have experienced since Khe Sanh or Con Thien, forty years ago. More than half the task force has served previously in Iraq or Afghanistan—some in both. Yet the unit's re-enlistment rate is 118 percent—among the highest in the U.S. armed forces.

FORWARD OPERATING BASE NOW ZAD, AUGUST 11–15, 2008

To link up with Company "F" 2/7 at this remote Forward Operating Base, we flew from Camp Bastion aboard a British CH-47 Chinook helicopter transporting a load of ammunition in a cargo net, slung beneath the bird. Several times during the flight it seemed we were going so low and so fast that either the rotor tips or the load of ammunition—or both— would hit the ground.

Loading up on a Brit helicopter at Now Zad

The ammunition, it turned out, was an emergency resupply of 81mm mortar rounds. The Marines and their British counterparts at this isolated NATO outpost were down to 18 rounds, split between two locations, saved for "final defensive fires" in the event they were being overrun by the Taliban.

As they have since arriving at Now Zad, the Marines and their British comrades in arms patrol day and night to keep the enemy off balance in this Taliban stronghold. Capt. Ross Schellhaas, the "Fox Company" commander, and the son of a Naval Academy classmate, says "Nothing in the field manuals could fully prepare us for this, but we adapt and overcome." And they have.

Over the course of the time we spent with "Fox" Company, Chris Jackson and I accompanied them on patrols into the deserted city. Once a "model agricultural settlement" for the UN and NATO, nearly 20,000 residents called Now Zad home before the Taliban drove them away.

Acres of almond and pistachio trees were planted. Irrigation wells and piping systems were installed. The town once had running water, electricity, medical and veterinary clinics, schools, paved streets, a busy bazaar, and a civic center.

Today it's a ghost town—devoid of human habitation. Except for the Taliban who slip into the deserted city to plant IEDs and snipe at the U.S. and British troops, it is an eerie, empty place.

A British officer, here on this third combat tour, described what happened, "When I arrived here in 2002, the city was thriving. We were told that the Afghan Army and National police were coming here and we were to train them. UN NGOs (non-governmental organizations) from all over the world came here to help the people. The army and police never came. But the Taliban did. They poisoned the wells, killed the livestock, burned the orchards, and told the people to leave—and they left."

Daylight patrols have become hunts for IEDs planted by the Taliban. On one such patrol, Chris Jackson and I watched as Marine SSgt Mark Randolph Smith, an Explosive Ordnance Disposal specialist, disarmed four of the deadly devices by blowing them up. His predecessor was killed while attempting to disarm an IED. Our videotape shows SSgt Smith placing the demolition charges. He has remarkably steady hands.

At night the Marines and the British send out sniper teams and ambush patrols to keep the Taliban from approaching the allied perimeters. Under NATO rules of engagement, the small U.S. and British forces in Now Zad aren't allowed to initiate contact. But, if they are fired on by the Taliban or see enemy combatants emplacing IEDs, they can declare "troops in contact"—a "TIC" in military vernacular—and they are supposed to get whatever support they need.

One night while we were in Now Zad, a Marine sniper team declared a TIC and called for close air support. It turned out that the only "air on station" was a B-1 "Lancer." From

60,000 feet, more than eleven miles in the sky, the USAF bomber put three 500 lb, laser-guided bombs directly on a dozen Taliban insurgents hunting for the outnumbered Marines.

Thanking Sgt Jace Halley for his service before we head back to Camp Bastion

Unfortunately, that kind of "back-up" isn't always available from NATO—particularly for helicopter support to units like "FOX 2/7" in remote locations like Now Zad. Because enemy contact has been so intense and casualty evacuation so tenuous, "F" Company now has its own shock trauma platoon headed by Commander James Hancock, a U.S. Navy surgeon.

To ensure the wounded receive immediate lifesaving treatment, he and his corpsmen mounted a steel container on the back of a flatbed truck and outfitted it as a mobile operating room. The "Doc in a box" already has saved more than a half-dozen lives. When I asked Dr. Hancock whether his battlefield innovations are being adopted as "doctrine," he replied, "Not yet, but I'm working on it."

These young Americans have responded to this difficult mission in Afghanistan with tenacity, selfless bravery, and creative resourcefulness. That's why Sgt. Maj. Matthew Brookshire, the senior noncommissioned officer in TF 2/7 refers to his charges as "the quiet professionals."

CAMP BASTION, HELMAND PROVINCE, AFGHANISTAN, AUGUST 16, 2008

We left Now Zad the way we came—in a British CH-47 helicopter. It brought us back to Camp Bastion where we arranged for delivery of equipment to replace the gear destroyed in the IED attack on August 3.

Returning to this big British base also allowed us to do some things we hadn't been able to do in Now Zad: remove our flak jackets, take off our helmets, take a shower, eat fresh food, take a shower, use a light at night, take a shower, sleep, and take a shower. Getting back to Bastion also permitted us to conduct interviews and file reports on the frustrations expressed by the troops we'd been covering.

Much of their dissatisfaction is aimed at the lack of accurate reporting by the U.S. media. It's a valid complaint. During our entire time in Afghanistan, we did not meet a single American reporter from a major media outlet.

Though American and coalition casualties have been nearly seven times higher in Afghanistan than in Iraq during 2008, the campaign against a resurgent Taliban remains widely underreported in the U.S. press. That's why so many of our countrymen are unaware of the courage, commitment, and sacrifice demonstrated by the 33,000 U.S. soldiers, sailors, airmen, and Marines serving and fighting in the shadows of the Hindu Kush. Their stories are profoundly stirring. Following are a few examples from our experience.

Cpl. Garrett Jones

On July 23, 2007, Lance Cpl. Garrett Jones was a fire team leader on patrol near Fallujah, Iraq, with 2nd Battalion, 7th Marines, when an IED detonated practically beneath him, shredding his left leg. At the hospital, surgeons amputated the shattered limb above the knee to save his life.

Today Garrett Jones is a Corporal, still with 2/7 and serving here in Afghanistan. In less than a year, he has suffered life-threatening wounds; recuperated from surgery; endured rehabilitation; been fitted with a prosthetic leg; proved he can perform in combat; and returned to the fight. An avid snowboarder, he plans to compete in the 2010 Paralympics in Vancouver, British Columbia.

Cpl. Jones could have taken a disability discharge and a pension for his wounds. Instead, he fought to stay on active duty and to return to a war zone with those he calls his "battle buddies." When I asked him why, he replied, "These are my brothers. I want to be where they are and continue to make a difference." He is.

While we were embedded with TF 2/7, the battalion suffered a dozen serious casualties. Three Marines, Lance Cpl. Juan Lopez-Castaneda, Lance Cpl. Jacob Toves, and Cpl. Anthony Mihalo were killed in action by improvised explosive devices. One of the wounded, Lance Cpl. Bryan Fisher, was flown to the British shock-trauma hospital at Camp Bastion. This is an excerpt from a message sent to me by the battalion's chaplain, Lt. Russ Hale:

"I went to the hospital to see LCpl Fisher, the 'E' Co. Marine who was wounded in the IED attack and had the unenviable task of sharing with him the names of the KIA from his platoon that were evacuated after him. Like any human, he broke down and began to weep at the loss of his friends and brothers-in-arms. We spoke for a bit about loss and grief and how these kinds of events are not something a person 'gets over,' rather, we 'get through' and with God's grace, we learn to cope in a healthy manner. As our conversation turned towards ways to honor the loss of his

Morale is surprisingly high despite the brutal conditions

friends and his own future, LCpl. Fisher floored me with his plans, 'I'm glad I'll be here at 'Bastion' for awhile before I go back to the field. This will give me time to process my re-enlistment paperwork to stay in 2/7 and then I can return to my guys.'

"Here is a Marine who just lost three of his friends, could easily have been number 4 of the KIA's, and his way of honoring his friends is to re-enlist to stay in the same battalion in order to return to the same place his friends were killed so that he can continue to carry the fight to the enemy. And what's most important is that his actions are not an act of vengeance but an act of love; a way to honor his comrades. He inspires me."

Stories such as these should inspire you, as well. Too bad the arbiters of the press so rarely bother to cover them.

SHINDAND AIRBASE, HERAT PROVINCE
AFGHANISTAN, AUGUST 17–19, 2008

Our FOX News *War Stories* team arrived at this former Soviet military base aboard a USAF MC-130 "Combat Talon." As usual, it was the middle of the night. Sitting in the cockpit wearing night vision goggles, I was actually looking up at the mountain peaks just off our wingtips as we soared through the valleys to this airbase built in 1980, about fifty miles east of the Iranian border.

We came here to embed with the 207th Afghan Commando Battalion and their U.S. Special Operations Command, Army,

With a Marine Special Operator and the Afghan Commandos

Marine, and Air Force counterparts. These U.S. "Special Operators," under the command of Combined Joint Special Operations Task Force-Afghanistan (CJSOTF-A) are nothing short of remarkable. All are volunteers and most have extensive experience in counterinsurgency campaigns. They had to prevail in an extraordinarily difficult selection process and then endure months of rigorous training just to be here.

As with their counterparts in the Philippines and Iraq, with whom our *War Stories* team has been embedded, we cannot show their faces or use their full names. For obvious reasons in a global fight against Islamic radicals, most of these Americans have beards—even the Marines. They often wear indigenous garb, use local vehicles, and employ non-standard weapons.

Though CJSOTF-A units conduct unilateral operations against high-value targets, their primary day-to-day mission here is to train, equip, advise, and support host-nation Special Operations forces. Here it is the 207th Afghan Commando Battalion, led by Lt. Col. Abdul Jabar, a professional soldier from the National Army.

Afghan Commandos at the firing range

Early in the morning of our first day at Shindand, the 207th and their U.S. Army, Marine, and Air Force advisors began preparing for a raid to capture or kill a high-level Taliban suspect alleged to be masterminding a rash of IED attacks. The target was believed to be hiding out in a valley about 15 km south of the base.

Intelligence reports and aerial photographs were used to construct a "sand-table" of the objective area and each member of the raid party was briefed on his assigned task during the operation. That afternoon the commandos conducted a full rehearsal for the mission and "zeroed in" their weapons on the range. At day's end the troops were told to be prepared to "mount up" at 0300 so they could be on the objective at dawn.

Preparation for the raid was near flawless to this old tactics instructor. There was only one problem with the mission. The following morning, as the commandos were closing in to surround and seal off the target area, the Afghan Interior Ministry in Kabul ordered them to halt about a kilometer short of the objective.

The U.S. Army and Marine Spec-Ops personnel launched furious objections over secure radio and data circuits to no avail. By the time the commandos received a "go ahead" order, the sun was high above the horizon and the element of surprise was lost. When they entered the walled compound where the Taliban kingpin and his supporters were supposed to have been, they were already gone.

Afterward one of the U.S. Special Operators said to me, "The biggest obstacle to success here in Afghanistan is the government in Kabul." At the time he said it, we didn't know how much more of a problem Kabul would become.

AZIZ ABAD, HERAT PROVINCE, AFGHANISTAN, AUGUST 22–28, 2008

A Taliban sentry fired the first shots shortly after 0230 as the Afghan commandos and U.S. Special Operations Command troops surrounded the compound at Aziz Abad. Though the Marine Special Operations Team employed a daring deception to achieve surprise, they were engaged by heavy gunfire from AK-47s and machine guns almost immediately after deploying at the objective.

For the next two and a half hours, the 207th Afghan Commandos and their U.S. Army and Marine counterparts were in a running gunfight with heavily armed Taliban fighters inside the walled compound. When enemy combatants on rooftops and in narrow alleyways could not be dislodged by fire from U.S. and Afghan troops on the ground, they were hit by supporting fire from manned and unmanned aircraft overhead.

Afghan Commandos and U.S. Spec Ops troops under fire at Aziz Abad

By dawn on 23 August, the commandos and their American advisers seemed to have achieved a stunning success. Credible information received after a town meeting with local tribal leaders revealed the timing and location of a Taliban gathering. The human intelligence was carefully confirmed and U.S. Special Operations Command officers sat down with their Afghan commando counterparts to carefully plan a raid to take several key Taliban leaders into custody—or if necessary—to kill them. Cameraman Chris Jackson and I accompanied the raid force.

To us and the U.S. and Afghan troops we were covering, it appeared they were victorious. Though one U.S. Marine Special Operator was wounded in the fray, a senior Taliban leader and twenty-five of his fighters were dead. A major Taliban arms cache was located and destroyed. Weapons, ammunition, communications equipment, materials for making improvised explosive devices, and thousands of dollars in cash were confiscated.

As the commandos withdrew from the objective shortly after sunrise, they gently treated and evacuated a woman and her child wounded in the crossfire. Our FOX News cameras captured the battle on videotape, including the careful treatment of noncombatants. Unfortunately, the good news quickly turned bad.

While we were en route back to the base from which the raid had been launched, the U.S. ground force commander received a report over the radio that pro-Taliban agitators were already asserting "the Americans (had) killed thirty civilians." The claims and alleged number of civilian casualties quickly escalated.

Shortly after noon, Iranian television reported, "A U.S. air strike south of Herat in western Afghanistan has killed more than fifty innocent civilians, including women and children." To counter these reports, U.S. aircraft transported Afghan and foreign reporters to the special operations base so they could see the confiscated weapons and other evidence for themselves. It didn't help.

That evening, as we filed our full story of the raid and an interview with a U.S. Special Forces officer, unnamed "sources" at the Ministry of the Interior in Kabul were telling reporters seventy-six civilians were killed. Little attention was paid to the destroyed Taliban arms and equipment at the objective or to the care provided to the wounded woman and her child.

Hamid Karzai called for an investigation of the incident

By the morning of August 24, little more than twenty-four hours after the operation, the international press wires and mainstream news outlets were carrying cell phone photos of damaged buildings and an Afghan human rights organization was charging that eighty-eight civilians—among them twenty women and fifty children—were killed by U.S. forces. Later that day President Hamid Karzai first called for an investigation and then denounced the operation. Though only eighteen new graves were evident in nearby cemeteries and no local civilians had sought medical treatment for wounds, the number of noncombatant casualties allegedly inflicted in the raid continued to rise.

On August 25, with several investigations underway but not yet complete, the commando battalion commander was "suspended." That evening, in a report on Fox News, I noted that neither cameraman Chris Jackson nor I saw any noncombatants killed and "the Taliban and their supporters are running a very effective propaganda campaign to discredit coalition efforts. Exaggerated claims of damage often result in demands for more money in compensation."

The next day, without ever visiting the village, the United Nations Assistance Mission in Afghanistan determined that ninety civilians were killed during the raid at Aziz Abad. Then, as we were departing for Herat, we were informed the government in Kabul was offering $200,000 to settle the claims and was planning new restrictions on Special Operations Command missions. None of the media coverage bothered to mention the civil-affairs projects, re-construction work, or medical support being provided by CJSOTF-A.

The furor over the Aziz Abad raid continued even after we returned home. Eventually an investigation by U.S. Special Operations Command concluded that thirty Afghans were killed in the raid. As is often the case in counterinsurgency operations, there are disputes as to who was and who was not a non-combatant before the shooting started.

KABUL, AFGHANISTAN, AUGUST 30, 2008

We're finally headed home, where there are paved roads, no Russian landmines, and the man standing at the next intersection isn't going to blow himself to pieces trying to kill me, my family, and my friends. At home, drinkable water comes out of a faucet, not just from a plastic bottle. Home is where meals come on plates, not in brown plastic bags, and we have air conditioning and fresh green vegetables, and showers last as long as we want. At home, we go to work in coats and ties instead of body armor and helmets. At home, our vehicles don't have turrets and if we drive after dark, we use headlights instead of night-vision goggles. At home, "overhead cover" is protection from the elements, not a defense from enemy rocket or mortar fire.

I lost fifteen pounds during the month in Afghanistan

In America, we take all these things for granted. Here in the shadows of the Hindu Kush, however, ignoring any of them could get a soldier, sailor, airman, Guardsman, or Marine killed. Unfortunately, the so-called mainstream media has ignored this fight for so long few in the U.S. are even aware of the challenges confronting our 33,000 troops in this always difficult and often dangerous place. For the benefit of those who care, here are some particulars the potentates of the press have overlooked. First, the bad news:

–Islamic radicals know their cause is lost in Iraq, so remnants of the Taliban, al-Qaeda and foreign fighters, intent on joining a jihad against the West, are flooding into Afghanistan from Pakistan and Iran. Factions in both neighboring countries are providing safe havens, training, and material support to those who want to overthrow the democratically elected government in Kabul.

–Despite seven years of United Nations and NATO "assistance" to Afghanistan, the Afghan National Army and Police have fewer than 65,000 troops and the country still has only one paved highway (Route 1, the "Ring Road"). As we were reminded firsthand on this trip, the dirt tracks passing for roads here are laced with landmines and improvised explosive devices, causing numerous U.S. and Afghan casualties and isolating the population.

–Illicit drug production—heroin/opium/hashish/ marijuana, the only real export commodity in the country—is an enormous criminal enterprise, generating more than $5 billion in cash to benefit the Taliban and corrupt officials in the Afghan government.

–The U.N.-led "economic reconstruction" of Afghanistan is a miserable failure. The number of displaced refugees, life expectancy, live birth rate, illiteracy, childhood disease, malnutrition, and unemployment all are getting worse instead of better because of incompetence, corruption, and the lack of coordination among "international donors." The Taliban insurgency thrives on ignorance and misery. As one U.S. officer in Afghanistan put it, "We're feeding the beast."

–There is no coherent command-and-control structure or common set of operating procedures among the Afghan National Army, the Afghan National Police, or the 40 nations in NATO's International Security Assistance Force. Nearly all of these entities have

Opium Poppies in the Hindu Kush

differing rules of engagement and national caveats on how they are employed. Though some U.S. units, such as the 24th Marine Expeditionary Unit and the 101st Airborne Division, have integral air support, others have to rely on ISAF. As a result, wounded Americans have waited hours for casualty evacuation that sometimes never comes.

Paved roads are essential for progress in Afghanistan

Now the good news. Though there are significant cultural and tribal differences between Afghanistan and Iraq—the military/security situation in Afghanistan is similar to what it was in Mesopotamia two and a half years ago. Both campaigns are equally "winnable" if we do the right things. Some repairs will take time, but these are urgently needed:

–Inform both the Pakistani and Iranian governments that insurgent cross-border operations will not be tolerated and if Taliban/terror bases on their territories are not closed, they will be attacked.

–Commence building paved roads throughout all of Afghanistan's thirty-four provinces, not just in urban areas. Such projects will generate tens of thousands of jobs, create lasting infrastructure, reduce casualties from IEDs and mines, and show the Afghan people their government cares about them.

–Stop illicit drug production from the top down, not the bottom up. Arrest and prosecute the kingpins and then go for eradication and crop replacement. It worked in Colombia, and it can work in Afghanistan.

–Fix the unity of command problem immediately. The NATO-ISAF command structure should be shut down. "Allied" forces that can't or won't fight should be thanked and sent home. More U.S. troops are needed in Afghanistan, but unless our new president gives Gen. Petraeus clear lines of authority to do what has to be done, the Afghan army and police never will get the equipment and training they need. Gen. Petraeus did it in Iraq. Now he needs to do it in Afghanistan.

The Afghan people don't want to be ruled by Islamic radicals. There is no real backing for the Taliban beyond what they can coerce from the civilian population. Afghan soldiers— properly trained, equipped, led, and supported—are brave and fight well, but they can't win unless these problems are fixed. As Brig. Gen. Khair Mohammad, chief of staff of the 207th Corps, Western Military Region, told me when we visited his headquarters, "We need to have America's help to win this fight. Your enemy is our enemy."

I MEF First Marine Expeditionary Force

AAV Amphibious Assault Vehicle; also LVT for Landing Vehicle, Tracked; carries eighteen to twenty Marines from ship to shore; serves as ground troop transport. Armament: .50-cal machine gun and 40-mm automatic grenade launcher

ABM Anti-Ballistic Missile

AGM Air-to-Ground Missile

AK-47 7.62-mm automatic rifle of Soviet design; now made in Russia, China, and North Korea, and formerly in most Soviet-bloc countries

Amn Al Khass Iraq's internal intelligence and security service; also known as SSS, Special Security Services

APC Armored Personnel Carrier

APU Auxiliary Power Unit

ASP Ammunition Supply Point

ATGM Anti-Tank Guided Missile

AWACS Airborne Warning and Control System (U.S. Air Force)

BMP A Soviet-made, tracked, infantry fighting vehicle; carries up to eight troops and is normally armed with a 73-mm or a 30-mm cannon and ATGMs

Bn Battalion

CAAT Combined Anti-Armor Team; consists of several Humvees equipped with TOW and Javelin ATGMs, .50-cal machine guns and grenade launchers

CAS Close Air Support

Cas-evac Casualty Evacuation

CENTCOM Central Command (Also USCENTCOM). U.S. Central Command, one of nine U.S. unified military commands; headquartered at McDill Air Force Base, Tampa, Florida. During Operation Iraqi Freedom, CENTCOM maintained a forward headquarters in Doha, Qatar.

CG Commanding General

CO Commanding Officer

CP Command Post

DASC Direct Air Support Center; provides a direct communications link between Marine air and ground units

EGBU-28 Enhanced Guided Bomb Unit; more accurate version of the "bunker buster" that uses GPS for guidance. See also GBU.

EOD Explosive Ordnance Disposal

EP-3 Lockheed EP-3E Aries II aircraft, designed specifically for Signals Intelligence (SIGINT) collection. The aircraft operates with a five-person flight crew and as many as twenty intelligence specialists.

EPW Enemy Prisoner of War

FAC Forward Air Controller; provides direction and control for aircraft firing or dropping ordnance in support of ground troops

FARP Forward Arming and Refueling Point

FO Forward Observer; provides fire direction and control for artillery or mortars

Frag Order Fragmentary Order; an abbreviated operations order that a commander uses to inform troops of information they need to carry out an assigned mission

G-3 Operations and training function for a military command of brigade or higher. See also S-3.

GBU Guided Bomb Unit; e.g., GBU-15, an unpowered, glide weapon used to destroy high-value enemy targets; the GBU-37 "bunker buster" is a five-thousand-pound laser-guided conventional explosive with a forty-four-hundred-pound penetrating warhead. The operator illuminates a target with a laser designator and then the munition is guided to a spot of laser energy reflected from the target.

GOSP Gas-Oil Separation Plant

GPS Global Positioning System

Gunny Slang for Marine gunnery sergeant

HARM High-Speed Anti-Radiation Missile; an air-to-ground missile, specifically the AGM-88 HARM

HEAT High Explosive Anti-Tank; armor-piercing, anti-tank ammunition

HET (U.S. Marines) Human Exploitation Team; helps collect and interpret intelligence

HET (U.S. Army) Heavy Equipment Transporter

HMLA Marine Light Attack Helicopter Squadron; flies AH-1J Cobras and armed UH-1N "Hueys"

HMM Marine Medium Helicopter Squadron; flies CH-46 "Sea Knight" helicopters

HUMINT Human intelligence, as contrasted with electronic, satellite, or other intelligence gathering

Humvee: High Mobility Multipurpose Wheeled Vehicle

HVT High Value Target

ICM Improved Conventional Munitions

ID In the context of a military unit, Infantry Division; also an abbreviation for identification

IFB Interruptible Feedback Line; allows a television producer, director, talent, and others to communicate with one another during a program, usually through an earpiece

IFF Identification Friend or Foe

JDAM Joint Direct Attack Munition; an unpowered, GPS-guided, one-thousand- to two-thousand-pound glide bomb

Jihaz Haneen Clandestine Baath intelligence and security organization

JSTARS Joint Surveillance Target Attack Radar System; a high resolution radar and command and control suite mounted in a modified Boeing 707 airframe

LAR Light Armored Reconnaissance Battalion; Marine unit equipped with LAVs for rapid ground reconnaissance forward and on the flanks of a larger force

LAV Light Armored Vehicle; LAV-25, wheeled light armored vehicle employed by Marine LAR battalion; carries six troops. Armament: 25-mm chain gun

LVT Landing Vehicle, Tracked. See also AAV.

LVTC Landing Vehicle, Tracked, Command. An LVT equipped with communications equipment and configured so that a commander can use an LVTC-7 as his command. Armament: turret-mounted .50-caliber machine gun

LZ Landing Zone

MAG Marine Air Group

MAW Marine Aircraft Wing. The 3rd MAW served as the Air Combat element of I MEF.

MAWTS Marine Aviation Weapons and Tactics Squadron

MEU Marine Expeditionary Unit; the smallest air-ground task force, consisting of a reinforced infantry battalion, a composite helicopter squadron, and a logistics support element

MIA Missing in Action

MOPP Mission-Oriented Protective Posture; designation for the protective suit, mask, and other equipment worn to shield troops from nuclear, chemical, and biological weapons. See also **NBC suit.**

MP Military Police

MPS Maritime Prepositioning Ship; large "roll-on roll-off" vessels full of military equipment, weapons, and ammunition; strategically placed to expedite the deployment of U.S. military units

MRE Meal, Ready-to-Eat

Mukhabarat The foreign intelligence service in Saddam Hussein's Iraq

NBC suit Nuclear, biological, and chemical protective gear

NCO Noncommissioned officer in the military services

NOK Next of Kin

NVG Night-Vision Goggles

OGA Other Government Agency; euphemism for CIA or other intelligence service personnel operating in Iraq, Afghanistan, and other places

Overwatch A base of fire from heavy weapons in support of a maneuver

PAO Public Affairs Officer

PAX (also "Packs") U.S. military abbreviation for passengers, usually in an aircraft

PFC Private First Class

POW Prisoner of War

QRF Quick Reaction Force

RAP Rocket-Assisted Projectiles

RCT Regimental Combat Team

Rein Reinforced

ROE Rules of Engagement

RPG Rocket-Propelled Grenade

RPV Remotely Piloted Vehicle; radio-controlled aircraft used to conduct reconnaissance and/or intelligence collection. See also UAV.

S-1 Staff officer who performs administrative record-keeping and personnel function for a battalion or regiment

S-2 Staff officer who performs intelligence and counter-intelligence function for a battalion or regiment

S-3 Staff officer who performs operations, plans, and training functions for a battalion or regiment

S-4 Staff officer who performs logistics, maintenance, and supply function for a battalion or regiment

SAD Special Activities Division

SAM Surface-to-Air Missile

SAW Squad Automatic Weapon, 5.56 mm; carried by one member of each Marine infantry fire team

SERE Survival, Escape, Resistance, and Evasion; plan followed in the event a pilot or other armed forces member is down or lost behind enemy lines

Sharqi Iraqi sandstorm

Sit Rep situation report

SOP Standard Operating Procedure

TAA Tactical Assembly Area

TF Task Force

TOC Tactical Operations Center

TOT Time on Target

TOW Tube-launched, Optically tracked, Wire-guided anti-tank missile

TRAP Tactical Recovery of Aircraft and Pilot

UAV Unmanned Aerial Vehicle; reconnaissance aircraft operated by remote radio control and or GPS

UN United Nations

UNSCOM UN Special Commission; the organization appointed by the UN to search for weapons of mass destruction in Iraq

V Corps U.S. Army forward-deployed headquarters for two divisions, a corps support command, and nine separate brigades totaling approximately forty-one thousand soldiers

VMU-2 Marine Unmanned Aerial Vehicle Squadron Two; operated RPVs over the battlefield for the Regimental Combat Teams. See also UAV.

WIA Wounded in Action

WMD Weapons of Mass Destruction

XO Executive Officer

Air Force

A1C Kenny Holston: 234
MSgt Andy Dunaway: 168
MSgt Coco Gunther: 223
MSgt Jim Varhegyi: top 224
MSgt Jonathan Doti: bottom 10
MSgt Lance Cheung: 33
MSgt Robert W. Valenca: 246
MSgt Val Gempis: bottom 44
SrA Brian Ferguson: middle 36
SrA Christina D. Ponte: 233
SSgt Aaron D. Allmon II: bottom 79
SSgt David Donovan: bottom 110
SSgt James L. Harper Jr.: 189
SSgt JoAnn S. Makinano: 114, 165
SSgt Michael R. Holzworth: top 44
SSgt Shawn Weismiller: 276
TSgt Andrew M. Rodier: 196
TSgt Brian Christiansen: top 253, 258
TSgt Dawn M. Price: 168
TSgt Maria. J. Bare: 225

Army

GS-9 Martin Greeson: 251
PFC James Matise: 74
PVT Daniel Meacham: 183
SFC Johancharles Van Boers: 184
SFC Robert C. Brogan: 113
SFC Todd Oliver: bottom left 250
SGT Ben Brody: top 282
SGT Curtis Hargrave: 164
SGT Jon Soucy: bottom 249
SGT Matthew Acosta: 208
SGT Mike Pryor: bottom 224
SPC David Marck Jr.: top 46, top 37, 48, bottom 52
SPC Kieran Cuddihy: 228
SPC Lorie Jewell: bottom 253, top 273
SPC Olanrewaju Akinwunmi: 158
SPC Patrick Weitekamp: 34
SSG Bronco Suzuki: 14
SSG Russell L. Klika: bottom right 250
William Glaser: 138

Chuck Holton

bottom 86, 99, 154, 174, top 219, bottom 220, bottom 231, 248, 263, 268, bottom 270, 279, 280, 282, 283, 284, 285, 286, bottom 290, 294, 295, 296

Department of Defense (DOD)

1, 8, top right 18, 23, 30–32, 35, top and bottom 36, top 41, top 47, 49, 54, 58, 60, 72, middle 76, top 80, 92, 94, 97, 98, top 110, 122, 125, 128, 131, 135, 136, 140, 142, 148, 155, 156, 158, 161, top 170, top 175, 185, 188, 191, 197, 202, 209, 218, 227, top 250, 256, 257, 259, 260, 275
Capt. Tom Bryant: top 38
Cherie A. Thurlby: 271
Cpl Jonathan K. Teslevich: 121
Don Dees: top 52
James McCauley: 200
Jane Marriott: 187
LCpl Brandon L. Roach: bottom 125
PFC Joshua Hutcheson: 108
R. D. Ward: 81
Sarah Underhill: 243
SFC David K. Dismukes: 78
Sgt Frank Magni: 51
Sgt Kevin R. Reed: 61
Shayne Johnson: top 66
SPC Jeremy D. Crisp: top 249
SPC Mason T. Lowery: 67
SPC Robert Woodward: 160
SPC Ronald Shaw Jr.: 193
SSG Craig Zentkovitch: 83, 85, top 101, 107, 118, 119, 126, 144, 152
SSG Mark Wojciechowski: 247
SSG Raymie G. Cruz: 88, 90
SSG Reeba Critser: bottom 135
SSG Scott Maynard: 100

FOX News

6, 21, bottom 25, top 27, 147, top 216, 254
Andrew Stenner: 93, 262, 291
Chris Jackson: 293
Griff Jenkins: 11, 65, 69, bottom 76, 93, 123, 124, 150, 153
Kelly Guernica: top 255
Mal James: bottom 66, 68, top 70, top 76, top 84, top left 86, top 89, bottom 100, 104, 109, 117, 129, 130, 133, top 134, bottom 149, 162, top 166, bottom 170, 179, 180, bottom 181, 194, 198, 207, 213, bottom 216, bottom 219, top 220, 221, 222, bottom 230, top 231, 245, 264, 265, 266, 267
Oliver North: top right 86, 91, 102, 103, 137, 139, bottom 172, 173, bottom 175, top 176, 212, 217, 229, top 230, 292

Marines

1st Lt. Barry L. Edwards: 214
Cpl Brian Reimers: top 10
Cpl Eric C. Ely: bottom 202
Cpl James M. Mercure: bottom 287, 288
Cpl Michael R. McMaugh: 199
Cpl Paul W. Leicht: top 79, bottom 89, bottom 176, 178
Cpl Robert R. Attebury: 215
Cpl Ryan C. Heiser: top 29
Cpl Shane S. Keller: bottom 282
Cpl Trenton E. Harris: 71
GySgt Daniel O'Connell: bottom right 55
GySgt Erik S. Hansen: 167
LCpl Brian L. Wickliffe: bottom 29
LCpl Lucian A. Friel: 203
LCpl Nicholous Radloff: 87
LCpl Sheila M. Brook: bottom 80
PFC Renato Lara: top 124
Sgt Adaecus G. Brooks: 116
Sgt Chad Simon: bottom 273
Sgt Joseph R. Chenelly: top 130
Sgt Kevin R. Reed, 157
Sgt Maryalice Leone: 141
Sgt Michael K. Kropiewnicki: 169
Sgt Paul L. Anstine III: 132
Sgt Ray Lewis: top 287, 289, top 290
USMC History Division: 24

Navy

AA Ricardo J. Reyes: 77
JO1 Mark D. Faram: 17
Joyce N Boghosian: 278
MCS1 Chad J. McNeeley: 239
MCS2 Nathan Schaeffer: 42
MCS2 Miguel Angel Contreras: 43
MCS2 Summer M. Anderson: 232
Michael W. Pendergrass: 19
PM1 Arlo K. Abrahamson: top 172
PM3 James Spiker: bottom 70
PM2 Jim Watson: 12
PM1 Tim Turner: bottom 47
PO1 Alan D. Monyelle: 186
SR Chad R. Erdmann: bottom 82

Perry-Castellano Library

top 25, bottom 39

Public Domain

64, 281

FREEDOM ALLIANCE

★ ★ ★ ★ ★ ★ ★ ★ ★ ★ ★ ★

SCHOLARSHIP FUND—Supporting the Children of America's Military Heroes

The Freedom Alliance Scholarship Fund honors the bravery and dedication of Americans in our armed forces who have sacrificed life and limb and provides college scholarships to their children. Through the generosity of the American public, the Scholarship Fund has awarded more than $1 million to the sons and daughters of American heroes.

Many of freedom's brave defenders who have lost their lives fighting terrorism have left behind young children. We believe it is our duty to help their children meet the rising costs of a college education, but more importantly to remind them that their parents' sacrifice will never be forgotten by a grateful nation.

SUPPORT OUR TROOPS—Honoring America's Armed Forces

The Freedom Alliance Support Our Troops program honors and supports our servicemen and women and their families—especially those who are serving on the front lines or who have been wounded and are recuperating at our military hospitals.

Freedom Alliance provides financial assistance and gift packages to these troops. The program also includes events such as Military Appreciation Dinners and special holiday activities. Freedom Alliance sponsors these activities to say "thank you" to our service members and their families.

Freedom Alliance, which was founded in 1990 by Lt. Col. Oliver North, USMC (Ret.), is a nonprofit 501(c)(3) charitable and educational organization dedicated to advancing the American heritage of freedom by honoring and encouraging military service, defending the sovereignty of the United States, and promoting a strong national defense.

For more information or to donate, contact:
FREEDOM ALLIANCE
22570 Markey Court, Suite 240
Dulles, Virginia 20166-6919
1(800)475-6620
www.freedomalliance.org   *"LEST WE FORGET"*